PERFORMING QUEER LATINIDAD

TRIANGULATIONS
Lesbian/Gay/Queer ▲ Theater/Drama/Performance

Series Editors
Jill Dolan, Princeton University
David Román, University of Southern California

TITLES IN THE SERIES:

Tony Kushner in Conversation
  edited by Robert Vorlicky

*Passing Performances: Queer Readings of Leading Players
in American Theater History*
  edited by Robert A. Schanke and Kim Marra

*When Romeo Was a Woman: Charlotte Cushman
and Her Circle of Female Spectators*
  by Lisa Merrill

Camp: Queer Aesthetics and the Performing Subject
  edited by Fabio Cleto

Staging Desire: Queer Readings of American Theater History
  edited by Kim Marra and Robert A. Schanke

A Problem Like Maria: Gender and Sexuality in the American Musical
  by Stacy Wolf

A Queer Sort of Materialism: Recontextualizing American Theater
  by David Savran

Margaret Webster: A Life in the Theater
  by Milly S. Barranger

*The Gay and Lesbian Theatrical Legacy: A Biographical Dictionary of
  Major Figures in American Stage History*
  edited by Billy J. Harbin, Kim Marra, and Robert A. Schanke

Cast Out: Queer Lives in Theater
  edited by Robin Bernstein

Queering Mestizaje: Transculturation and Performance
  by Alicia Arrizón

*Bulldaggers, Pansies, and Chocolate Babies: Performance, Race, and
Sexuality in the Harlem Renaissance*
  by James F. Wilson

Lady Dicks and Lesbian Brothers: Staging the Unimaginable at the WOW Café Theatre
  by Kate Davy

A Menopausal Gentleman: The Solo Performances of Peggy Shaw
  edited by Jill Dolan

Performing Queer Latinidad: Dance, Sexuality, Politics
  by Ramón H. Rivera-Servera

PERFORMING QUEER LATINIDAD

Dance, Sexuality, Politics

Ramón H. Rivera-Servera

THE UNIVERSITY OF MICHIGAN PRESS

Ann Arbor

Published in the United States of America by
The University of Michigan Press
Manufactured in the United States of America
⊗ Printed on acid-free paper

2015   2014   2013   2012   4   3   2   1

A CIP catalog record for this book is available from the
British Library.

Library of Congress Cataloging-in-Publication Data

Rivera-Servera, Ramón H., 1973–
    Performing queer latinidad : dance, sexuality, politics / Ramón H. Rivera-Servera.
        p.   cm. — (Triangulations: Lesbian/Gay/Queer Theater/Drama/Performance)
    Includes bibliographical references and index.
    ISBN 978-0-472-07139-5 (cloth : acid-free paper) — ISBN 978-0-472-05139-7
(pbk. : acid-free paper) — ISBN 978-0-472-02864-1 (e-book)
    1. Gay theater—United States.   2. Hispanic American theater.   3. Homosexuality
and theater.   4. Gays and the performing arts.   I. Title.
PN2270.G39R58   2013
792.086'640973—dc23   2012019745

The Northwestern University Research Grants Committee
has provided partial support for the publication of this book. We
gratefully acknowledge their assistance.

For Joel,
In celebration of the Grand Pas de Deux
that is our life together.

ACKNOWLEDGMENTS

Performing Queer Latinidad is a project written in travel throughout the United States during the 1990s and into the early 2000s. I first ventured into this research as a doctoral student in theater at the Graduate Center of the City University of New York and then at the University of Texas at Austin. I continued fieldwork and archival research while on the faculty ranks at Arizona State University and Northwestern University. Critical support for this project was provided by fellowships and grants from the Ford Foundation, the Woodrow Wilson Foundation, the Herberger College of Fine Arts at Arizona State University, and the School of Communication at Northwestern University. The preparation and publication of this manuscript is made possible in part by a publication subvention grant from Northwestern University.

Across the terrain I have encountered an incredibly generous, creative, and inspirational community of artists, scholars, activists, and friends who have become my extended family. This project would have been impossible without their presence in my life.

Arthur Aviles welcomed me to Hunts Point with open arms and generously shared with me his passion for the neighborhood and his faith in how the arts could help this embattled but resilient pocket of creativity feel like home. His artistic work and his vision for the role the arts could play in his community inspired me in the first place to pursue the research that became this book. I thank Charles Rice-González, Elizabeth Marrero, Jorge Merced, and the many fierce dancers, performers, and *teatreros* who have graced the stages of BAAD!, the Point, Pregones, and many other gathering spaces in the Bronx with deliciously queer humor and intelligence.

A little bit farther south, between Loisaida and Fourteenth Street, I came to know a world of art practice and queer community that sustains me to this day. Among the many artists that populated my experience of the Lower East Side, Alina Troyano and Marga Gómez articulate for me the politics of pleasure and laughter.

In 1999, the good people of the Esperanza Center, especially Graciela Sánchez, opened the doors of their cultural center. They allowed me access to their extensive archives, introduced me to key collaborators in their struggle to protect their funding and their dignity, and taught me that feminist and queer politics and Latina/o politics can coexist in creative friction. Esperanza staff and volunteers, especially Antonia Castañeda, Virginia Grise, Peter Haney, Amy Keastly, Herminia Maldonado, René Saenz, and Manuel Solis, were generous with their time and stories. Their conviction and enthusiasm made hope for justice palpable, even possible.

I thank Adrián, Clara, Gerry, Gina, Héctor, José, Josué, Juan, Lena, Linda, Luis, Marisa, Michael, Néstor, Nilda, Rosalinda, Tomás, Yadira, Victor, Wilbert, William, and the many other club patrons, dancers, bartenders, bouncers, promoters, and performers I have talked to and danced with in New York, Rochester, San Antonio, Austin, Phoenix, and Chicago over the past two decades. I am especially grateful for those who agreed to participate in this study. You have not only taught me a step or two on the dance floor but have transformed my life with your comradeship and creativity.

I am fortunate to have worked with an incredible group of mentors throughout my academic career. At the University of Rochester, Michael Ann Holly, Douglas Crimp, Claudia Schaefer, and Sharon Willis offered a strong foundation from which to build my scholarly, artistic and political interests. Allen Topolski taught me how to integrate theory and practice in the arts. Lisa Cartwright introduced me to the field of performance studies and offered critical early encouragement and guidance. Rosemary Feal challenged me to think interartistically and interdisciplinarily and was an enthusiastic endorser of my venture into a scholarly career. Ondine Chavoya, Tina Takemoto, Karen Kosasa, Tarek El-Ariss, and Briget R. Cooks served as role models and allies. Rishad Lawyer and William Estuardo Rosales became my brothers, Jessica Gerrity my sister. Garth Fagan, Norwood Pennewell, Steve Humphrey, Bit Knighton, Natalie Rogers-Cropper, Valentina Alexander, Christopher Morrison, Lavert Benefield, Sharlene Shu, Sharon Skepple, and the rest of the dancers at Garth Fagan Dance became and continue to be my dance family. At the City University of New York, Marvin Carlson, Jane Bowers, and Eve Kosofsky-Sedgwick were transformative pedagogues who pushed my engagements with performance. At the University of Texas at Austin, Ann Daly, Stacy Wolf, Charlotte Canning, and Richard Flores provided key methodologies for the development of my research agenda and many hours of dedicated mentorship.

I began my career as a university professor at Arizona State University, where Tamara Underiner was an incredibly supportive and generous collaborator. Our work together on Theatre and Performance of the Americas has been as intellectually generative as it has been pleasurable. Stephani Woodson, Margaret Knapp, Linda Essig, Lance Gharavi, Guillermo Reyes, Roger Bedard, Johnny Saldaña, Amira de la Garza, John J. Leaños, Arthur Sabatini, Chris Danowski, Shelly Cohn, Colleen Jennings-Roggensack, and Jeff Macmahon made a social and artistic oasis out of the Arizona desert.

Many scholars have influenced and supported my career over the course of this research. I am especially indebted to Ric Knowles and Diana Taylor for being scholarly models and generous senior colleagues. I have been inspired by the work of many other scholars and friends. Among them: Marlon Bailey, Melissa Blanco Biorelli, Bernadette Marie Calafell, Ernie Capello, Harry Elam Jr., Licia Fiol-Matta, Cindy Garcia, Marcial Godoy, Patricia Herrera, Josh Kuhn, Larry La Fountain-Stokes, Jill Lane, Irma Mayorga, Raquel Monroe, Shane Moreman, José Esteban Muñoz, Deborah Paredez, Rachel Perlmeter, José Quiroga, Ricky Rodríguez, Jon Rossini, Margaret Savilonis, Susan Tenneriello, Maurya Wickstrom, and Tomás Ybarra-Frausto.

Eng-Beng Lim, Josh Abrams, and Jennifer Parker-Starbuck have been anchors throughout this journey. Their intellectual engagements and friendship have meant the world to me.

Amelia Malagamba-Ansótegui has been a constant presence in my life since I first enrolled in her doctoral seminar in Austin. The many hours spent conversing about the arts over a home-cooked meal have sustained me over the past decade. *Gracias por hacer familia conmigo.*

Marvette Pérez is a brilliant scholar, curator, and artist. I thank her for bringing humor and hopeful anger into my everyday.

Emma Velez-Lopez has been listening to my ideas, both academic and artistic, since we were sixteen years old. She has always provided perspective on where we come from and encouragement when the going gets rough. I am honored to be part of her life.

Jennifer Brody, Dwight McBride, Alejandro Madrid, Agnes Lugo-

Ortiz, Dianne Miliotis, Sharon P. Holland, and Frances Aparicio welcomed me into Chicago and introduced me to the intellectual, artistic, and life pleasures that lie within this wonderful city. Thank you.

Ana Aparicio listened to countless versions of this book recited over the phone and always offered fresh and incisive commentary. She motivated me with her words and fried green tomatoes and *pernil*.

It is a pleasure to work in a campus where performance is taken seriously and where the humanities remain central to our educational mission. The Dean of the School of Communication at Northwestern University, Barbara O'Keefe, has created the intellectual environment and provided the critical resources that have made my teaching and scholarship possible. My colleagues in the Department of Performance Studies—Joshua Chambers-Letson, Marcela Fuentes, Carol Simpson-Stern, Paul Edwards, Margaret Thompson-Drewal, and Mary Zimmerman—have been encouraging and supportive. D. Soyini Madison and Sandra Richards have been inspiring mentors, colleagues, and friends. My colleagues across the Northwestern University campus have made my life rich and my thinking stronger. I thank Susan Manning, Tracy Davis, Nitasha Sharma, Traci Burch, Henry Godinez, Victoria De Francesco-Soto, Ivy Wilson, Emily McGuire, Gerry Cadava, and John Alba Cutler for their deep collegiality. Harvey Young has been a wonderful collaborator and confidant.

Working with my students at Northwestern University has been one of the most rewarding experiences of my career. I am especially thankful to my doctoral students Victoria Fortuna, Elias Krell, Kemi Adeyemi, and Colleen Daniher for their research assistance and their engagement with my ideas.

E. Patrick Johnson has been a blessing in my life. His leadership in our department has been visionary and I owe much to his counsel and protection. He and Stephen Lewis have made Chicago feel like home. *Gaia!*

Patricia Ybarra has been an incredible travel companion, scholarly partner, and friend. *Mi comadre* Alicia Arrizón has been a wonderful supporter and always served as a sounding board for my ideas and career decisions. David Román has been a much-needed critical voice since I entered the profession and has provided deep and challenging comments on my scholarship. His comments on earlier versions of this manuscript and his own scholarship have significantly influenced the work here presented.

Alberto Sandoval-Sánchez inspired me to become an academic. He has been a constant presence in my development as a scholar. *Muchísimas gracias por tu apoyo, nuestro intercambio intelectual, y tu amistad.*

LeAnn Fields has been unwavering in her support throughout the process of writing this book and encouraged my work in more ways than she would recognize. Our field is in excellent hands under such curatorial and editorial mastery. Anonymous readers provided careful and thought-provoking assessments of this project. I thank them for their insight and generosity. Scott Ham, Marcia LaBrenz, and the rest of the staff at the University of Michigan Press have been a joy to work with. They made the process of publishing a first book a joy.

I am most grateful to Jill Dolan for providing visionary pedagogy, intellectual guidance, career counsel, and love for so many years. My life has been forever touched by her wisdom and political commitments to performance and what it might make possible. This book has been shaped in conversation with her scholarship and in appreciation of her friendship. Thank you for believing in me and my work.

My family has always been a fountain of love and support. My mother and siblings, Carol Servera, Natalie Bonaparte-Servera, Dennis Rivera-Servera, make me feel at home and in family even when far away. *Gracias por su paciencia, entendimiento, y amor.*

Joel Valentín-Martinez has been my dance and life partner for the totality of the journey this book documents. His insights as an artist, his work as a choreographer, and his rigorous engagement with my work have influenced my thinking about dance and movement. He has provided care in every imaginable configuration. I thank him for sustaining me and for making me feel loved. I look forward to the rest of our dance together. One, two, three . . . step.

An earlier version of chapter 4 appeared as "Choreographies of Resistance: Latina/o Queer Dance and the Utopian Performative," in *Modern Drama* 157.2 (2004): 269–89. An excerpt version of chapter 5 appeared as "Dancing Reggaetón with Cowboy Boots: Social Dance Clubs and the Politics of Dance in the Latino Southwest," in Alejandro Madrid, ed., *Transnational Encounters: Music and Performance at the U.S.-Mexico Border* (London: Oxford University Press, 2011): 373–92.

CONTENTS

LATINA/O QUEER PERFORMANCE

A Critical Travelogue

WE ARE RAIN OR SHINE . . . COME ON BY . . . WE'RE HERE!
—Orgullo en Acción[1]

Queer Latinidad in Public

It is an overcast summer morning on June 13, 2009, as I prepare to attend Orgullo en Acción's Fourth Annual Latina/o LGBTQQ Pride Picnic at Chicago's Humboldt Park.[2] The clouds look menacing and last night's heavy downpour makes me hesitant about attending the outdoor event. I am about to give up and stay in for the day. A message pops up on my Facebook screen: "We are rain or shine . . . come on by . . . we're here!" I am hailed by this statement of resilience by a group eager to celebrate their queer latinidad despite the possibility of inclement weather or broader societal obstacles that render the simple act of gathering in a public place a heroic feat. The very phrasing of the pronouncement "we are rain or shine," as opposed to "we are here rain or shine," showcases the social and cultural dynamics central to this book. Queer Latinas/os at the picnic "are" or "become" a collective by "being here" in public and participating in acts of performance that range from the social to the theatrical. The simple, and I would speculate purposeful, slippage of the Internet communiqué advances a theory of performance's world-making powers by collapsing the idea of "being" Latina/o and queer with the practice of "being there" at the site of Latina/o queer public enactments. And it is precisely my interest and investment in performances of queer latinidad that beckons me to this event in a city I am still getting to know and with a group of strangers who find pleasure in performing their Latina/o queer selves as public interventions. I quickly ready for an afternoon of fellowship in Latina/o queer pride.

I arrive at Humboldt Park and walk west on Division Street to encounter a section of the picnic area demarcated by two giant rainbow flags. The flags echo the space-making practices performed by Puerto Ricans throughout the neighborhood. A historically working-class enclave in Chicago's near west side, Humboldt Park has been the symbolic, cultural, economic, and political center of Puerto Rican Chicago for over five decades. Since the early 1990s the community has organized against the westward push of gentrification as formerly low-income neighborhoods transform into hipster heavens for young up-and-coming mostly white middle-class families.[3] The Puerto Rican flag is prominently displayed everywhere: on windows, murals, business awnings, T-shirts, baseball caps, and the monumental steel arches that cross the street as gateways into the Division Street business district, popularly referred to as Paseo Boricua or La División. This showcase of the Puerto Rican national icon marks territory for a community that struggles to maintain its sense of place in a fast-changing Chicago human landscape.[4]

The Latina/o Pride Picnic extends the visual gestures of the neighborhood with proud rainbows that plant the flag of queerness upon a Puerto Rican urban geography. The stage itself displays banners advertising Latina/o queer organizations that sponsored the picnic: Orgullo en Acción, the Association for Latino Men in Action (ALMA), and Amigas Latinas.[5] The use of rainbow flags and banners cites visual strategies typical of post-Stonewall gay and lesbian liberation movements. Flags from all Latin American countries, including Brazil and Puerto Rico, are planted on the ground in a sequence that travels from the edges of the platform stage onto the picnic area. This temporary public transformation of the Puerto Rican park into a pan-Latina/o space acknowledges the shifting demographics of neighborhoods like Humboldt Park itself, where Latinas/os of Mexican, Salvadoran, and Dominican descent represent an increasingly significant portion of the population.

This diverse group of queer Latinas/os and their allies use flags and performance to produce an alternative public event in Humboldt Park. The picnic site is just a few yards from a cruising site where Puerto Rican and other men in the neighborhood search for sexual encounters. The picnic's location may serve as recognition, even legitimization, of the queer routes created by the traffic of cruising men in the park. Nonetheless, the picnic as an event is markedly different from the more discreet act of having sex behind the bushes. Instead of the tacit nature of the men cruising, who do not necessarily affirm a queer identity in public or

Fig. 1. Paseo Boricua. Chicago, IL. Photo by the author.

at home, the performances that take place at the picnic rely on explicit and at times spectacular displays of Latina/o queer sociality and aesthetics.[6] The difference between these two ways of inhabiting the same site does not lessen the equally performative and public ritual of gay cruising. I recognize both of these activities—the dramaturgically amplified strategy of occupying the park with the explicit intent of staging an intervention, and the quotidian rituals of gay cruising—as performance. I will outline the broad spectrum of activity that enacts queer latinidad below.

At the picnic, drag queens and kings, poets, dancers, singers, and community organizers take to the stage to assertively perform their carefully crafted numbers. The choices in performance genre vary from Mexican pop ballads to club music and from formal gowns and crowns to hip-hop attire. The audience is equally diverse, and during the brief period I spend at the event I meet gay, lesbian, bisexual, and transgender folk from all over the Latina/o diaspora. Queer latinidad is palpable, even if temporarily, as an affective tie among friends, family members, and even strangers who chose to travel to this site for the single motive of experiencing, celebrating, and feeling a community in pleasure.

The Latina/o Pride Picnic pursues the collective effort of performance practice to instantiate pan-Latina/o queer social networks. It provides a

Fig. 2. Orgullo en Acción,
Annual picnic flyer, Chicago

temporary shared space in hopes that the encounters experienced over the course of a few hours might yield longer relationships with potentially political implications. Latina/o and queer agendas circulate in these events shaped by the increasing threat of development and gentrification and the hypermasculine heteronormativity of Puerto Rican resistance to it. For the six hours this event lasts, this section of Humboldt Park is transformed into a pleasure-filled intersection of Latina/o queer subjects who "become" a collective by the sheer act of "being" and performing "here" together "rain or shine."

Home, hope, utopia, and friction emerge as the contours of a collective affectivity born of an insistence on "being" or rather "becoming" a queer and Latina/o community in the practice of performance. The efficacy of this event relies on the emotional optimism that instituting community often requires. Affirmations such as "we are" and "we're here" insist on the hopeful utopianism that performance might model ways of being in place with others despite the frictions intimated by "rain or shine," a statement that opens to the possibilities and contingencies of a social encounter where not all variables can be determined a priori. The

Fig. 3. Orgullo en Acción, Annual picnic flags, Humboldt Park, Chicago. Photo by the author.

statement, as much as the event itself, are invitations "to be" or "to be there" by "coming by." We are invited to show up to the park as a practice of becoming a "we" in the "here" of the event. That is, performance trans- forms the park into a home to queer latinidad through the embodied spatiality of the event. Occupying public space together in the practice of performance constitutes an effort that requires both an investment in the possible, what might become of the exchange promised by the event, and a realization that pursuing that possibility entails as many pleasures as it invokes risks.

In *Performing Queer Latinidad* I chart Latina/o cultural affinities or latinidad in queer spaces.[7] I do so by attending to the ways gay, lesbian, bisexual, transgender, and other nonnormative sex practitioners of Latin American descent with greatly differing cultures, histories of migration or annexation to the United States, and contemporary living conditions encounter each other and build social, cultural, and political bonds. Through examining a variety of performance case studies ranging from concert dance and street protest performances to the choreographic strategies deployed by dancers at nightclubs, this book documents the emergence of a Latina/o queer public in the United States.

In this book I argue that performance played a critical role in the development of Latina/o queer public culture in the United States at the dusk of the twentieth and the dawn of the twenty-first centuries. The fifteen-year period of cultural activity covered in this book (1996–2011) saw the simultaneous dramatic increases in the Latina/o population in the United States and their presence in the national public sphere and challenges to and surveillance of the public spaces where latinidad could circulate. I contend that at a time when latinidad ascended to the national public sphere in mainstream commercial and political venues and when Latina/o public space was increasingly threatened by the redevelopment of urban centers and a revived anti-immigrant campaign, queer Latinas/os recurred to performance to claim spaces and ways of being that allowed their queerness and latinidad to coexist. *Performing Queer Latinidad* demonstrates how the social events of performance and its attendant aesthetic communication strategies served as critical sites and tactics for creating and sustaining queer latinidad.

The goals of this book are as much historical as they are theoretical. I am as invested in documenting the remarkable cultural activity of queer Latinas/os who coalesced in the publicity of performance during the 1990s and early 2000s as I am in arguing for the critical praxis this cultural activity constitutes as conceptualizations of and interventions in the social and political realms of the United States. For these reasons, I attend to the political economies that these particular performances emerge from and engage, the strategies of communication they model, and the theories of identity, community, and citizenship these practices articulate. The various case studies that comprise *Performing Queer*

Latinidad—in New York, Texas, and Arizona—provide evidence of the national spread of the material conditions and representational politics that queer Latinas/os encountered and intervened in during this period. While full coverage of the Latina/o queer national map would prove impossible, I engage a wide range of work and locations in order to position queer latinidad properly as a national phenomenon. The book is divided into two parts: one focused on arts organizations and the other on social dance clubs. I attend to the dance work of choreographer Arthur Aviles in the Hunts Point neighborhood of the Bronx (chapter 2), the art and activism collective at the Esperanza Peace and Justice Center in San Antonio, Texas (chapter 3), and dance clubs in Rochester, New York City, Austin, San Antonio, and Phoenix (chapters 4 and 5). Each of the case studies focuses on specific critical aspects of queer Latina/o life across the nation: from the difficulty of finding and instituting places to live and be together (chapter 2), and the struggle to defend Latina/o queer public culture from attacks by religious moralists or commodifiers of Latina/o culture (chapter 3), to the politics of cohabitation inside the social realm of Latina/o queer performance (chapters 4 and 5).

At every turn I argue that performance became an important vehicle for queer Latinas/os who negotiated what anthropologist Micaela di Leonardo has termed the "new landscapes of inequality" or the "immense social suffering" occasioned by neoliberal economics and policies in the United States.[8] Each of the cities I visit in this study experienced significant changes in its economic, political, and cultural landscapes between the 1990s and early 2000s. After a period of national urban renewal begun in the mid-1960s when these cities attempted to delay rapid suburbanization and the violence of civil rights turmoil with architectural facelifts halted with the early 1980s recession, cities entered a period of degentrification or the devaluation of gentrified property built in expectation of growth. By the 1990s, following within the national trend, all of them struggled with diminishing sources of revenue, strategic adjustments and development programs geared toward addressing income shortages, and a growing dependency on competitively attracting investments by pitching their assets to investors. At the same time, each of these cities saw the growth and diversification of the Latina/o population. These new conditions encountered very particular local contexts as each locale negotiated histories of economic, political, social, and cultural relations that shaped the ascendancy of latinidad and its potential queering in a myriad of different ways. My reference to the "new" or "recent" nature of these arrangements and inequalities is not meant to suggest a detachment from history. In fact, history governs my understanding of the theoretical and practical innovations Latina/o queer performance introduces throughout this book.

As I write in the year 2011, the temporal specificity of this study focuses my analysis in what we may term the recent past. However, I argue that there are important connections to earlier historical precedents in the social and cultural phenomena that I attend to in this book. I take heed from performance scholar David Román's observations that "contemporary performance is itself already embedded in a historical archive of past performances."[9] For example, my interpretation of the 2010 Latina/o Pride Picnic at Humboldt Park above can only account for the significance of the event as intervention when placed in perspective relative to the history of economic and political struggle of the Puerto Rican and Latina/o communities in Chicago. It also must consider their employed strategies and aesthetics for engagement, the heteronormativity of antigentrification activism in the neighborhood, and the historical marginalization of queers from the broader public articulation of Latina/o community and family. The recurrence to the flags as a space-claiming strategy relies on the significance of ethno-national iconographies as repertoires of resistance to assimilation in the transmigrated context of the U.S. city. The onstage presentations are equally in conversation with Latina/o and queer performance traditions from popular music to cabaret performance.

These past performance histories, however, need not always be explicitly acknowledged or valued by participants, both performers and audiences, in order for their enactments to offer significant pleasures and effects in the very moment they unravel. Many participants in Orgullo en Acción event and the performance sites I visit throughout this book present a keen awareness of history. However, not all participants in the event are motivated in their participation by a knowledge of or emphasis on these historical contexts. In some instances it could be argued that the pleasure of being among peers during the elsewhere in time and space created by the event as performance constitutes a conscious escape from the very contexts that structure my critical analysis and evaluation of the picnic. That is, the communicative force of the performance event, while depending on an assumed familiarity with the historically significant signs and symbols employed, may be also garnered from the social situation it constitutes in the present. Performance's value, I suggest, relies as much on its historical reach as it does on its investment in the present as deeply embodied and social experience.[10]

While I reach back from the recent past to earlier historical contexts and performances, I also contend that the approaches to engaging queer latinidad modeled in this study offer useful entry points to the analysis of Latina/o queer and other cultural practices beyond the particular period and locations of the book's frame. The material, representational, and affective economies articulated below and addressed throughout this book as constituting aspects of queer latinidad are likely to remain critical components of how Latina/o queers and other groups institute community at other times and in other places. However, I do not mean this model to be prescriptive of a predictable futurity for queer latinidad. Instead I offer approximations to the study of this constantly evolving public culture that attends to the emergence of Latinas/os into an increasingly influential economic and political collective while accounting for the disappointing patterns of recent history. In this sense, the public circulation of aspirations and expectations about Latinas/os and the backlashes it prompted from conservative nationalism in the United States during the 1980s, were repeated with refined and reinforced precision in the 1990s, and then again in the early 2000s. Similar patterns have characterized the emergence and circulation of queer subjectivities in the United States.

This pattern of emergence and conflict demands a turn to performance that is as aware of its spatiotemporal specificity as it is of its reiterative force. For instance, it is the constancy of the pushback by Puerto Rican activists in Humboldt Park, and not the totality of a successfully completed single strategy or gesture, that has retained or delayed gentrification's westward push in Chicago. Similarly, it is the traditions of flag waving and space claiming in the Humboldt Park community, as well as the historical antecedents of "gay pride" celebrations popularized throughout the United States in commemoration of the 1969 Stonewall riots in New York City, that inform and fuel the Latina/o queer claims on public space that the Orgullo en Acción event performs annually.[11] "We're here" as the rallying statement of the Facebook invitation reperforms the claims to space and to presence of the "We're here, we're queer" affirmative slogan as much as the "We're here. We're not going anywhere" chant of the antigentrification and immigrant rights movements. Thus, the repetition of performance techniques and their accompanying insight and emotional force, especially Latina/o cultural repertoires explicitly cited and variously queered by the cultural actors introduced in this study, informs my interconnection of past contexts and performances to the specific case studies discussed in this book.

Latin Explosions, Pink Dollars, and Conservative Pushback

During the period that comprises this study, representations of Latinas/os proliferated in far-ranging venues from popular music and film to news media and museum exhibitions. Popularly referred to as the "Latin Boom" or the "Latin Explosion," the mid-1990s into the early 2000s marked the largest gain in mainstream market share for Latina/o pop culture in commercial media in the United States. It also saw dramatic growth in the Latina/o population, incremental influence and gains in local and national electoral races, and the development of a national Latina/o niche market for media, goods, and services. However, the rhetoric of Latina/o rise into national prominence was not unique to this period. In fact, the focus on the Latina/o community as "booming" or "exploding" in the United States could be described as a recapitulation of the story of Latina/o ascendancy previously circulated under the "Decade of the Hispanic" label in the 1980s.[12] The eponymous naming of the 1980s as Hispanic or as belonging to Hispanics sought to mark the growth in the Latina/o population of the United States. In doing so it forecast political and economic adjustments or opportunities posited to the multicultural image of the nation under the Jimmy Carter presidency and the market growth needs of U.S. corporations. At the same time the "Decade of the Hispanic" sounded a warning to the nation about the Hispanic Other rising from within. This fear was turned into the increased xenophobia materialized in legislative and activist measures of the Right, but also into the opportunism of corporate interests that exploited both the labor and the consumer markets Latinas/os represented without much regard for their quality of life or dignity.

The 1980s precedent to the 1990s Latin Explosion has much to teach us of the multiple interests invested in the definition, management, and exploitation of *lo latino*.[13] It also presents a key historical antecedent to the conceptual figuration of Latinas/os as both the future of the nation and its purported demise. The origin of the phrase "Decade of the Hispanic" has been attributed to a comment by Maria Elena Toraño cited in a 1978 *U.S. News and World Report* story about the push by the His-

panic Congressional Caucus for more Latina/o federal government officials in the Carter administration. Toraño, a Cuban-American entrepre-
neur and Carter appointee to the Community Services Administration,
predicted that while Latinas/os had historically suffered from "a lack of
leadership," the 1980s would be their moment to rise and make claims
on the nation.[14] In this sense, the "Decade of the Hispanic" aspired to
develop Latina/o political power through direct appeal to governmental
institutions. Interestingly, the phrase has also been credited to an early
1980s niche-marketing campaign for the Adolph Coors Company. As
the conservative family-owned brewery settled employment discrimination charges from Latina/o and African-American communities and a
boycott from labor unions, it launched an unprecedented and expensive
public relations campaign designed to save the company's prestige and
expand its share of the market in the growing Latina/o community.[15] The
corporation's mobilization of a Latina/o market is here the result of a
remediation strategy designed to at once avoid litigation and evaluate a
potential consumer base. The circulation of the story of Latina/o emergence broadcasts growth under the logic of corporate capital gain.

The concurrence of Latina/o mainstream political aspirations and
corporate interests in prognosticating the story of "Hispanic" arrival into
the realm of the national during the 1980s depended on a rhetorical discourse of growth and potentiality that situated latinidad as an imminent
futurity. The 1980 census data inaugurated the use of Hispanic as an official category for identification and corroborated the story of dramatic
growth of the Latina/o population.[16] The increase in the "Hispanic"
population allowed activists like Toraño and corporations like Coors to
validate their claims and influence the design of business or lobbying
plans directed at Latinas/os.[17] The 1980s marks the birth of an intimate
relationship between Latina/o politics and corporate sponsorship that
set not only the infrastructure but the rhetoric of market growth that fueled the Latin Explosion of the 1990s.

The announcement of a second Latina/o arrival during the 1990s,
made more spectacular by the frenzied coverage of the Latin music explosion and its spread into all aspects of corporate media, further consolidated the enduring and growing presence of the Latina/o population in
the United States.[18] The Latin Explosion continued the story of Latina/o
"entry" into the nation but raised the stakes by centering Latinas/os further as commodities in the broader national popular culture. Selena,
Ricky Martin, Jennifer Lopez, Marc Anthony, Salma Hayek, Enrique Igle-

sias, Shakira, and many other artists saw their careers in popular music, film, and television skyrocket during this period and became household names across a diverse demographic that far exceeded Latina/o-specific markets. Despite cultural critic Licia Fiol-Matta's appropriate warning that the Latin Explosion "was primarily a media event, a product carefully tailored to fit the American market and to buttress American cultural supremacy globally, in the guise of diversity and multiculturalism," it was also during the 1990s and into the early 2000s when Latinas/os in the United States became a measurable and palpable reality in the everyday life of most Americans.[19] The sheer growth and dispersal of the Latina/o population and the media attention provided by the explosion made quotidian exchanges with Latinas/os routine across the nation.

This second arrival of Latinas/os into the mainstream was also accompanied by a reinvigorated xenophobic and anti-immigrant backlash that sought to protect a revived USAmerican exclusionary nationalism. Right-wing anti-immigration groups argued that immigrants were stealing jobs and draining resources from U.S. citizens. Anti-immigrant groups and government officials like the Light Up the Border and Governor Pete Wilson of California in the 1990s and the Minute Men and Maricopa County, Arizona, sheriff Joe Arpaio in the early 2000s organized highly mediatized campaigns that honed the rhetorical approaches that would fuel the public anger against undocumented immigrants and aggressive legislative measures during the 1990s and well into the first decade of the twenty-first century.[20] Most notably, the 1994 Propositon 187 in California sought to deny public benefits to undocumented immigrants and Arizona's SB 1070 (2010) attempted even harsher measures that included the legalization of state police intervention in matters of border security and immigration.[21] While both measures were defeated or weakened through legal or political challenges, their influence in the national discourse and policy about Latinas/os continues to be significant. Over the fifteen years of history reflected in this study, anti-immigrant sentiments and practices specifically targeted at Latinas/os offered a sobering counterpoint to the hip-swaying, percussive rhythms, and glittery sexuality of the Latin Explosion stars.

Queer communities encountered similar degrees of commoditization and attack in the United States. Coming straight out of the 1980s struggles with the AIDS pandemic, the beginning of the 1990s saw a motivated and increasingly organized queer activism coalescing around demands for medical research and services, fighting against homophobic discriminatory measures imposed under the pigeonholing of all gay men as potentially infectious, and outrage at the lack of governmental action on behalf of the community.[22] The networks of care and activism developed around AIDS during the 1980s, in part critical reactivations of early queer activism in the 1970s, provided the infrastructure through which queers in the 1990s made broader claims as a political community. However, the efforts of grassroots organizations focused primarily at the local and regional levels were overshadowed by the emergence into prominence of a highly visible national network of organizations. Groups like the Gay and Lesbian Advocates and Defenders (GLAD), Gay and Lesbian Alliance Against Defamation (GLAAD), Human Rights Campaign (HRC), and Lambda Legal—all founded in the 1970s or early 1980s—catapulted into the national scene as the institutionalized voice of queer politics in the early 1990s. By the mid-1990s they consolidated into a visible national cluster of organizations governed by corporate-style boards. While the work of these organizations to defend basic civil rights for lesbian, gay, bisexual, transgender, and queer folk in areas of employment, housing, education, and public accommodations and the community's representation in popular media has been significant, the orientation of their politics have been suspiciously aligned to a neoliberal logic of capitalist citizenship. These politics have often been more focused on the development of consumer identities over attention to the macro- and microeconomic obstacles to the fair and ethical distribution of rights and resources.

Similar to the story of Latina/o emergence, queer communities became identified as a niche market.[23] The "pink dollar," or queer purchasing power, became the preferred currency of transaction for corporate and governmental interests in the hunt for the largely mythologized expendable income of affluent gays and lesbians. As the queer community became increasingly visible in the public sphere through media saturation in television, film, and popular culture, the narrative of queer mainstreaming or homonormativity came to the fore. Homonormativity, as queer theorist Lisa Duggan explains, is "a politics that does not contest dominant heteronormative assumptions and institutions, but upholds and sustains them, while promising the possibility of a demobilized gay constituency and a privatized, depoliticized gay culture anchored in domesticity and consumption"[24] It assumes the goals of a gay politics to be largely dependent on the standards of heteropatriarchal capitalism and its definitions of "the good American life." The politics of queer mainstreaming, focused as they are on the institutions of marriage, the military, the corporation, and the media networks, became the primary objective of the national gay movement from the 1990s and into the twenty-first century. Much like how the Latin Explosion paraded its cast of celebrities as evidence of an arrival into the realm of the national, queer celebrities, from Ellen DeGeneres and Rosie O'Donnell to Elton John and Neil Patrick Harris, signaled a mainstream queer presence in the nation's public sphere. In television, the increased visibility of gays and lesbians in shows like *Will and Grace, Queer Eye for the Straight Guy,* and more recently *Glee* and *RuPaul's Drag Race* presented a view of gays and lesbians as key figures in the commoditization of lifestyle and aesthetics for both queer and straight folk alike. However, the glossy veneer of queerness in popular media during the period of this study parallels the case of the Latin Explosion in a less festive manner.

Despite attempts at mainstreaming the political ambitions of queer politics to be in alignment with the values of the nation, including marriage and the military, queer politics received sobering compromises and pushbacks in the form of legislative measures and mandates like the "Don't Ask Don't Tell" policy in the military in 1993 and the Defense of Marriage Act (DOMA) in 1996.[25] The period also saw the reawakening of an aggressive antigay movement comprised of religious conservatives intent on stalling what they saw as the potential takeover of the Christian-Protestant nation by homosexual depravity.[26] Fed by the hysteria of AIDS phobia cultivated since the 1980s and reinforced by emboldening successes in influencing electoral politics, the religious Right pressured legislators at local, state, and national levels and demonstrated against the recognition of rights for gays and lesbians and the representation of sexuality in the arts, media, and public culture.[27] As queers circulated in mainstream media and in everyday life as standards of consumer identity, their detractors found fodder to strengthen their opposition. The antigay activism of conservative organizations became increasingly professionalized, drawing on the very strategies for mass communication modeled by corporate America and developing a cadre of lawyers, lobbyists, and legislators ready to pursue homosexuality across the nation.[28] In the same way the Latin Explosion shared space with rising anti-immigrant sentiments, queer ascendancy into popular culture encountered a highly organized and hostile antigay movement.

In attending to queer latinidad in the United States during the 1990s and early 2000s, *Performing Queer Latinidad* traverses the historical trajectories of ascendancy into the national public sphere and the conservative pushback that sought to prevent both queer and Latina/o communities from "exploding" into the nation. Key to my analysis is the understanding that in the lived experience of queer Latinas/os, queerness and latinidad have rarely occupied separate spheres. What might on the surface read as parallel accounts across a shared timeline are overlapping and intersecting materialities, intimacies, and frictions that render the focus on a single identitarian or communal category at best partial and at worst simply misleading. There is ample evidence of historical precedents to the presence of Latinas/os within mainstream and even elite queer culture in the United States. These include the often forgotten presence of Puerto Ricans at the Stonewall riots and the significant influence of Latinas/os on queer cultural production from disco music to the artwork of Keith Haring, Andy Warhol, and Madonna.[29] Similarly, the archives of specifically Latina/o queer social and cultural scenes across the United States have been the focus of work in the academic fields of Latina/o studies and queer studies.[30] However, it was not until the 1990s that the Latin Explosion became a central commodity for pink dollar purchasers. The rise in influence of Latina/o queer cultural production permeated mainstream queer culture during this period. Nowhere was this presence more palpable than in the nightclub scenes I attend to in chapters 4 and 5. From the enduring presence of Latin rhythm and choreography in the soundscapes and choreoscapes of urban nightlife to the proliferation of Latina/o characters in queer theater, film, and television, queer latinidad became a key aesthetic to queer culture during this period. As cultural studies scholar José Quiroga has observed, Latin toys circulated extensively within the mainstream queer 1990s—from the "anatomically correct" Carlos doll (the Latina/o companion to Billy who was sold at gay bookstores and novelty stores nationwide) to Ricky Martin, who before his coming out in 2010 was already regarded as queer celebrity and commodity nationwide.[31] Similarly, queer Latinas/os engaged mainstream queer cultural productions in circulation at the time, often turning to rainbow flags and pink dollars to exercise their own queerness.

From the 1990s onward, queer Latinas/os experienced both the proliferation of commodified queerness and latinidad and the reinvigoration of anti-immigrant and antigay activism and policy. They traversed Latina/o, queer, and queer Latina/o geographies shaped by the multiple pleasures and frictions, interests and necessities that shaped their lives. These worlds were at times brought violently together as the rapid transformation of urban environments throughout the country pitted working-class Latinas/os pushed out from gentrifying neighborhoods against upwardly mobile queers touted as key agents of urban renewal.[32] Not all queers were welcomed in the slick urban renewal either. For example, the transformation of New York City into a family entertainment mecca during the 1990s forced venues of queer public social and sexual exchange outside of the city core. Arguably, this is also the time when inter-Latina/o relations and cultural influences rose to new levels as changes in the national demographic, mediatic, and political maps of the United States increasingly bridged communities and enabled new collective identities to emerge.

Intersections on the Ground

The panethnic cultural affinities this book documents result from shifts in the makeup of the U.S. Latina/o population over the past two decades. These shifts are due in large part to the diversification of the national, ethnic, and racial composition of communities of Latin American descent in the United States. Since the 1980s new migratory waves from the Dominican Republic and Central and South America have begun to interact with older settlement communities of Mexicans, Puerto Ricans, and Cubans in ethnic enclaves at the country's major urban areas. These inter-Latina/o connections also result from the ongoing dispersal of the Latina/o population from historical settlement areas to other regions of the country, including suburban and rural geographies and the American South, and the emergence of commercial, media, and political networks addressing this large segment of the population (the largest minority aggregate population in the country as reported in the 2000 census). These changes have resulted not only in gained political clout and cultural visibility for Latinas/os but in new social and cultural formations as Latinas/os of increasingly diverse backgrounds negotiate their lives together.

Contemporary approaches to the Latina/o population by popular media in the United States have generally assumed that these intersections lead to a coherent and easily identifiable social group whose collective behaviors or opinions can be predicted or swayed.[33] Such a view is most evident in corporate marketing and political campaigning strategies employed across the nation throughout the 1990s. The identification of what marketing experts label as a "niche market" and political strategists a "voting bloc" operates by the assumption that all Latinas/os share the same values, interests, and cultural traits. Media and political strategists use essentialized notions/descriptions of latinidad in promotional materials ranging from television, radio, and print advertising to political campaign rhetoric in order to secure the successful sale of a product, candidate, or legislative measure.[34] A cursory survey of the representations these courtships of a Latina/o public circulate shows the overwhelming emphasis on an imagined, aspirationally middle-class, light-skinned, heterosexual, and reproductive family unit. Erased from this imagined public image are Latinas/os of a darker hue, those with less mainstreamed class aesthetics, those with queer sexual or gender identities, and those who participate in alternative kinship configurations.

I further contend that Latina/o studies as an academic field of inquiry has followed similar suit for its own particular goals. Attempting to establish latinidad as a viable research agenda and unit of coalitional political mobilization has often led to facile generalizations of what in fact constitutes this "new" American demographic. A "light brown" identity and its formation in the history of *mestizaje* has become the dominant paradigm of inquiry for understanding a population with a much more diverse profile of racial and ethnic experience that includes both historical and contemporary Afro-diasporic and indigenous experiences.[35] The reproductive heterosexual family on which the narrative mixture of *mestizaje* depends has been established as the center of research in the field. Queerness has traditionally remained at the margins of this definition.[36] Alternatively, queer studies as a field of inquiry in U.S. academia has rarely approached Latina/o subject matter.[37]

Performing Queer Latinidad argues against the homogenizing and often normative assumptions of a Latina/o public but does not do away with the potential of latinidad as an intersectional category that might bring diverse groups together under a shared, if partial, ethnic imaginary. In fact, it argues that these intersections are already part and parcel of the experience of queer latinidad in the United States. Attending to the embodied acts of performance culture, this book models a focus on on-the-ground quotidian manifestations of latinidad that highlight the ways in which this social category is emergent and lived in local contexts. More specifically, this study examines embodied expressive practices that articulate latinidad to queer ends. It advocates for an understanding of the critical intersections of sexual, gender, racial, and ethnic identities as a growing and critical element of Latina/o experience in the United States. Additionally, *Performing Queer Latinidad* comments on the overwhelming focus on a Latina/o middle class in corporate, political, and entertainment media by highlighting the ways queer latinidad in the United States has been historically constituted and presently grounded in working-class aesthetics and sensibilities.

My approach to the sites of performance discussed throughout this book combines scholarly theories with vernacular concepts articulated within the expressive practices under question. I document and describe public spaces where both latinidad and queerness were being constituted in new and significant ways during the 1990s and early 2000s. It is in the particular articulation of nonnormative sexualities and ethnicity together that I argue Latina/o queer performance imagines and practices new social formations and modes of being in the world. In attending to these critical imaginaries I identify the historical and contemporary contexts of each performance. I also pursue the theoretical and political interventions that emerge from these practices. I prioritize the knowledge produced by and within performance, what I term theories in practice. I focus my analysis on conceptual categories that originate from the performances themselves and explanations and testimonies by artists and participants. Theories in practice refer to situated forms of knowing that emerge from live embodied contexts, what Chicana feminist writer Cherríe Moraga terms "theories in the flesh."[38] While Moraga's term authorizes historical experience as a critical component of our orientation to the world, the concept of theories in practice also pursues the generative world-making power of performance. By theories in practice I seek to identify and define the enfleshments and experiences produced in laboring together in the shared time-space of performance. This does not represent a refusal of traditional conceptions of theory as an exercise of rational thinking but proposes a model that privileges the body and its actions as conduits of knowledge about the world. It is in the acts of performance that I situate both the theory and the potential interventions queer latinidad can make in the public sphere at large. These theories in practice have been culled from a decade of observation as an ethnographer, spectator, participant, and at times collaborator in the artistic, political, and academic projects that I describe in this book.

Performing Queer Latinidad offers a multisited ethnographic portrait of queer latinidad as it manifested in performance during the 1990s and

early 2000s. I draw my evidence from extensive formal and informal interviews conducted with artists, activists, and social dancers with whom
I have interacted in these spaces, from the material culture of the various
field sites, and from archival documentation of the performances I address here in the form of video and audio recordings, scripts, and photo-
graphs. However, it is primarily in my interactions with members of the
communities where I document most successfully the thoughts and feelings, concepts, and techniques that govern participation in Latina/o queer
performance. I follow an approach to the ethnography of performance
grounded in the exemplary work of the late Dwight Conquergood, who
proposed we enter the research situation not as participant observers but
as "co-performative witnesses."[39] For Conquergood, as well as for me,
the labor of research requires embodied participation in and attentive
witnessing to the performance events before us. It demands an orientation to the social exchanges that constitute ethnographic engagement
as performance. In pursuing my research for this book co-performance
has meant cohabitation in communities that were or became also my
own. Because the queer Latina/o social scenes I research in this study are
also the sites where I as a queer Latino sought my own social, cultural,
and emotional replenishment during the fifteen years of researching and
writing this project, I have danced along with others, both in the literal
sense of partnering on the dance floor and in the sense of being attuned
bodily and emotionally to those around me. In this sense, the theories I
bring into my analysis have been practices in performance; experienced,
learned, and felt on my own body.

Each chapter in this book identifies, documents, and analyzes a specific theory in practice. I argue for the concepts of home, hope, utopia,
and friction respectively as approximations to the vernacular knowledges
of performance by the artists, activists, and social dancers whose lives
and work I discuss in the pages that follow. Taken individually, none of
these concepts offers a universally applicable theory of queer latinidad.
The value of each of these conceptions lies in its specificity. However,
taken together, the theories in practice I outline here offer an engagement with queer latinidad that is attentive to the range of experiences,
material conditions, and creative strategies that characterize contemporary Latina/o USA. These theories in practice are not the only ways
into the analysis of Latina/o queer sociality during this period either.
For example, as Latina/o studies scholar Deborah Paredez demonstrates
in her analysis of popular music performer Selena Quintanilla, mourn-

ing may also serve as a mode of engagement for Latina/o collectivities.[40] In approaching Latina/o queer performance I also recur to contemporary theories in cultural studies, performance studies, Latina/o studies, feminism, and queer studies. While these areas of academic inquiry have been historically committed to the critical understanding of identity, beginning in the late 1990s they turned to less definitive notions of group culture by referencing affect as an equally powerful element of collective experience. José E. Muñoz's writings on Latina/o affect suggest, following Raymond Williams, that there is a "structure of feeling," resulting from Latina/o ways of being, that might bridge communities-in-difference. He argues, "What unites and consolidates oppositional groups is not simply the fact of identity but the way in which they perform affect, especially in relation to an official 'national affect' that is aligned with a hegemonic class."[41] Latinidad is presented here less as a programmatic political articulation and more as a performative modality that counteracts the negative marking of Latina/o cultural practice as outside the realm of the nation. While latinidad seeks to coalesce without erasing the trajectories and histories of specific groups, these encounters are not always achieved in neutral grounds or without conflicts resulting from those very different specificities. Moving away from a notion of identity as the end-all of individual and collective experience, I consider how affect compels social actors to specific practices or desires without requiring absolute fidelity to an anchoring script. For example, a social actor might enter the space of performance called by a particular investment in Latina/o musical practice or desirous of queer companionship without having to formulate any particular loyalty or politics to any such category. Just the notion of satisfying such an interest or desire, feeling good through participation in a specific event, or sharing in the collective mourning of a public figure or even political effort, might offer a social actor an experience in queer latinidad that remains at the level of feelings without landing in the narrative of identity. Home, hope, utopia, and friction, I argue, allow us to approach some of the contours of this affective economy. From the 1990s and into the early 2000s, queer Latinas/os developed personal and collective dispositions about themselves and their environment based on their ability to be in shared time and space (home) immersed in the possibilities (hope) of experiencing being together in the moment of performance (utopia) despite the pressures, risks, and conflicts that governed the very likelihood of their assembly as well as their interactions within (friction). It is precisely these affective economies that I argue lead to the Latina/o queer public sphere I discuss below. I do not suggest doing away with identity as a focus of analysis but propose affect as a parallel realm through which identity may or may not manifest itself. That said, my goal is to document the circumstances out of which a Latina/o queer affect arises. I supplement my inquiry with a careful contextualization of performance sites in relation to both contemporary lived experience and the historical past. I situate these practices and their governing logics within the broader scenario of contemporary USAmerican culture.[42]

Critical Triangulations

Latino/Queer/Performance

The three key terms that comprise the title of this book—Latina/o, queer, performance—map a circuitry of activities and practices of world-making that are geographically and politically complex. As I will explain below, the social and cultural categories, the identities, imaginaries, and affects assumed within umbrella terms such as queerness or latinidad are ever-expansive and in the process of becoming. Performance as an object of study allows a snapshot of moments when these social and cultural coordinates are at play in particular contexts. And yet the notion of what these concepts encompass can never be fully arrested much less narrated in absolute terms. Much like performance itself, queerness and latinidad evade ossification or fixity. *Performing Queer Latinidad* is less invested in cataloging identity banners than in approximating the worlds that identities and affects, in performance, might make possible. I bring the reader close to the action, understanding this proximity to be partial, even elusive.

Latina/o

In my usage throughout this book the term "Latina/o" refers to populations of Latin American descent born, currently residing, or with a history of residence in the United States. In proposing this definition I adjust performance scholar Diana Taylor's own defintion, which includes only U.S.-born Latinas/os and foreign-born Latin Americans "living permanently in the United States."[43] I do so in order to account for the increasingly circular patterns of migration from Latin America that have brought large numbers of temporary visitors in proximity to settled Latina/o communities. Additionally, I heed sociologist Juan Flores's recent account of the diaspora's return and its cultural remittances to places of origin.[44] Latinidad, in turn, refers to the ethnic and panethnic imaginaries, identities, and affects that emerge from the increased intersection of multiple Latina/o communities. If, as literary scholar Paul Allatson has surmised, ethnicity "designates the set of characteristics (cultural practices and traditions, language, shared ancestry, religion, national or regional origin or location) that combine to define or identify a particular group,"[45] panethnicity points to new intersections among previously constituted ethnicities, as provisional as these might be, that result in an expanded notion of community based on perceived common interests or desires. Latinidad articulates such a point of contact between Latinas/os of diverse backgrounds who find themselves increasingly sharing common cultural material and lived experiences, be it from representations in media—produced in the United States or imported from Latin American sources—or from actual physical proximity to one another in places of work, residence, religious practice, or leisure.

There is as well a material history to the emergence of Latina/o as a category that needs to be accounted for in this narrative and that places inter-Latina/o connection beyond a simple narrative of cultural affinity. Latinidad cannot be properly addressed without attending to the political economies that have shaped both the living conditions of Latinas/os living in the United States and their available strategies for making sustainable and pleasurable lives. These conditions have been significantly shaped by the increased reconfiguration of world economies through globalization. Globalization serves as an umbrella term for a large variety of changes shaped by the worldwide reorganization of financial, political, and cultural infrastructures that have characterized late capitalism at the end of the twentieth century. These changes can be primarily attributed to the neoliberalization of the world economy.[46] Brought about by policies of financial deregulation, technological advancement in manufacturing, the rise of information technologies, and the increased reliability and affordability of transportation networks, this economic model has resulted in "the rapid and massive movement of capital, goods, people, ideas, institutions and images across the globe."[47]

The rapid growth of the Latin American–descent population in the United States is in large measure caused by the shifts in the world economy since the early 1980s. But they are also the result of an older, yet equally global, history of U.S. interventionism in the economic and political affairs of Latin American nations.[48] Both historically and in the contemporary, these interventions have been driven by an interest in securing consumer markets, labor forces, and natural resources for transnational corporations.[49] The resulting instability created by this uneven economic development[50] and unstable political infrastructures has especially affected indigenous, black, and working-class communities who find it increasingly difficult to gain access to the skills and technologies necessary to participate fairly in the global economy at home. While some regions have benefited economically from an influx of manufacturing jobs, especially *maquiladora*-style assembly plants along the U.S.-Mexico border and elsewhere, the overall impact has resulted in skyrocketing gains for the elite and the devastation of farming and other entrepreneurial sectors that have been flooded with competition from primarily U.S.-based transnational business. Labor conditions in the receiving ends of the global manufacturing networks have deteriorated significantly leading to largely exploitative conditions under NAFTA and other free trade agreements. Large groups of disenfranchised communities have become nomadic, traveling from town to city and abroad in search of opportunities to make their living.

Latinidad also results from contemporary patterns of migration and settlement—Mexicans in New York and Puerto Ricans in Austin, for example—which have significantly altered what were previously perceived as homogenous concentrations of diasporic or border communities. The settlement patterns of the three largest Latina/o populations in the United States remained generally stable until the early 1990s: Mexicans in the Southwest, Puerto Ricans in the Northeast, and Cubans in the Southeast. However, these patterns have begun to shift. The Latina/o population in New York City, for example, was primarily Puerto Rican until the 1980s. Mass migrations from the Dominican Republic changed the composition of this population significantly. More recently, Mexican settlement in the city has increased dramatically as well. As measured by the 2000 census, the Mexican population in New York skyrocketed almost 50 percent over ten years, from 4.9 percent of the total Latina/o population in 1990 to 9.1 percent by 2000.[51] Preliminary reports from the 2010 census demonstrate that this pattern has not only held but precipitated. In the case of Florida, the growth of the Puerto Rican, Mexican, and Central American population has been so rapid that by the 2004 presidential election the *New York Times* and other mainstream publications had begun to speculate about their impact on the assumed Republican-leaning Cuban voting bloc.[52] Similar trends can be observed in large cities throughout the United States, with new settlement patterns also bringing increasingly diverse Latina/o populations into new regions such as the South, Midwest, and the Great Plains. In Chicago the Latina/o population has been historically constituted as a dynamic intersection of Latina/o origins, with Mexicans and Puerto Ricans being the largest, where eth-nonational identities intermingle and at times collide.[53]

Because latinidad in the United States is so closely tied to global historical and contemporary connections, the commonalities called forth by the term "latinidad" are in need of further qualification. As both Diana Taylor and queer theorist Juana María Rodríguez explain in their respective works, there are a multitude of differences and interests that must be considered when assuming such a collective banner. In her introduction to the first critical collection devoted to a joint examination of Latina/o and Latin American performance, Taylor proposes "Latin/o America" as a category that explores "the historical, political, ideological, and artistic connections between these areas that all but disappear when we divide them in two, oppositional blocks."[54] This intersection is immensely fruitful, as it acknowledges within its realm the circuitries enabled by travel, media, and other forms of cultural sharing that continue to connect Latinas/os to Latin American communities to date. Rodríguez also extends her definition of latinidad beyond the U.S. national boundaries. She proposes a model of latinidad based on philosophers Gilles Deleuze and Félix Guattari's concept of the rhizome whereby the identitarian and expressive possibilities of this label emerge and regenerate from multiple sites and influences without having to yield a coherent narrative or trajectory.[55] Based on this understanding, latinidad is about "the 'dimensions' or 'the directions in motion' of history and culture and geography and language and self-named identities."[56] Rodríguez arrives at this processual, dynamic definition after accounting for the myriad of differences (from race to language to differences in migration and citizenship conditions) that interfere in the constitution of Latina/o unity in the United States and beyond. Most importantly, both Taylor and Rodríguez remark upon the shared histories of colonialism and neocolonialism (including slavery) from Spain, Portugal, and the United States as experiences that have shaped power differentials across a multiplicity of axes but which may constitue one of the central points of intersection for both Latinas/os and Latin Americans within and outside the United States.

Similarly concerned with the shared experiences of colonization that latinidad encompasses, performance theorist Alicia Arrizón turns the term into a political strategy where a "strong, positive group identity—one that recognizes and embraces heterogeneity" might aid in "escaping the shackles of colonized subjectivity."[57] Cultural theorist Alberto Sandoval-Sánchez also embraces the promise of a relational politics offered by latinidad in affecting social change. Identifying latinidad as an agentive gesture markedly different from the commercially oriented practice of what he labels Latinization, Sandoval-Sánchez observes, "'Latinization' differs from 'Latinidad' in that the latter results from Latina/o agency and interventions when U.S. Latinas/os articulate and construct cultural expressions and identity formations that come from a conscious political act of self-affirmation."[58] Both authors go on to present examples of Latina/o theater and performance where latinidad figures as strategically counterdiscursive relative to the homogenizing machinations of an oppressive U.S. state or culture. Understood in this way, latinidad produces a mark of heterogeneity against the erasure of difference by dominant discourses in U.S. corporate and political media, which tend to bundle up Latinas/os into undifferentiated and often stereotypical masses.

Frances Aparicio encourages the decolonial[59] orientation of latinidad and warns against simple dichotomies in positioning its potential gestures. She defines latinidad as "a concept that allows us to explore moments of convergences and divergences in the formation of Latina/o (post)colonial subjectivities and hybrid cultural expressions among various Latina/o subjectivities."[60] This move is critical. It allows us to attend to both positively construed intersections and the tensions, misunderstandings, and frictions that emerge from inter- and intra-Latina/o encounters. Additionally, Aparicio's turn to latinidad in all its complexities articulates the ways in which Latinas/os are both resistant to and at times complicitous with dominant positions of power. For example, Latinas/os may contribute to stereotypical representations in the media at the same time that they consume those representations strategically to different ends. Aligning myself with the open-endedness and multifarious nature of latinidad, I examine its material presence in particular queer communities, including instances of disagreement and dissent.

Latinidad highlights the process-based nature of identity and articulates the ways in which identitarian categories are both social constructs and performative effects of cultural practice.[61] That is, latinidad is an identity-in-process and it is through serial acts like the performances (theatrical and quotidian) that I examine in this book that it becomes an approachable, although fluid, position. A central tenet of this book is that although cultural interconnectedness results from the discursive practices of dominant institutions such as corporate media or national political rhetoric, it also arises from on-the-ground exchanges among Latinas/os in the United States. In following Aparicio's exhortation to understand the "moments of convergences and divergences," I undoubtedly prioritize performance as a category of cultural activity where latinidad is manifest both as representational force and as immediate lived experience. Communications scholar Angharad V. Valdivia has explained that "if we understand Latinidad to mean the set of practices and subjectivities that cohere, albeit dynamically and temporarily in relation to a range of Latina/o peoples and their histories and experiences, then once more we are right back at the point where we must consider historical and regional specificity."[62] The ethnographic mode of analysis adopted throughout this book furthers such a strategy as I look at the material and contextual specifities from which latinidad is performed. Moreover, I posit that practices of latinidad may be further enabled by queer identification.

Queer

I use the term "queer" to refer to sexual and gender identities and practices that operate outside the logic of normative heterosexuality. This umbrella category brings under its banner gays, lesbians, bisexuals, transexuals, S-M practitioners, among other sexual and gender practices. In her survey of linguistic references to queer sexuality and gender among Latinas/os, Rodríguez demonstrates that there exists a vast and ever-growing number of discourses, used both colloquially and academically, that seek to name these practices and desires from specifically Latina/o contexts. *Divas, atrevidas, entendidas, tortillera, buchota, marimacha, mariquita, maricón, vestida, papi* are but a few of the words she identifies as currently in circulation. These namings have specific origins and historical usages, but they are also shared among Latinas/os who engage in acts of translation and communal pedagogies that cross such particular locations. Rodríguez further explains that "Latinas/os in the United States also make full use of English words" to name queerness.[63] Yet, the term "queer" itself as a marker of identity rarely appears as a referent in the Latina/o queer contexts I examine in this book. In this context, my usage of the term serves more as a generalizing strategy as well as a theoretical tool.

As a theory, I use queer to approximate the ways in which individuals engage, produce, and consume culture shaped by their positions as sexual and gender marginals. Thus, I assume queer as both a position and a strategy. As a position, "to be queer" describes the lived experiences, identities, desires, and affects of subjects who practice or entertain the possibility of practicing sexual or gender behaviors outside heteronormative constructs. As a strategy, "to act queer" refers to the set of practices engaged by queers themselves in their creative navigation of everyday life in a heteronormative society; although being queer is not a precondition to acting queerly. These two usages concur with queer theorist Michael Warner's statement that "queers do a kind of practical social reflection just by finding ways to be queer."[64] This book works from the premise that "finding ways to be queer" requires engaging in queer acts. Put more simply, being queer is never a completed journey but a continuous process of becoming queer that requires queer acts. These strategies may range from a queer approach to everyday practices such as dress, speech, gesture, and, of course, sex, to more formal presentations of self in public contexts such as the theater or the dance club. Queer acts may also include ways of reading or seeing the world from a queer perspective.[65] Queerness may or may not lead to more explicitly political interventions in the public sphere, but, following the important feminist edict that the personal is political, the very act of acting queerly may be construed as a political one.

I engage the open-ended promise "queer" as an analytic offers. I am also fully aware of the limitations that queer theory has historically presented to understanding the experiences of queers of colors. As I seek to articulate queerness relative to latinidad I assume performance theorist E. Patrick Johnson's "quare" strategies.[66] In his critique of queer theory, Johnson points to the overwhelming privileging of the experiences of white gays and lesbians as the focus of study and the tendency not to engage the knowledge produced by scholars of color. Most alarming still is queer theory's turn away from the materiality of experience as it races to champion a theoretical posture that deconstructs the very notion of identity as a viable project.[67] In addition to the suggestion that queer theorists pay attention to work by and about queers of color and their experiences in formulating new theoretical knowledge, Johnson also suggests a turn to theories of performance, for it "not only highlights the discursive effects of acts, it also points to how these acts are historically situated."[68] In devoting this book to Latina/o queer performance practices, I seek to focus precisely on the critical acts—the vernacular praxis Johnson calls for outside the academy—that performers are already engaged in under the rubric of queer latinidad. This is precisely the strategy undertaken in the work of theorists like Johnson, who argue for the ways in which the citationality of performance works in tandem with its experienced material grounding, and José E. Muñoz, who positions performance as a "world-making" practice by queers of color.[69] In the works of Johnson and Muñoz performance is both the theory and the doing. These are the theories in practice I call attention to in my writing. Therefore, my engagement with queerness (theoretically and materially) throughout this book centers Latina/o experience as the context from which sexuality is performed and vice versa.

Pursuing the interconnections between queerness and latinidad requires an understanding of migration and movement.[70] Queer subjects are oftentimes also traveling subjects[71] as many move away from their homes into urban centers and other locations within their own countries or venture abroad in search of "sexual freedoms."[72] For Latin American queers, travel into the United States can be motivated by their economic, political, or personal situation but also by a search for sexual liberation.[73] If gender and sexuality do not figure explicitly as a cause or motivation for migration, they still shape the itineraries as well as the obstacles through which to traverse the social realm. Queer Latinas/os struggle through the material exigencies of travel as marginals based on their ethnic, racial, and class positions and encounter, with equal intensity, the homophobia of the multiple communities through which this travel occurs. As the late sociologist Lionel Cantú Jr. concludes in his discussion of Mexican gay immigrants to the United States, arriving in a new environment and dealing with the social and economic limitations of migrancy presents particular stresses to queers, who more often than not encounter marginalization of their sexual identity at home from their families or other traditonal support structures. He explains that "sexuality influences households, the very spaces that these migrant men come to call home. And sexuality also shaped the spaces where Mexican gay men try to form communities."[74] Finding spaces in which to develop queer social relations becomes a survival strategy for queer migrants often marginalized from heterosexually oriented Latina/o (and most other) establishments and the whiteness of the mainstream queer scene in the United States.[75]

Despite marked differences between communities with imposed U.S. citizenship (Puerto Ricans), those with privileged access to it (Cubans), and others, the specter of migration shapes the perception of latinidad in the United States. Migration and travel are just as important to the lives of U.S.-born Latinas/os, even if they have never left the national, city, or town borders. In the xenophobic and anti-immigrant climate of contemporary U.S. culture—especially since the terrorist attacks to New York City's World Trade Center on September 11, 2001—all Latinas/os regardless of their citizenship status may become suspect inhabitants of the American public sphere. Being Latina/o in the United States thus implicates negotiating the assumption of criminality not just in terms of citizenship status but in reference to myriad other xenophobic, racist, and classist stereotypes and sentiments in circulation about what Latinas/os as a group are like.[76] These (mis)representations of Latinas/os as suspect citizens travel as well. They permeate and influence social spaces along with the equally mobile images, narratives, choreographies, sounds, and discourses of and about latinidad—and queerness—that move with equally powerful force through radio, television, film, print and electronic media, and embodied cultural transfers nationwide. This suggests that even when the Latina/o queer subject remains in place, she is never static.

The Latina/o queer establishments that I discuss in *Performing Queer Latinidad*—cultural centers, theaters, and dance clubs—are equally shaped by travel, but also offer important sites of arrival: home. Because of their explicit investments in Latina/o queer affect and desire, these spaces allow for a grounding, at least temporarily, for subjects at the margins of a heteronormative and white cultural geography. The cultural work that takes place in these spaces, especially those performance practices I highlight throughout this book, help displaced communities find homes, both in the sense of places of dwelling, jobs, and basic needs, and in the sense of building community. I argue that performance functions as a site where marginalized communities, such as queer Latinas/os, make home by participating in embodied experiences with others in the midst of travel to collectively devise strategies of being and being together.

Latina/o queer spaces are not always physical structures dedicated exclusively to such an identity. They are oftentimes claimed through practices of quotidian as well as activist intervention. If, as Michel de Certeau has explained, space is "actuated by the ensemble of movements deployed within it,"[77] many of the Latina/o queer spaces I explore in this book are constituted in and through performance practice. The Bronx Academy of Arts and Dance in the South Bronx, New York City, and the Esperanza Center for Peace and Justice in San Antonio, Texas, which I discuss in chapter 2 and chapter 3 respectively, are both arts organizations that rent or own a permanently dedicated space in established Latina/o neighborhoods where their identity as Latina/o queer institutions is well known. Yet performers, audience members, activists, and other participants alike must negotiate their travel back and forth from these buildings, even if just walking down the street, in ways that extend the spatial demarcations of queer latinidad well beyond the safe havens awaiting inside the architectural structures. Approaching these spaces entails a conscious dramaturgy that presents multiple alternatives. For example, I can flaunt my queerness in an act of pride or defiance, or I can choose to neutralize my walk so as not to disturb passing foot traffic by advertising my effeminate gender performance. I might instead rush my walk hoping for a quick entrance and avoiding being identified by family or neighbors. In all three instances, out of many more approaches available, I do not only choose a route that is most convenient or comfortable depending on my purpose, but I also assume a performance approach that might involve choices not only in dress and styling but in movement, gesture, and speech.

Most of the Latina/o queer dance clubs that I visit in New York City and Rochester, New York, in Austin and San Antonio, Texas (chapter 4), and in Phoenix, Arizona (chapter 5) are situated within the urban core of their respective cities, although not always near Latina/o neighborhoods, affording some anonymity and freedom for those who might not be comfortable being "out" in proximity to their communities. Nonetheless, unless you have the luxury of an automobile or live nearby, getting to these places often requires traveling via public transportation. This transitional journey between the place of living and the club requires equal awareness of quotidian dramaturgies, as the fashion codes that shape the social playfulness of the club might be differently perceived in your house, your neighborhood, the bus or train, or even down the block between the bus stop and the building's door.

But not all the queer dance clubs I visit are exclusively Latina/o either. Entering the white queer club presents a whole new set of considerations to queer Latinas/os who seek admission and at times acceptance into these privileged establishments. The choices upon arrival are many and oftentimes enacted in the space of the dance floor. As I discuss in chapter 4, some Latina/o dancers assume their choreographic practices on the dance floor as claims to the public sphere of the white queer club. For instance, I might travel across the dance floor forcefully, extending my arms in grand gesture to mark my space relative to others, or I might stay put in one place; defiantly, I might articulate my buttocks in intense repetitive isolations so as to push away anyone in proximity. The space of the club is also built around the possibility of contact, so I might choose instead to sway my hips suggestively, extending my arms in an open embrace as I approach a fellow dancer. Whatever the choices, queer Latinas/os like myself negotiate our travel to the club and our experiences within it through performances that draw from the social contexts, at times disciplinary ones, we traverse en route to our experiences of pleasure. In doing so, dancers make Latina/o queer space through performance.

Performance

While this book is not conceived exclusively as a dance studies project, it devotes most of its analysis to dance cultures. This book is the first single-authored monograph devoted primarily to the cultural study of U.S. Latina/o dance in theatrical, social, and political contexts.[78] However, as I explained above, it is the broader understanding of movement that I find most useful in addressing the various theories in practice that animate the "social choreographies" of queer latinidad. Literary scholar Andrew Hewitt uses the term "social choreography" to approach both theatrical and quotidian choreography as a "medium for rehearsing a social order in the realm of the aesthetic."[79] I am similarly interested in engaging how approaches to movement on the stage, the street, or the dance floor rehearse both normative and interventionary notions of embodiment.

Dance scholar Randy Martin has also remarked that a critical engagement with movement might offer a more accurate picture of political participation that is aware of the fact that despite the overwhelming emphasis in political analysis on representation (how a political message is communicated) it is not until bodies are mobilized into action that the very possibilities of the political materialize.[80] This notion of mobilization and embodied participation is crucial to my case study in chapter 3, incidentally the only chapter in the book not devoted to dance. At the Esperanza Peace and Justice Center, queer Latina/o cultural activists took to the streets to mobilize the largely working-class *mexicano* community to support their struggle against the City of San Antonio after their funds were cut because of the queer content of their work. Their strategy was to create performance situations where audiences became implicated bodily and moved emotionally into action. In my analysis of this case study I focus on how embodied practices elicit the kinds of affective forces required to instantiate political change. In doing so I do not mean to evoke a metaphysics of the body but attend to what dance scholar Susan Leigh Foster has described in her analysis of the movement training and practices of nonviolent protest groups as a "perceptive and responsive physicality that, everywhere along the way, deciphers the social and then choreographs an imagined alternative."[81] In attending to the work of queer Latina/o choreographers, activists, and social dancers I approach performance as both a social situation always already embedded in the political and a technology for achieving political interventions.

In this book I offer an account of the routes through which Latina/o queers like myself travel to public spaces in search of connections and communion with others not like us or a lot like us. I do so driven by the excitement, the joy, and the pleasures that spectating or participating in these events might allow me and those around me to feel. Performance as both a social phenomenon and a technology is paramount to this equation.[82] In understanding queer latinidad as and in performance, I call attention to performance's dual function as a social situation and a set of expressive techniques. As a social phenomenon, performance in the contexts I examine refers to the presentation of stylized and purposeful behaviors before an audience. At its most basic definition this model of performance entails a communication scenario whereby a performer acts in expectation of recognition and feedback from her spectators. The relationships that shape the experience of traditional Western theater are perhaps the most rehearsed, if conventional, examples. Here, audiences arrive at the theater to spectate quietly the representations before them and be entertained, enlightened, or emotionally moved by the event on stage. At the end of the performance the acting ensemble will approach the stage and will be, ideally, applauded by a grateful audience.[83] That is, both actors and audience members enter the theater in full knowledge of the expectations, codes, and conventions of the encounter they have agreed to partake in. But performance, as I understand it and use it throughout this book, is not the exclusive realm of the theater event.

As I noted above in my description of the considerations for travel by audience members and dance club patrons, a performance relationship can be established or assumed in everyday life as well. Audience members preparing to attend a performance, for example, also assume specific approaches to dress code and comportment when approaching the theater. Their choices, conscious or not, call upon specific repertoires of self-presentation that conform or challenge not only the expectations of propriety within the theater but also outside it. Turner defines these less structured performances as "social performance." My argument is that although social performances tread a thin line between social actors knowing and not knowing what motivates and directs specific choices about their daily practices, they are imbued with the possibility of agency. Queer Latinas/os—because of their experiences of marginalization before a patriarchal, xenophobic, and homophobic society—are acutely aware of the ways their "presentation of self in everyday life," to borrow sociologist Erving Goffman's expression, is of great consequence to the ways they traverse the social realm.[84] The realm of unconscious habitual behaviors shaped by cultural convention since youth, assumed in the work of sociologist Pierre Bourdieu, is not so readily available to minoritarian subjects like queer Latinas/os.[85] We are hyperaware of how we traverse our worlds and how we are perceived or surveilled by others. Where others might fall into the routines of behaviors, we are often in the mode of performance, purposeful and strategic in our quotidian dramaturgies of survival.

Performance practitioner and scholar Richard Schechner's formulation of performance, like my own, posits that performance ought to be understood as a larger social phenomenon far surpassing its duration on the stage.[86] That is, he merges the conventions of cultural performance to the contexts of social performance to extend the reach of what performance analysis entails. In doing so he suggests that the study of performance should include an analysis of the process and context under which formal events like the theater occur as well as their consequences or aftermaths.[87] For Schechner the theater experience exceeds the duration of the event on stage; he suggests that "surrounding a show are special observances, practices, and rituals that lead into the performance and away from it."[88] These rituals include preparation and travel to and from the theater as well as numerous other activities, from approaching the ticket booth to discussing the performance with friends over a drink or dinner. Casting a social performance frame to cultural performances allows us to more accurately describe and understand the work of performance in the larger public sphere. It also opens up our possibilities to the creative enactments that take place in our daily lives, including those that lead to our experiences of cultural performance, as significant and potentially political practice.

Performing Queer Latinidad approaches the local environs of Latina/o queer performance as social phenomena. I understand these spaces as intersections or crossroads, sites where the impulses for a Latina/o community in the United States at large are negotiated and queered at the level of the local, the immediate experience. I document the sociocultural contexts of particular performances historically situated in given relations of power. I attend to the labor that precedes their enactment by attending to the motivations, visions, and ideas of artists and social actors involved in the making of performance and documenting their rehearsal process. I analyze the performance enactments on the stage, the street, or the dance floor, not as texts but as events. These particularly positioned events as lived experience are inclusive of the audiences sitting or dancing about me and breathing life into the social process that unravels in the darkness of the theater or the strobe lights of the club. Finally, I seek to identify the theories in practice achieved in these performances, especially in their constitution of a Latina/o queer public sphere.

Now, performance as a technology refers to the material resources, techniques, and creative thinking that makes these events happen. It seeks to understand the labor undertaken by performers, designers, directors, curators, scholars, administrators, activists, and audiences in creating and transforming spaces where Latina/o queer communities congregate and participate in social and cultural performances. It asks how performance is done, understanding that this doing is the result of social relations. But it also asks, what does performance *do* to shape or change the social realm?[89]

In looking at performance's doings, I explore the strategies deployed by Latina/o queer performers in the United States as they seek to make sense of and affirm their position within a heavily overdetermined public sphere with age-old assumptions about both latinidad and queerness. The performances examined in this book archive these complicated negotiations and devise counterpublic alternatives.[90] They dare to imagine different social arrangements and instantiate new communitarian configurations in the moment of performance, in the work performed to make it happen, or at a later time when participants critically or emotionally awakened by its insight draw from its force for their own ends. As such, Latina/o queer performance may produce moments of what performance theorist Jill Dolan has termed "utopian performatives": moments in performance that allow us to experience or feel the world as it should be.[91]

As Dolan explains, "Utopian performatives describe small but profound moments in which performance calls the attention of the audience in a way that lifts everyone slightly above the present, into a hopeful feeling of what the world might be like if every moment of our lives were as emotionally voluminous, generous, aesthetically striking, and intersubjectively intense."[92] Utopian performatives work in between the rational and the emotive. They emerge out of moments where the aesthetic event becomes, temporarily, a felt materiality that instantiates the imaginable into the possible. Utopian performatives bank on the heightened emotional states that performance makes possible. Performance technologies ranging from the virtuosity of the performer to the sheer beauty with which language is spoken on the stage may elicit such moments of elation. Lastly, Dolan explains how utopian performatives depend on performance as a social phenomenon. For her, the relations among the performers on the stage or with the audience, even the experience of sitting next to others equally mesmerized by a moment of performance, can achieve such emotional effects.

I share Dolan's enthusiasm for what performance can do. I always enter the scene of performance hopeful that such a moment as a utopian performative might happen. I retain vivid memories of those instances where I have experienced them and recall them whenever I ready for my travel to the theater or the dance club. One such memorable experience occurred to me and my companions in 1999 when we found ourselves emotionally moved by Arthur Aviles's solo dance *Puerto Rican Faggot from the South Bronx Steals Precious Object for Giuliani's East Village.* At the time, as I mentioned above, the New York City queer community could still hold a public grudge against a pre-9/11 Rudy Giuliani for the "clean up" that gradually displaced sex-oriented businesses from most of Manhattan. These spaces, important cruising sites for gay men, were targeted via a myriad of restrictions imposed by city government to make areas such as Forty-second Street desirable for development by the Disney Corporation and other "family oriented" businesses.[93] We were an angry bunch when it came to discussing Giuliani and perhaps that is why we were so enthusiastic about attending a performance that by its title promised to be critical of the mayor.

We made our way to the Bronx Academy of Arts and Dance and sat in the audience for over an hour. When the time in the program came, Aviles entered the stage wearing a gold cape and pants. He began twirling, arms extended and head tilted back to the sound of a drum played by Angel Rodríguez. The fabric of the cape seemed to grow as he gracefully opened it with his arms to allow the resistance of the air created by his fluid movements about the stage to amplify his body. Halfway through the piece, Aviles removed his cape and pants and exposed his naked light-skinned body as he gracefully continued his dance: soft rounded arm gestures that traveled above his head, quick small steps, a few sudden jumps, and the piece was over.

My two companions—both Latino gay men—and I found ourselves in tears throughout the whole performance. We could not speak to each other at the time. We silently made our way to the subway station en route to our neighborhood in Brooklyn. I was touched by the performance. Despite the absence of an explicit critique of Giuliani, perhaps more so because of it, I was forced to encounter my own anger. I had to surrender to the sheer beauty of the flowing fabric and the simplicity of Aviles's movement. As I think about this event years later, I can still recall vividly the moment in the performance when I felt I had to give in and release my tension in a profoundly felt cry.

I now think it was the simple experience of being there in the South Bronx, participating as members of a queer public witnessing the beauty of a Latino gay man's assertive performance of self in all his nakedness that truly took us. Seeing such a public display of queer embodiment at a time when our spaces for public sex were quickly disappearing, and seeing queerness articulated so proudly and eloquently in the Puerto Rican enclave of the South Bronx where I experienced firsthand the homophobia of my own family, gave me a chance to feel queer latinidad as a utopian performative. These are the memories that compel me back into the spaces of performance that I turn to throughout *Performing Queer Latinidad.*

As much as I am inspired by the possibility of experiencing the utopian performative, I am also always fully aware of its provisional state,

Fig. 4. Arthur Aviles performs *Puerto Rican Faggot from the South Bronx Steals Precious Object from Giuliani's East Village* (1999), Hostos Community College, New York. Photo by Tom Brazil.

even as I surrender to its seductive embrace. In analyzing the experiences of inter-Latina/o encounters in performance I am also mindful of the need to attend to the tensions and frictions that emerge within social spaces that are structured around difference and inequality. The spaces of Latina/o queer performance offer many such moments when competing agendas, misunderstandings, or quite simply disagreements shape the resulting performances. In accounting for these less joyful or less coherent moments I seek to present a fuller picture of what the intersections of queerness and latinidad truly entail. It is no easy task to live in proximity to each other. And still, I believe that these frictions have much to teach us about being and being together. I follow in the footsteps of anthropologist Anna Lowenhaupt Tsing in suggesting that intersections that are constituted in friction might still lead to productive, if at times compromised, ends.[94]

Convivencia Diaria: Introducing the Case Studies

The various chapters that comprise this book offer accounts of what anthropologists Milagros Ricourt and Ruby Danta have termed *convivencia diaria,* or "daily-life interactions." In their ethnography of inter-Latina relations in Queens, New York, they observed a sense of panethnic community arise from daily exchanges between women of diverse backgrounds who met and interacted at work, the local businesses they patronized, from the coin laundry to the supermarket, and places of worship and leisure. Working-class and poor Latinas often encounter similar experiences of discrimination in housing and work opportunities despite their differences in ethnic or national background. They frequently find themselves drawn or pushed into the same neighborhoods, not necessarily as the result of a choice based on their identity, but by other factors such as housing affordability or availability of jobs. Traversing similar routes in their day-to-day routines, these women developed a sense of familiarity with each other. Spending time together in public spaces gradually led to the establishment of relations of intimacy and collaboration. But these relationships, as Ricourt and Danta note, also developed from the labor of community activists and cultural workers who actively sought to shape Latina/o panethnicity through the organization of community programs, political coalitions, or activist campaigns.[95] That is, latinidad may result from circumstantial encounters as well as intentional proximities. Through these quotidian interactions, Latina/o women came to identify their commonalities—in language, history, culture, and other factors of experience—and created bonds that translated into active support networks. The resource sharing that resulted from these ties ranged from giving out information about jobs, housing, or other basic opportunities to actual assistance such as babysitting and economic and emotional support.

Anthropologist Arjun Appadurai has discussed a similar set of social dynamics and practices emergent among communities historically marginalized from the financial resources, technologies, and political access generally enjoyed by corporations, nation-states, and their affiliates in the current neoliberal global economy. He explains:

> A series of social forms has emerged to contest, interrogate, and reverse these developments and to create forms of knowledge transfer and social mobilization that proceed independently of

the actions of corporate capital and the nation-state system (and its international affiliates and guarantors). These social forms rely on strategies, visions, and horizons for globalization on behalf of the poor that can be characterised as "grassroots globalization" or, put in a slightly different way, as "globalization from below."[96]

Grassroots globalization refers to survival strategies developed by or on behalf of disenfranchised communities outside the global corporate infrastructure that connect like-minded groups across national borders. Appadurai's primary examples are not-for-profit organizations, or NGOs. These organizations develop transnational networks around particular issues such as workers' rights, water, food supply, and the environment. Working collaboratively to secure funds, material goods, labor, and public support for their causes, these organizations model ways in which sharing resources and knowledge may activate new economic, political, and social networks that seek to ameliorate experiences of disenfranchisement globally. A sense of interconnection between communities at great distance from one another is key to the important labor these groups perform.

In my own analysis I offer a more localized understanding of grassroots globalization by arguing for its emergence in *convivencia diaria*. I see the quotidian exchanges among queer Latinas/os of diverse backgrounds in spaces of social and cultural performance as potentially transformative events that yield equally powerful notions of community, resource sharing, and potentially collective political action. I approach Latina/o queer performance as grassroots globalization by attending to the multiple scales of relations and influences (local, national, transnational, global) that shape the contexts in which performance takes place. The Latina/o queer performances examined throughout this book are positioned as cultural practices that negotiate global interests with local necessities. They serve simultaneously as spontaneous meeting places and as purposeful interventions in the public sphere. Latina/o queer performance enables *convivencia diaria* by creating spaces where queer Latinas/os gather to participate in performance. It also labors to imagine and circulate specific representations of latinidad or activate aesthetic and social practices that promote it, not as a narrative of identity, but as a feeling, an insight or an embodied experience of who we are or who we might become in the collective social sharing of the performance event.

The chapters that comprise *Performing Queer Latinidad* model a journey through the affective landscapes of queer latinidad. We traverse through feelings of home and hope to arrive at the utopian doings of performance. In doing so we must realize how each of these emotional states and social orientations emerge out of circumstances of friction, not naive collectivism. Understanding home, hope, utopia, and friction as theories in practice asks us to attend to the labor of performance. Consequently, in each of my critical forays into queer latinidad I highlight significant practices contributing to the emergent public lives of queer Latinas/os through performance. Performance here is not understood as an inherently progressive or radical venture. It fulfills its potential in the contexts and practices of queer latinidad—from the formal choreographies of concert dance and the political movements of street protest to the quotidian dramaturgies of the dance club. Thus, I pursue how performance, with its emphasis on *convivencia diaria* and its arsenal of techniques for engaging the world and others corporeally, might help us reach those moments and movements of critically engaged, affectively rich, and politically promising interconnection. It is those feelings of intimate proximity in the public spaces where I locate queer latinidad.

Performing Queer Latinidad provides a comparative map of Latina/o queer public cultures that addresses the unique characteristics of the various locales I engage while accounting for their interconnections as part of the nation. As such, the five cities I visit as the primary research sites of this study offer an unprecedented opportunity to think about queer latinidad comparatively across a vast geographic expanse—from New York City to Phoenix—but also in relation to significantly different configurations of urban economics, daily life, and history. New York and San Antonio are both cities with long histories as centers of Latina/o life—Puerto Rican and Dominican in the former and Mexican in the latter. Rochester and Austin, as smaller cities in relative proximity to New York and San Antonio respectively, offer a different scale of engagement but also sites where Latinas/os do not count with the iconic presence and clout they enjoy in their neighboring locations. Phoenix presents a more recent model of Latina/o ascendancy. It counted with a historic Mexican community but it grew precipitously from the 1990s onward. This growth was largely immigrant labor from Mexico. During the period of this study New York City, San Antonio, Austin, Rochester, and Phoenix have all experienced dramatic shifts brought forth by major economic and social events—from 9/11 in New York to economic collapse of the high-tech industries in Austin, the old industrial sectors in

Rochester and San Antonio, and the housing market in Phoenix. The adjustments undertaken to stage a recovery in each of these cities have affected Latina/o queer livelihoods.

I look at large global cities as much as medium-sized secondary urban outposts in order to offer an account of queer latinidad that moves beyond the expected maps of coastal urbanity in the United States. Even when looking at New York, I do not drop magically into Chelsea, the more visible and iconic gay neighborhood in the city, but approach on foot from Hunts Point or Williamsburg, which as I will argue have been plenty imaged as urban dumpsites in the midst of renewal but rarely accounted for as homes to queer latinidad. My move here is partly academic and partly political. I want to offer a pool of evidence diverse enough to make my claims about queer latinidad relevant beyond a specific neighborhood, city, or region, but I also want to document the labor of cultural workers and social actors who have received limited attention from scholars. The marginal position of this work should not stand as a judgment of the quality or significance of their work or lives, but as the result of their distance from already focused-on locations. I argue throughout this book that queer latinidad in performance can be experienced as profoundly, and be of equal consequence to a group of hundreds of activists rallying on the streets of a primarily Latina/o city, and to a single dancer moving across the dance floor in a primarily white dance club.

We begin our journey through this vast expanse in chapter 2, "Building Home: Arthur Aviles's Choreography of the Public Sphere." Here I examine the artistic and activist work of "New York Rican" choreographer Arthur Aviles. At a time when the South Bronx was experiencing an expansion of its industrial businesses and the residential core of Hunts Point remained neglected, Aviles oriented his dance practice toward the creation of a meeting space or home for the articulation of Latina/o queer lives. In this historically Puerto Rican neighborhood, frequently dismissed as an industrial wasteland or a sex trade back alley, Aviles employed performance as a community-building practice. I argue that his homemaking, challenged and queered definitions of latinidad circulated in mainstream popular culture, as well as within the neighborhood. I demonstrate how his efforts to develop a Latina/o queer dance scene at the Point Cultural Center and the Bronx Academy of Arts and Dance—two arts organizations dedicated to cultural and economic development and activism in the Bronx—resulted in the development of a critical Latina/o queer counterpublic. In my analysis of Aviles's work I attend to the process of making performance (the labor of finding or building spaces, accessing audiences, conceiving and rehearsing work) as well as to the subject matter of performance (the actual representations presented on the stage) as equally critical components of what constitutes dance as a public practice. I turn to Aviles's choreographic oeuvre to explore how his work advocates for and practices the intersection of Latina/o and queer interests, aesthetics, and communities. I analyze three of his choreographic projects and works—"A Community That Dances Together" (1998), *Arturella* (1996), and *This Pleasant and Grateful Asylum* (1999)—as examples of Latina/o queer homemaking. The chapter conceptualizes home, as both material goal and emotional space, as one of the theories in practice of queer latinidad.

If chapter 2 focuses on the labor of building spaces for queer latinidad, the next chapter is concerned with the labor necessary for maintaining them when they come under attack. Chapter 3, "Movements of Hope: Performance and Activism," looks at the Esperanza Center for Peace and Justice, a cultural organization in San Antonio, Texas, targeted by conservative activists and legislators for its involvement in the production of Latina/o queer arts. I examine the cultural and political climate that led to defunding of the Center by the City of San Antonio in 1997, including the economic downturn that textured the city's decision making about arts funding and its turn toward a tourist industry, based as it is on Mexican folk traditions, as a potential savior. I demonstrate how right-wing activist networks circulated fear as an affective strategy to rally conservative allies and to pressure city officials to defund the Center. The chapter focuses on grassroots efforts undertaken by the Esperanza Center in order to persuade the broader San Antonio community, especially *mexicano* families not generally aware of and at times hostile toward queer latinidad, to respond to their defunding and provide support as they ventured into a historic legal battle in defense of their First Amendments rights to express their sexuality in public. In their campaign to save Esperanza, queer Latina/o art activists and their allies drew from and queered the aesthetic and affective expectations of folkloric Mexican happiness in the tourist-oriented image of San Antonio. This chapter proposes hope as a theory in practice that, although sometimes mocked by critics, continues to fuel the coalitional politics of queer latinidad.

Chapter 4, "Quotidian Utopias: Latina/o Queer Choreographies," moves from performance in a theatrical framework to performance in everyday life. It focuses on club dancing by queer Latinas/os in primarily gay establishments across the United States in the late 1990s. The chapter is organized differently than the preceding ones as I center on the dancerly strategies of the performers and their understanding of them to evidence ways in which performance articulates agency in space. I look at choreographic practices in improvised social dance as acts that localize the global sounds of Latina/o popular music. I present social dance choreography as articulate embodiments that negotiate in their seemingly pleasurable abandon both the possibilities and the risks of assuming queer latinidad. I offer an understanding of dancing in the club as a practice of what I term "choreographies of resistance," embodied practices through which minoritarian subjects claim their space in the social and cultural realms of the dance floor. I argue that these vernacular knowledges, already available within the community, expertly showcase utopia as a theory in practice.

Chapter 5, "Dancing Reggaetón with Cowboy Boots: Frictive Encounters in Queer Latinidad," returns to the space of the dance club, this time in Phoenix, Arizona, and almost a decade after my first entry into the establishments I engage in the previous chapter, to pursue the frictions that so shape queer latinidad. In doing so I demonstrate the ways performance cultures travel across social settings. I attend to how notions of class distinction mark critical differences within queer Latina/o cultural enclaves and how these are in turn grounded on transnational exchanges that are both historical and contemporary. I chart the arrival of reggaetón—a Puerto Rican dance music genre developed out of the mixed influences of Panamanian reggae, Jamaican ska and dance hall, Dominican merengue, pan-Latino salsa, and hip-hop—into the queer geographies of latinidad in the United States. As reggaetón crossed over from a Puerto Rican geography to a transnational popular music market, it was quickly taken up in Latina/o queer dance clubs in Phoenix. In these spaces, Mexicans danced to Puerto Rican sounds and rehearsed new vocabularies, both linguistic and choreographic, that translate reggaetón into queer latinidad. Club patrons appropriated the words and accents of Puerto Rican Spanish and the steps and rhythms of reggaetón dancing to perform their own queer identities. I argue that these performances serve as harbingers of new social arrangements across Latina/o queer communities in the United States that materialize pan-Latina/o imaginaries while highlighting friction as a significant element, a theory in practice, of queer latinidad.

In my closing epilogue, "Moving Forward: Between Fragility and Resilience," I return to each of the sites visited throughout the book to offer a second visit, an opportunity to see what has become of these places and artists a few years after my initial engagements. These visits, check-ins as they are described in ethnographic parlance, are not meant to offer an update into the now. The ethnographic present slips quickly into its pastness the minute it is experienced, despite our insistence in writing as if we were experiencing it once more. Instead, I offer this return to the sites in order to demonstrate the temporal and spatial fragility of performance and the communities it creates. But this is by no means a pessimistic look at what happens in the aftermath of performance or social movements. What I offer in closing is an engagement with the ephemerality of performance that seeks to grasp onto what remains, the theories in practice and their affective economies, as available resources for what might come next.

There is significant overlap between the time periods each of the case studies focuses. While the book is organized according to my entry into fieldwork, it also follows the chronological progression of the cultural events discussed—from Arthur Aviles's return to the Bronx in 1996 to Esperanza Center's defunding in 1997, and onto my arrival into the dance club scenes of Rochester and New York in 1998, San Antonio and Austin in 1999, and then in Phoenix in 2004. As mentioned above, the sites have been selected in order to offer a broader sample that evidences the widespread phenomenon of queer latinidad. But I was also drawn to these locations by a desire to map alternative locations where queer Latina/o public culture thrives but has been little engaged in academic scholarship. The various locations in this travelogue through queer latinidad in the United States became possibilities as research sites because of my own personal encounters with their social, artistic, and political work as a spectator, activist, and dance club patron who sought his own queer latinidad in the arts organizations, street performances, and dance floors presented in this study. It is in search of my own pleasures that I ultimately stumbled upon the complex map I relate in this book.

While I do not make any promises as to the pleasures this text might provide, it is my belief that this is indeed a project centered on pleasure, sexual and otherwise, as the source from which Latina/o queer performance enacts its identities and affects. In describing her goals in exploring performance and utopia, Jill Dolan says, "I want to perpetuate experiences of utopia in the flesh of performance that might performatively hint at how a different world could feel."[97] Throughout this book I seek to model such a practice, looking at the ways in which Latina/o queer performance has offered these experiences to me, hoping that these and other performances might have the same effects on others.

Lastly, in researching and writing this book I have become increasingly convinced that our current models for understanding Latina/o public culture in the United States in the humanities require significant rethinking. So much of the work in Latina/o studies and American studies about Latinas/os relies on the propping-up of a singular critical voice exercising know-how over culture rendered as text. I want to model a different approach to this scholarship. In doing so I want to argue for performance studies as a model for conducting, analyzing, and reporting scholarship about queer Latinas/os that invests in the interpretation of culture as experienced embodiment. For this reason, my analysis, while displaying my own critical engagements with the cultural material before me, also seeks to showcase the experiences of the very social actors who have shared their motivations, aspirations, visions, and frustrations about their lives and their practices with me over the course of the past fifteen years. Performance studies, I argue, provides a critical methodology and an orientation to research as practice that privileges our cohabitation with others as a way of understanding culture. It is my hope that the chapters that follow will honor the shared time and space that performance made possible for me across so many diverse communities I claim here under the rubric of queer latinidad.

2

BUILDING HOME

Arthur Aviles's Choreography of the Public Sphere

Here is to you Hunts Point
with your hos strolling, your pimps rolling
your used parts, broken hearts
auto glass, hos showing ass
scrap metal, right foot on the pedal
Banknote, ho's hopes
Hell's gate, the goat's wait
asthma's high, babies cry
fishmarket smells, meat markets sells
produce buy, truckers fly
hookers on the stroll, pimps on the roll
sunrise, celebration, The Point
it's The Point, Hunts Point.
            —Brent Owens, *Hookers at the Point: Five Years Later*[1]

Art spurs investment, and then investment spurs displacement.
That's a paradigm we have been trying very hard to avoid.
            —Paul Lipson, former director of the Point, cited in
            The Village Voice[2]

Once upon a time in a far away land there was a tiny ghetto,
peaceful you know, with the occasional crime, and the *gangas*
and knifes, *pero* peaceful all the same.
            —Elizabeth Marrero as Maeva, in Arthur Aviles's *Arturella*[3]

In this chapter we visit the primarily Latina/o neighborhood of Hunts
Point in the Bronx Borough of New York City. We will look at the work
of dancer-choreographer Arthur Aviles. I focus primarily on the initial
three-year period of activity from his arrival to the Bronx in 1996 up to
his development of the Bronx Academy of Arts and Dance (BAAD!) in

1999. I demonstrate how his performance work negotiated the introduction of a viable queer public culture within a Latina/o neighborhood and functioned as a practice of queer Latina/o homemaking. The cultural activity addressed in this chapter unraveled at a time when industrial development took precedence over the quality of life of the residents in the neighborhood and when the sex and drug trades saw growth as the result of Mayor Rudy Giuliani's "cleanup" of neighboring Manhattan. In response, artists and cultural workers like Aviles set out to create sites of social and cultural exchange where residents could develop relationships with one another and to their community. Aviles's queer-specific work went further by developing a queer-affirmative and sex-positive alternative to the heteropatriarchal orientation of the housing activism in the neighborhood and its villification of the sex trade as the culprit of the neighborhood's neglect. I consult material culture and archival sources about the neighborhood, interviews with Aviles, live and recorded versions of his choreography, and fieldnotes from three years of initial visits to Hunts Point between 1997 and 2000 and another four years of periodic check-ins in order to evidence my argument about his role as a Latina/o queer homemaker. In relating the strategies employed by Aviles and his collaborators to develop a Latina/o queer home in Hunts Point, I argue that his performance work modeled practices of engaged cohabitation critical to the viability of a queer presence within the broader South Bronx.

I explained in the previous chapter that the contexts and conditions confronted by queer Latinas/os in the United States have local specificities but also shared national contexts. During the middle to late 1990s urban centers across the United States ventured into urban renewal projects focused on the development of new revenues following the national recession of the early 1980s and the dramatic economic rearrangements that ensued. At a time when most of the traditional urban infrastructure built around industrial labor had gone obsolete, economic growth migrated to the corporate managerial and service sectors. Neoliberal policies for manufacturing increasingly relocated labor outside the United States. In response, cities invested on high-end residential projects, corporate headquarters, and tourism to incentivize their local economies. For many working-class and poor Latina/o communities concentrated at urban centers nationwide, this meant significant push away from their historic neighborhoods. Investors and city officials closed down affordable housing units in order to clear the cities for new high-end tenants.

For queer communities this also meant similar pressure to relocate since formerly queer districts were decimated by development master plans wanting to create "family friendly" living, entertainment, and retail environments or were upgraded into built-up queer destinations meant to court the pink dollar with chic restaurants and trendy shops. Cities showed their new face to potential corporate relocators or tourist marketers in the form of refurbished theater districts and loft buildings, high-rises with glass facades, and newly installed street lighting while simply ignoring the many people displaced to make way for the new Starbucks or Disney stores. Neighborhoods in the periphery of this new development were equally affected. Many received displaced communities or became identified as ideal locations for the massive infrastructure needed to support the urban core—from water treatment plants and distribution centers to cheap housing for laborers. Hunts Point is one such neighborhood, and its subsidiary history relative to Manhattan's protagonism harks back decades before my fieldwork commenced.

The epigraphs above, all statements commenting on Hunts Point by cultural workers active during the 1990s and early 2000s, suggest that visions of this neighborhood are as varied as they are creative. While the first quote celebrates the decadence and decay of the urban environment, the second warns against the risks of development. Homemaking in the South Bronx is not an easy task to achieve. It requires purposeful navigation and awareness of the quotidian violences and structural limitations that have positioned this neighborhood, like many others across the United States, in such a marginal position. It also asks us to consider the risks that gentrification or industrial development might bring to a fragile residential district. Ultimately, I am invested in the strategies intimated by the third epigraph. The words are part of the opening to Arthur Aviles's Latina/o queer dance adaptation of the Cinderella story, *Arturella*, which I discuss in this chapter. Spoken by Maeva, a sassy butch matron, at the opening of the piece, they flaunt an ability to find pleasure and comfort without losing critical edge or political stance. Maeva humorously and ironically invokes peacefulness. In doing so, especially within the context of a dance piece where the stories of the fairy tale's kingdom are transposed onto the Latina/o ghetto, she makes peacefulness happen as a felt and embodied experience for spectators who despite encountering the very violences mocked and pointed to in her statement find each other in the shared laughter of the queer performance space. Maeva's "peaceful ghetto" confronts and puns a representational economy that has positioned Hunts Point between a story of industrial potential and social blight, never quite accounting for those who strive to survive or make home, at times even pleasurably, from within. Her proud and resilient attitude echoes the welcoming iconographies of Hunts Point's main business drag.

Food Markets and Flesh Trade: Imag(in)ing Hunts Point

It is a hot summer afternoon in 2003 as I exit the Hunts Point Avenue stop of the Number 6 New York City subway line en route to the Bronx Academy of Arts and Dance. I walk down Hunts Point Avenue and cross under the Bruckner Expressway toward Garrison Avenue. As I emerge from the shadows of the enormous concrete elevation into the blinding brightness of the Bronx open sky, I encounter a lively neighborhood buzzing with foot traffic. An old Cass Gilbert[4] railroad station points to the area's past as home and playground to some of Manhattan's most affluent families up to the end of World War I.[5] At present, this dilapidated building no longer stands as a symbol of leisurely escape for the city's well-to-do, nor does it evidence the history of working- and middle-class Jewish, Irish, and Italian communities that urbanized the area up to the mid-twentieth century. The cluster of businesses tightly crowded into its structure announce a much different demographic.[6]

Advertising signs for Tormenta Restaurant, Torres Fruits & Vegetables, Bella Vista Fried Chicken and Bella Vista Gyros, a hair salon, El Coche bar and restaurant (one of the neighborhood's four strip joints), and a travel agency cover the old station. They also offer a visual preamble to a worn but enthusiastic billboard on the adjacent building welcoming me and fellow walkers-by into the Hunts Point neighborhood of the South Bronx. The weathered and graffitied surface of the billboard reads in bold multicolored hand-painted block letters: "¡Bienvenidos!" The gesture is translated and repeated in English, albeit in a smaller plain black font: "Welcome to the Village of Hunts Point."

As the billboard's linguistic hierarchy reveals, Hunts Point is now a primarily Latina/o community with approximately 80 percent of the population in the neighborhood identifying as Hispanic.[7] The colorful and proud image of a Latina/o Hunts Point announced in the welcoming

Fig. 5. Cass Gilbert train station, Hunts Point, NY. Photo by the author.

pronouncement of the billboard is probably not the first image to come to mind when thinking of this neighborhood. Many other narratives and images have shaped the public perception of contemporary Hunts Point.

To some readers Hunts Point may be best known as the largest food distribution and processing center in the United States. The complex of warehouses and processing plants that comprise the Hunts Point Cooperative Market employ over ten thousand workers who process, pack, and distribute meat, poultry, fish, vegetables, and soft drinks to a New York metro market, serving a population of well over ten million.[8] Since its development in the 1960s, the industrial park and food market districts of Hunts Point have been touted throughout the city and nation as examples of economic development. Historical as well as more recent accounts throughout the 1990s and early 2000s mark it as a hopeful sign of local activity at a time when manufacturing and other jobs in this sector of the economy have fled the northeast United States for the southern United States or the global South.[9]

The story of industrial Hunts Point is an extention of New York City's transformation into a center of management for the global economy, a trend that has since influenced urban development processes through-

Fig. 6. Welcome sign, Hunts Point, NY. Photo by the author.

out the United States.[10] At the midpoint of the twentieth century, urban developers and city officials alike became invested in the infrastructural transformation of Manhattan to accommodate new offices and housing for the financial and corporate industries increasingly assuming the city as world headquarters. The South Bronx stood on the receiving end of much of the relocated "undesirable" operations that supported the transformation of Manhattan during this period, including the development of the World Trade Center site into a modern financial district. The corporate story of Hunts Point is thus one of spectacular ascendancy as its role as destination for the food distribution industries displaced from Lower Manhattan positioned the neighborhood at the center of a critical market in contemporary global economics.

In contrast to the portrait of industrial prosperity represented by the food businesses, Hunts Point may also come to mind as the subject of film director and Bronx native Brent Owens's documentaries on prostitution. These films were featured in HBO's America Undercover series from the release of *Hookers at the Point* in 1996 up to his *Hookers at the Point: Five Years Later* in 2002.[11] The films offer footage of prostitutes walking the streets of Hunts Point, approaching their johns, and negotiating their tricks. Hidden microphones allow the viewer to listen to the moaning and groaning of sexual exchange as the camera shoots from a safe distance the bouncing vehicles parked in dark alleys. These images are juxtaposed with on-camera interviews, frequently in tight close-ups, with prostitutes and pimps who offer their personal narratives of drug addiction, economic struggle, and experience in the trade. Often to the background of slick jazz brass or piano sounds, the deep voice of an invisible narrator, Owens himself, offers surface commentary about the women in a stylized two-beat rhythmical delivery reminiscent of the spoken word performance poetry tradition. Through these quasi-ethnographic documentary portraits of prostitution in the neighborhood, Hunts Point appears as a wasteland of junkies and sex traders.

While the documentaries offer unprecedented insight into the labor routines, the emotional conundrums, and the quotidian struggles of the women who practice sustenance prostitution to support themselves, their families, or their drug habits, they rarely offer a critical view of the social, economic, and cultural dynamics that have positioned the neighborhood and the women who labor on its streets at such a marginal existence. It is not until Owens's closing sequence at the end of his third film in the series that a broader picture of Hunts Point is even suggested. This closing scene juxtaposes footage of the women walking the streets with shots of Hunts Point's deteriorated landscape from architectural landmarks and cargo trucks to back-alley murals on warehouse walls. This visual collage is matched to the text that opens this chapter, spoken as it is by an omniscient and judging narrator. And it is here also where queerness as nonheterosexual desire is insinuated in the figure of the "goat," a slang word for transsexual prostitute, who waits at "hell's gate" for their johns. But focused as this film is on an overwhelmingly heterosexual and male point of view, the transsexual prostitute is summoned in coded language but never materializes bodily on screen. While this brief closing sequence suggests that there are more complicated factors at play in the neighborhood, especially those having to do with economic blight, it nonetheless tends to subsume Hunts Point metonymically to the body of the prostitute as both protagonist and culprit of the disaster before us. What is more, the success of the documentary in directing the attention of the national cable network viewers to Hunts Point as a destination can be attributed to the voyeuristic experience of witnessing the prostitute's sexual performance. The narrator's voice-overs fuel this dynamic by assuming an aggressively seductive attitude when describing them, often relying on the drawn-out delivery of a basic pimp rhyme. Much like the women in the documentaries, Hunts Point is here pimped out for the immediate pleasures of a paying viewer who may care little for the off-screen life experiences of the bodies in sight while in pursuit of quick and easy satisfaction as spectators.

At the time of their release in the 1990s, Owens's films were but the latest in a long tradition of sensational media representations of the South Bronx that include Daniel Petrie's 1981 film *Fort Apache, The Bronx,* which featured none other than Pam Grier in the role of a prostitute, and also countless newspaper, radio, and television newscast accounts of the area as a no-man's land. This image was not just a regional story but a prepackaged urban drama for international export. For example, the tagline in the UK theatrical trailer to Petrie's film introduces the South Bronx thusly: "15 minutes from Manhattan there's a place where even the cops fear to tread." The film stars veteran Hollywood actor Paul Newman as a police officer fighting the chaos of a drug-infested, prostitution-heavy, gang warfare-ridden Forty-first Police District in the South Bronx and gave Hollywood-style circulation to the image of the neighborhood as an apocalyptic void that endures in the present.

In its televisual circulation as a prostitution and drugs hub, Hunts Point is offered as a story of contrasts to the success of the food industries. The very identity of the neighborhood as a socially and economically marginalized area is collapsed into facile portraits of spectacular criminality that suggests that the conditions of the neighborhood are derived from the suspect activities of its residents. That is, while the sex and drug trades emerge in these representations as the Achilles's heel to the neighborhood's exemplary status as a center of commerce, the material conditions that have led to its decline all but disappear from the viewer's realm. What results from these stereotypically negative and violent representations of Hunts Point is by no means a balanced account of the residents' experiences of the neighborhood or an opportunity to voice their needs relative to the industrial development stories that accompany them. Moreover, the overwhelming focus on the area's blight, especially when it is always called forth relative to a portrait of criminal ethno-racial collectivity, make it increasingly difficult for residents to imagine themselves otherwise, to think of a future where their livelihood is not only viable, but also hopeful.[12]

The formulation of counternarratives to these representational tendencies through performance and their possibilities as interventions in the material conditions of Hunts Point have been central motivations in the work of dancer-choreographer Arthur Aviles since his arrival in 1996 to make the neighborhood his home. I use the term "home" here literally as a site of dwelling and in the more emotional sense of affiliation to place. Performance has played a central role in his efforts to create a liveable Hunts Point. It has functioned as both a communication technology and a social phenomenon that enacts community. Aviles's performance events invite neighbors to come together to see themselves critically imag(in)ed on the stage. This alternative mode of socialization through the arts assists in the instantiation of collective identities and affects. As I argue throughout this chapter, these interventions achieve such collective imaginaries by circulating homegrown representations that counter outsider views of Hunts Point. They are also realized by providing public spaces, structured around the performance event, where residents experience durational encounters with each other that might lead to a developed familiarity of and commitment to living in proximity to one another. This sense of belonging, a feeling of togetherness relative to place, fuels the idea of shared needs and interests. Such heightened sense of collective interconnection and responsibility, what social scientists have come to understand as social capital,[13] is paramount to the more immediate and material goals of improving the conditions of a neighborhood that to date constitutes one of the poorest congressional districts in the United States, annually records one of the highest levels of violence in New York City, and has a disproportionately large incidence of health problems from asthma to HIV/AIDS.

This chapter takes a queer turn into the understanding of development in this Latina/o neighborhood. I propose Arthur Aviles as an example of the ways in which queers might, and increasingly do, participate in the broader politics of Latina/o homebuilding. The queer latinidad I chart throughout this chapter emerges out of a desire to make daily living possible, perhaps even pleasurable, for queer Latinas/os who encounter the macroeconomic pressures that shape neighborhoods like Hunts Point nationwide. It also registers the moralistic discourse around sexuality that can result from a rejection of the neighborhood's image as a prostitution hub while racing toward the kinds of "respectable" representations that might attract development. Queer latinidad offers an alternative to the heteronormative logics of economic development by challenging the exclusive focus on the traditional reproductive nuclear family and introducing different social and cultural configurations as equally significant components of the community and its future. Before we turn to the creative strategies modeled in Aviles's Latina/o queer homebuilding in Hunts Point it is important to get a more grounded view of the neighborhood outside of the representational short-sightedness that the industrial development and prostitution narratives afford.

Community Renewal: Housing (as) Story

Hunts Point is one of the largest industrial parks in the New York City metro region and also an iconic location for the sex and drug marketplace and its representation in popular culture. The neighborhood is also home to over ten thousand New Yorkers, mostly Latinas/os, whose lives are affected by the economic and social dynamics described in the two widely circulated depictions above.[14] The experience of this community cannot be reduced to financial reports of the growth of commerce or to fetishistic portaits of sex workers. Hunts Point, a peninsula surrounded by the East River on three sides and cut off from the rest of the Bronx Borough by the noisy expressway, remains a primarily low-income Latina/o residential enclave.[15] It also has a significant African-American community estimated at 21 percent of the overall population.[16] It has been this way for over fifty years, since Puerto Ricans and African-Americans began to relocate to the area in large numbers. Many of these new arrivals at Hunts Point were communities displaced from low-income housing in Manhattan as New York City pushed for its position as a center for global economics during the interwar years and tenements and other low-income housing were torn down to accomodate the white-collar labor force and the corporate infrastructure that accompanied the growth of the managerial economy.[17]

The arrival of Latinas/os and African-Americans to Hunts Point in the 1950s occurred in tandem with accelerating white flight as incentivized suburban developments enticed middle-class movement further away from the city center. Divestment in the historic housing stock encouraged the move to the suburbs and the inevitable decline of the area. The neighborhood was soon transformed from a thriving and diverse residential and commercial enclave featuring printing presses, garment factories, domestic-use gas production, and the then-developing food-processing businesses into an increasingly desolate industrial zone. The construction of the Cross Bronx Expressway and the Bruckner Expressway dealt violent blows as well by destroying thousands of residential units that stood along their paths. The expressways effectively cut the South Bronx off from the rest of Manhattan and Hunts Point from the rest of the Borough, significantly reducing the value of properties in proximity to the monumental structures and polluting traffic.

It is estimated that between 1970 and 1979, roughly twenty years since the first communities of displaced Puerto Ricans and African-Americans made their way into the housing districts of Hunts Point and the broader South Bronx, more than forty thousand housing units were demolished or converted into nonresidential use in the area.[18] Over 250,000 residents were eventually displaced from the South Bronx by the early 1980s.[19] With their departure came the decrease in critical city services, including education and health care. Hunts Point became an illegal dumping ground and gained national notoriety for drug and gang violence, prostitution, and a plague of arson that spread across the abandoned infrastructure during the 1970s and early 1980s.[20] By the 1990s enforcement of zoning laws in Manhattan intent on clearing the way for gentrification and expansion of the tourist entertainment industry pushed out adult sex-related businesses such as video stores, theaters, and peep shows.[21] The city also increased its policing of public sex and prostitution in neighborhoods such as Times Square in midtown Manhattan. This rezoning represented an additional pressure on the Hunts Point sex trade as both sex workers and their clients were pushed to the periphery of the city core.

Despite the difficult circumstances they have encountered during the economic downturn, residents of Hunts Point have demonstrated remarkable resilience in their attempts to make this neighborhood their home. Since the mid-1960s community organizations have struggled to ameliorate the increasingly desperate conditions of the neighborhood, especially in regards to housing. Many of these efforts were outgrowths of the housing/tenant movement spearheaded by activists organizing in urban areas across the United States. They received further economic and organizational support from federal programs such as the Community Action and Model Cities programs.[22]

The People's Development Corporation (PDC) is perhaps one of the best known early efforts in the South Bronx. The PDC worked as a collective of organized residents to claim abandoned properties and develop them into affordable housing. Organizations such as the PDC relied on participatory governance and skill sharing in order to make collective decisions, invest labor and resources, and acquire state, private, and foundation funding for the strategic transformation of their neighborhood. Members of the group participated in the actual rehabilitation of properties they would eventually go on to occupy and were active in charting the organization's goals and activity plans. This hands-on experience with the work of conditioning the properties offered residents an opportunity to develop a greater appreciation of and commitment to their places of dwelling. Most importantly, it created a window of time that allowed neighbors-to-be to work and spend time together investing in their mutual goals of building their homes and the community at large.[23] Similar community efforts focused on the development of green spaces in the heavily industrialized neighborhood. Two remarkable examples took place on Baretto Street, where neighborhood organizing persuaded city government to demolish an abandoned building to turn the plot into a community garden[24] and transformed an empty lot into green space.[25] Assuming stewardship of abandoned private property allowed community members to improve, albeit often temporarily, their surrounding areas.[26]

The story of housing activism in Hunts Point and the greater South Bronx became a frequent headline in New York City media beginning in the late 1960s. At a time when the city struggled to keep up with the fast-growing number of abandoned and repossessed properties that came under its control as private owners hit by the economic downturn abandoned or lost their buildings to creditors, housing development activists became beacons of hope that could turn blighted or burned-down buildings back into community assets. Not-for-profit organizations that focused on the housing issue proliferated.

While development has indeed exploded in Hunts Point over the past twenty years, at the time of writing in 2011, the economic stabilization of the residential areas has proven more difficult to achieve. This discrepancy may have much to do with the organizational models currently in operation at nonprofit organizations throughout the neighborhood. As urban studies scholar Brian Sahd has observed, activist organizations that worked on housing and development were transformed by their own success. The influx of financial resources offered by government and private sectors required appropriate administrative capabilities, governing boards, and other organizational restructuring. Community development corporations evolved into bureaucratic institutions that by the late 1990s constituted a third sector of power next to the government and the private corporations in the area. No longer grounded in the collaborative efforts of citizens, these large organizations continued to mind the interests of the community but did so through the paid labor of professional staffers.[27] Community participation in life-shaping decisions in the neighborhood receded significantly from the integral role of hands-on governance and labor of early efforts, giving way to a corporatized delivery of social services.

This distance from the more intimate and interactive model of community participation has also affected the potential integration of queer Latinas/os in significant ways. It is important to consider here that the model of community most generally advocated for in the more institutionalized tenant and housing movements as well as in much organizing in the Hunts Point neighborhood relies on the family as the foundational unit for community formation. The predominance of family values does not result exclusively from the moral codes advanced by religious organizations heavily involved in social activism in the area. The heterosexual nuclear family has been similarly naturalized in the discourse of social service and economic development agencies who assume this configuration as the basic economic and social unit from which to build up the community. The heterosexual reproductive nuclear family is the protagonist of much Latina/o and African-American resistance to the story of development. An examination of promotional brochures for social services and other opportunities in the neighborhood, websites for the corporate as well as nonprofit sector, and even the rhetoric circulated at neighborhood meetings, public festivities, and political demonstrations in Hunts Point shows an almost exclusive focus on the nuclear family and especially on the story of parenting. Rarely do these events acknowledge single-parent households, much less queer kinship. More so, the rhetoric circulated by Latina/o organizations in the South Bronx, including many of those involved in arts and culture, relies on an appropriation of masculine swagger, often aestheticized in hip-hop fashion, as a forceful performance of difference before the corporate sector. There is also a general attitude of disdain toward speaking of sex altogether, with the exception of traditional family planning. As I mentioned earlier, prostitution is frequently cited as the primary cause of neighborhood deterioration in Hunts Point. To formulate sex-positive alternatives or to circulate queer sexual identities within the broader public sphere of this neighborhood entails engaging with the overwhelming focus on the reproductive heterosexual family and an overall negative attitude toward sex grounded in the experience of the sex trade.

In his performance-based work Arthur Aviles recovers the social intimacy of collective participation and opens up the possibilities for ways of knowing community that move beyond rigid scripts of corporate development or heteropatriarchal formulations of activism. He practices Latina/o queer homemaking through the arts. As the scaling-off paint on the welcoming sign on Hunts Point Avenue suggests, the story of the neighborhood cannot be understood in a simple or singular narrative of economic progress or social blight. Much as the billboard attempts to perform as a warm gateway into the neighborhood despite its quickly decaying conditions, the community of Hunts Point struggles to become a home to a small but highly concentrated residential district that is entirely represented neither in the narratives of progress of the industrial park nor in the nighttime geographies of the sex trade. In working toward building a collective future in the South Bronx, Hunts Point residents must and often do engage with dominant narratives about their neighborhood as they try to secure their participation in the economic gains of the region and seek to transform their neighborhood into a more liveable environment for their families. Nevertherless, the collective effort to make Hunts Point a home requires a different narrative focus, one that I argue has been appropriately articulated and inscribed in the performance work of Arthur Aviles and his collaborators.

Dance as Public Practice: Artur Aviles's Homecoming

How can the arts, and dance in particular, contribute to the collective development and betterment of Hunts Point? What might perfomance as a collaborative artistic practice do to model community awareness and participation in the day-to-day concerns of the neighborhood? How might Latina/o queer cultural workers engage in what performance theorist Jill Dolan has termed "performance as public practice," or the ability and force of performance to affect, even change, our social imagination and arrangements?[28] In Hunts Point, arts organizations and artists like Arthur Aviles have focused on the development of sites of conviviality and exchange from which collective efforts might in turn emerge. A bright yellow caption on the welcoming billboard on Hunts Point Avenue announces the neighborhood as "The New Spot for Arts and Entertainment." On the right-hand side of the billboard directional signs guide the viewer to three of the leading arts and culture institutions credited with giving Hunts Point such a reputation as an emerging arts center in the city: BAAD, the Point Community Development Corporation, and the Bronx Charter School for the Arts. Arts and cultural institutions in Hunts Point operated during the mid-1990s and into the early 2000s in the midst of a major transitional period for the local residents as the industrial sector expanded in an attempt to ward off competition from other New York metro locales in pursuit of the food distribution business. Hunts Point cultural institutions worked to ensure the fair participation of local community members in the development of the neighborhood.[29] To achieve this goal, their identity campaigns advanced a proud identification with the area by promoting an understanding of its history and makeup, education on the issues involved in the efforts of the corporations, and activist organizing. And it is precisely the contributions that the arts made and may continue to bring to the practices of community building, awareness, and action that I wish to showcase in my discussion of Hunts Point resident and cultural worker Arthur Aviles.

To some, focusing on Latina/o queer performance might seem tangential at best, or trivial at worst, especially when addressing a period when the Hunts Point neighborhood was undergoing significant economic developments ushered in by federal and state government-funded tax incentives and while local communities organized to negotiate their survival in the midst of these rapid changes. However, cultural workers such as Aviles demonstrate how queer latinidad might in fact be central to a critical standpoint relative to development in Hunts Point. Dancer-choreographer Arthur Aviles, along with his collaborators playwright and novelist Charles Rice-González and performance artist Elizabeth Marrero, worked to create a queer home within this Latina/o neighborhood. They invested in creating a space where queer Latinas/os could gather publicly and encounter themselves on and off the stage. Their performance work offered a refreshing alternative, a moment of rest, to the busy itineraries of living Latina/o queer lives in less hospitable public contexts.

For Aviles the labor of culture is inextricably linked to his personal search for community and home. In many ways his search for community embodies the migratory history of this neighborhood. Born to Puerto Rican migrants in Queens, New York, Aviles was raised in

Brooklyn and the Bronx. He grew up surrounded by the Puerto Rican diaspora. Yet, as literary critic Lawrence La Fountain-Stokes has noted, "In Arthur's house, everything Puerto Rican was frowned upon; as he puts it, his home was a constant battlefield in which American values and customs were presented as superior even while Puerto Rican traditions and habits were observed. This explains why Arthur does not speak much Spanish."[30] Aviles's parents encouraged him to become versed in the language and culture of the United States as a strategy to secure his success and social mobility. Proficiency in English and knowledge of US-American culture were equated with access to wealth and power. Despite this assimilationist notion of the experience of migration, Puerto Rican culture, if slightly undervalued, remained an ever-present influence in Aviles's life. It was evident in the quotidian practices of the family, from food preparation and musical preferences to personal style and speech patterns.

The simultaneous assumption of two seemingly contradictory positions toward cultural valuation in the home is not unique to the Aviles household. As sociologist Juan Flores has observed,

> Puerto Ricans in the United States are tending toward neither as-
> similation nor uncritical cultural preservation; they are neither
> becoming Americans nor continuing to be Puerto Rican in any
> handed-down or contrived sense. Their historical position as a co-
> lonial people at the lowest level of the North American class struc-
> ture makes either option unfeasible. But what is left is not simply
> confusion, or cultural anomaly, or a "subculture of poverty," as a
> wide spectrum of commentators including René Marqués, Edu-
> ardo Seda-Bonilla and Oscar Lewis conclude. It is a delicate bal-
> ance, "a tight touch," as [Tato] Laviera calls a remarkable short
> poem.[31]

Aviles's upbringing displays the "tight touch" of the Puerto Rican experience in diaspora. Laviera's poem, included in his critically acclaimed collection *La Carreta Made a U-turn,* describes the subterranean marginalities of Puerto Rican experience through the metaphor of the crevice, a narrow opening, "deeply hidden in basement land." This margin is also an opening that ushers in "the scratching rhythm of dice / percussion like two little bongos / in a fast mambo." And it is this sensorial awakening into music that ushers in the light "struggling to sneak in" and the "echo of the scent" allowing the marginal to become the possible. As the poem affirmatively announces, "we are beautiful anywhere, you dig?"[32] Much as Laviera's poem embraces the contradictory elements of an abject geography with the performatively invigorating force of diasporic aesthetics, Aviles's experience showcases the negotiations between an assimilationist discourse maintained in proximity to a tacit Puerto Rican habitus, demonstrating—consciously or not—what theorist Homi Bhabha has characterized as "cultural hybridity."[33] For example, Aviles identifies as New York Rican instead of the more commonly used Nuyorican to strategically mark his distance from an idealized "authentic" Puerto Rican subject. Assuming this label allows him to claim his difference as a non-Spanish-speaking queer artist of Puerto Rican descent who grew up in a family that at once dismissed and embodied Puerto Ricanness. These identificatory hybridities are paralleled by Aviles's equally eclectic dance education.

Aviles trained as a dancer at Bard College in upstate New York with an emphasis in dance techniques developed by notable choreographers José Limón and Merce Cunningham. He learned both narratively oriented forms of modern dance and the irreverent formal experimentation of the postmodern tradition. He graduated into an eight-year career with the internationally acclaimed Bill T. Jones / Arnie Zane Dance Company. Touring with the Jones/Zane company, he put to practice the emphasis on cultural identity he found so present in the Limón repertoire and the formal playfulness with movement characteristic of the Cunningham tradition. More profoundly, Aviles learned to use performance as a tool for social engagement as modeled by the politically invested works of the Jones/Zane company, including the much discussed *Still/Here* (1994): a full-length dance piece developed out of a series of dramaturgical workshops with participants experiencing terminal illnesses including HIV/AIDS.[34] Jones's *Still/Here* was at the center of debates about the state of the arts in the 1990s. At the time, the *New Yorker* dance critic Arlene Croce, a staunch critic of the development of politically assertive art during the rise of multiculturalism in the 1980s, dismissed Jones's staging of the real-life experiences with illness and the testimonies of his collaborators through the medium of dance as a move away from the universal "art for art's sake" address she expected of the genre. Croce labeled Jones's work "victim art" and refused to attend the performance. Despite not having seen it, Croce published a diatribe against Jones's work.[35] Aviles experienced this debate firsthand as a soloist in the Jones/Zane company and a participant in the development of *Still/Here*. He bore on his body the stories of interlocutors with whom he interacted during the dance workshops from which the piece was developed. Moreover, encountering the controversy over Jones's work presented him with the realization that the work he deemed of most significance or relevance as a queer man of color was not necessarily the work being welcomed by the arbiters of culture in established publications like the *New Yorker*. *Still/Here* represents a significant lesson for Aviles on the marginal nature of the work he found most compelling. If we assume Croce's dismissal to be representative of a hegemonic dance public, then Jones's *Still/Here* and the public it imagines and creates in performance might be considered under the rubric of what queer theorist Michael Warner understands as a counterpublic, or an alternative public aware of its marginal stance. Jones's counterpublic is one that, aware of its subordinate position, broadcasts with urgency to a community constituted by dancers and audiences alike, as well as those whose solidarity with or affinity to the concerns, the aesthetics, and the labor of his work become oriented toward his art from the distance.

The idea of a counterpublic offers an appropriate entry point into Aviles's own practice as a homemaker through dance. Michael Warner understands publics as emerging from "the circulation of texts among strangers who become, by virtue of their reflexively circulating discourse, a social entity."[36] Warner's definition of the public is based on German sociologist and philosopher Jürgen Habermas's influential theorization of the public sphere in *The Structural Transformation of the Public Sphere*.[37] In his study, Habermas approximates a phenomenon of social exchange that emerged in eighteenth-century Europe. With the rise of the bourgeoisie and their communication through quotidian exchanges in public spaces such as the square, the café, and the salon and via printed sources, communities of opinion emerged. These exchanges resided in a realm distinct from the private spaces of the home and the authoritative spaces of the state or the church. Habermas's publics are endowed with the critical ability to democratically engage in open debate over their socioeconomic and cultural worlds and collectively shape both their sense of being in those worlds and the imagination and construction of new ones. Feminist critic Nancy Fraser identifies the historical exclusions present in and constitutive of the Habermasian concept of the public sphere and advances the concept of the "subaltern counterpublic" as an alternative social phenomenon under which marginalized communities—variously defined by class, gender, race, sexuality, and so on—engage in public social exchanges that are both cognizant and oftentimes critical of the hegemonic or dominant publics of bourgeois society.[38]

Warner in turn engages Fraser's critique to champion the possibilities of queer counterpublics. Counterpublics, in his understanding, are endowed with "world-making" capacities that do not necessarily depend on prior identitarian assumptions (although they are certainly influenced by them). They have the capacity to performatively enact new orientations into collective social configurations. As he explains:

> A public or counterpublic can do more than represent the interests of gendered or sexualized persons in a public sphere. It can mediate the most private and intimate meanings of gender and sexuality. It can work to elaborate new worlds of culture and social relations in which gender and sexuality can be lived, including forms of intimate association, vocabularies of affect, styles of embodiment, erotic practices, and relations of care and pedagogy. It can therefore make possible new forms of sexual citizenship—meaning active participation in collective world making through publics of sex and gender.[39]

Approaching queer latinidad as a counterpublic entails strategic movement across varied geographies in order to explore the many experiences, interests, and desires that coalesce under such an intersectional communicative event. In lived experience, attending to each of these identitarian or collective investments often requires the temporary separation of membership from one public for another: I should be gay in Chelsea but Puerto Rican in El Barrio.[40] For many queer Latinas/os, finding a meeting place to encounter each other in the public realm requires travel, oftentimes outside Latina/o communities, where queerness is often marginalized, and into "queer districts" characterized by white-oriented rainbow-flag aesthetics and social conventions where latinidad is not always welcomed. Despite this, there is a growing number of Latina/o queer spaces, including temporarily transformed spaces, such as the Orgullo en Acción Latino Gay Pride Picnic in Chicago's Humboldt Park with which I open this book, that insist on transforming assumptions about the Latina/o public sphere as antithetical to queerness.[41] Since the mid-1990s Aviles has labored to establish such a queer home within Hunts Point.

The ethos of participating in counterpublic art-making and the no-

tion that communities are constituted in the efforts of dance labor resonate with Aviles's own understanding of his practice as a cultural worker
after retiring from the Jones/Zane company. His approach to dance is
founded on the idea that the exercise of dance making results in significant community development. As Aviles explains:

> When I was leaving his company [Bill T. Jones] it was like I was
> part of one community, which was almost a fantastical commu-
> nity, and the reason I say that is because we toured all over the
> world as, in a sense, as a community. That's what companies do.
> You get to know these people. You go here and there with them.
> You learn how to deal with their personalities in different situa-
> tions. You know they are not your sisters, your mother, they are
> not even your ethnicity. So I learned to communicate in a wide
> range. So that community was one thing that was extremely im-
> portant for me.[42]

The social negotiations encountered during the shared routine labor of
the dance company result in social practices that, as performance theorist Judith Hamera has demonstrated in her ethnography of dance communities in Los Angeles, dance communities into being.[43] In recognizing
the socially generative potential of dance making (from technique class
to rehearsal to performance), Aviles assumes community dramaturgy as
central to his practice. Through detailed attention to the material elements of making performance, Aviles enters the labor of producing work
with a commitment to process as an important and often the primary
component of performance.

The investment of time in shared space dedicated to engaging collectively in ideas and desires through movement is the substance of Aviles's
process. If we consider once again that this sense of community is developed relative to a climate where critics like Arlene Croce and her stand
on "victim art" represent a powerful sector in the mainstream, then the
labor of politically aware Latina/o and queer dance-making, and the
community it creates inside and outside the studio, can be considered
to constitute a counterpublic. And it is from this investment in counterpublics as viable alternatives to social and aesthetic practice that Aviles's
homecoming to the Bronx ought to be understood as both a return to his
Puerto Rican (or New York Rican) roots and a commitment to creating
new paths, queerly.

In his work, Aviles attempted to build the home he sought to find when he returned to the Bronx. He did not seek to re-create representational formulas of what a Puerto Rican Bronx should traditionally look or feel like. Instead he populated it with equally passionate performers, characters, and audiences that produce home, Bronx or otherwise, in the embodied collectivity of performance. When he decided to venture into Hunts Point to develop a new dance company, he went explicitly in search of this home. As he says, "I went to Hunts Point with the exclusive purpose of building a relationship to my community, a relationship to my ethnicity." He approached this through a literal relocation of his life. He further explains, "For me one of the changes in philosophy in relation to Bill's [Bill T. Jones] company is that I said that when I left the company I was going to set up a situation right around the corner from where I lived, because after all that traveling around I found it very difficult to focus. And I needed some focus then."[44]

Focus for Aviles meant self-focus, an engagement with his personal quest for identity. Furthermore, Aviles's desire to develop his own work involved an investment in a local sense of place. After eight years of belonging to the mobile community of the dance company, Aviles relocated to Maneida Street in the Hunts Point neighborhood to live around the corner from his studio.

Aviles's move to Hunts Point in 1996 resulted from an invitation by Bard College alumni singer-songwriter Mildred Ruiz and performance poet Steven Sapp to join them at the Point, a community center on Garrison Avenue cofounded by the couple with current director Maria Torres and former director Paul Lipson. His work with other cultural workers invested in effecting changes in the quality of life in Hunts Point provided a critical community and learning experience that shaped the development of his own space three years later. The mission of the Point is to bring art, culture, and economic development to Hunts Point. Its mission statement reads:

> The Point Community Development Corporation is a non-profit organization dedicated to youth development and the cultural and economic revitalization of the Hunts Point section of the South Bronx. We work with our neighbors to celebrate the life and art of our community, an area traditionally defined solely in terms of its poverty, crime rate, poor schools, and sub-standard housing. We believe the area's residents, their talents and aspirations, are The

Point's greatest assets. Our mission is to encourage the arts, local enterprise, responsible ecology, and self-investment in the Hunts Point community.[45]

The Point adopted a cultural development model that sought to build the community from below, allowing residents of the area to participate fully in the transformations taking place in Hunts Point. As Don Adams and Arlene Goldbard explain, "In community cultural development work, community artists, singly or in teams, place their artistic and organizing skills at the service of the emancipation and development of an identified community, be it one of proximity (e.g., a neighborhood or a small town), interest (e.g., shipyard workers, victims of environmental racism) or any other affinity (e.g., Latino teenagers, the denizens of a senior center)."[46] The Point followed this model closely. It offered education in the arts including theater, dance, creative writing, and visual arts in combination with after-school programs, technology proficiency courses, and the Activists Coming to Inform Our Neighborhood program (ACTION), an activist program that trains teenagers to select, organize, and execute social change projects in the Hunts Point neighborhood.

The organization was founded on the belief that culture, and the arts specifically, are practices of community empowerment and thus vehicles for economic development. In an interview for the *Bronx Times* Mildred Ruiz explained, "It's been our experience that where art thrives in a community, the economy of the community also thrives. Look at the Apollo in Harlem: it's a world famous performance center and all sorts of businesses have grown up around it."[47] The Point's building, formerly an abandoned bagel factory remodeled in 1996, houses the Live From the Edge theater, a Bessie and Obie Award–winning one-hundred-seat flexible space and the only professional theater space in Hunts Point until Aviles's opening of the Bronx Academy of Arts and Dance in 1999.[48] In addition to the theater and arts facilities, the Point offers affordable retail and office space to local entrepreneurs that has included the only dance apparel store in the South Bronx, a soul food restaurant, a woodcarver, a public relations agency, a catering company, and Strange Fruit TV, New York City's longest-running gay soap opera.

Arthur Aviles joined the center to develop a dance program that would reflect the scope and focus of the Point's mission. He taught modern dance technique and worked incessantly to develop a dance scene in the Bronx. The efforts to make home in Hunts Point thus entail both a physical relocation into the Bronx and a reembodiment of the everyday as the dancer negotiates his return to his community as home and develops practices of being, most clearly articulated in the act of choreographing movement that require cohabitation with others in performance.

Aviles's approach to dance making as a practice of community development can be most clearly identified in one of his first and most successful projects: "A Community That Dances Together," an annual talent showcase where community members were invited to display their creativity in a fun and supportive environment. "A Community That Dances Together" was performed annually at the Edge Theater from 1998 to 2000. Aviles rounded up a diverse group of community members: business people, the homeless, local kids, and parents of different races and ethnic backgrounds. The performances were organized in a talent show format without the competition that generally governs them. Despite the investment in individual presentations, Aviles insisted that all participants in the production work together to learn a group dance that would frame the evening's performances. Aviles explains,

> We had some common dance material, very easy, some very basic patterns, and circle dances, stomp phrases. And I introduced something, so that if someone in the community wanted to come up and display their talent, if they wanted to sing, read some poetry or do a dance, it was still connected to this one big dance piece that kind of moved a talent show along from beginning to end.[49]

The choreography was relatively simple, emphasizing basic rhythmic step counts and large easy-to-follow floor patterns. Framing the individual performances with a collaborative dance piece also shifted the focus of the event from competitive display into one of community practice. But what was most significant about the group choreography was the time commitment to shared space required to rehearse it. Participants who would have otherwise worked in isolation had to commit sufficient time to learn and rehearse Aviles's choreography. In doing so they had to commit to engaging each other.

What might all of this have to do with queer latinidad? If we return to the concept of counterpublics as understood by Warner, we find that publics can be understood as "stranger relationality."[50] These are relationships among strangers who come together not so much under a prescripted identitarian premise, although these too are possible entry points into such encounters, but participate in the very constitution of the public as a performatively achieved becoming. This becoming, the collectivity that is the public, is facilitated through the mediations of cultural phenomena that may assume but not always predict its targeted collective or audience. If a counterpublic is a doing, a verb rather than a noun, then we find ourselves in the midst of a model of social engagement less invested in the continuation of traditional models of kinship and more open to improvisational, at times accidental, routes to the formation of community and home. Latinidad, queer latinidad in particular, figures as the aesthetic and social form through which the stranger relationality of Aviles's counterpublicity emerges.

The shared time and space of the dance studio or the dance theater may be understood thus as an important site for *convivencia diaria*. As anthropologists Milagros Ricourt and Ruby Danta explain about their fieldwork on Latina panethnicity in Corona, Queens:

> Convivencia diaria extends from homes to the interactions established in stores, workplaces, and a variety of public spaces. Products sold in stores and interconnections and collaboration in workplaces and public spaces all lead to cultural exchanges among Corona's Latinos as people of many diverse nationalities exchange vocabulary, foods, music, folk remedies, information and so on. These intra-Latino cultural exchanges form the content of an ongoing experiential panethnicity.[51]

The quotidian social intimacies that Ricourt and Danta understand as *convivencia diaria* parallel the emergence of community Hamera identifies in the labor of dance training and dance making. Bringing together a multigenerational and diverse group of performers that included working-class or middle-class heterosexual nuclear families as much as their queer, sex worker, homeless, and poor neighbors expanded notions of who belongs to Hunts Point. These collaborative gatherings worked to counter the affective evictions other representations, like Owens's films, might provoke.

Furthermore, Aviles's enactments of home constitute a theory in practice that brings to fruition the kinds of alternative modes of affiliation Chicana scholar Cherríe Moraga describes as "making *familia* [family] from scratch."[52] Moraga's notion of queer *familia* emerges from a Chicana feminist standpoint that accounts for the tensions her ethnicity, gender, and sexuality introduce to her relationships with her biological family, the feminist movement, and the Chicano movement. Like "stranger relationality," "making *familia* from scratch" means entering into a social formation influenced by traditional family kinship but open to the potential that others might join with whom equally and sometimes more powerful intimacies may develop. Moraga's notion of *familia* and homemaking has been central to Latina/o queer cultural criticism— from Richard T. Rodríguez's critical assessment of the heteropatriarchal foundations of *la familia* as a formative grounding of Chicana/o cultural production to Marivel T. Danielson's critical analysis of Chicana and Latina "queer homecomings."[53] While Rodríguez works through an archive of representations inspired by the Chicano movement and created by Chicano men and Danielson attends to the work of Chicana and Latina queer cultural workers, they both demonstrate the pressures imposed by a history of Chicano and Latino heteropatriarchal models of kinship and the possibilities of their queer reworkings. At the heart of both projects is an understanding that in figuring community, queer Chicanas/os and Latinas/os, as Rodríguez concludes in his study, "will undoubtedly continue to critically assess and negotiate their relationships with the families to whom they are born as well as to those with whom they are joined by necessity."[54] I understand Aviles within this genealogy of cultural work that seeks to engage and interrogate Latina/o family, home, neighborhood, and community through creative counter-representations of Latina/o queer sociality. But what Aviles so masterfully performs in his work is also a collectivizing of the process of homemaking by extending the process beyond the biography or representation of a single cultural worker and into a participatory engagement with dance for all involved, either as artistic collaborators or as audiences. In performance, as a commitment to sharing time and space, participants temporarily become *familia.*

Aviles's dance invites negotiations of difference across national, ethnic, racial, gender, and sexual orientations, first by calling them into being as predetermined characteristics, what would result in a diverse but formulaic casting call, and then by suspending the certainty of their governance over the collective constituted in the rehearsal room. Aviles sees these, at times difficult, exchanges as necessary steps into the exploration of his own sense of self, intersected with multiple sites of identification. That is, to be New York Rican with its reference to many localities and trajectories of migration, to be light skinned in a Puerto Rican community marked by the history of racialized discrimination,[55] to be queer in a community that is traditionally homophobic, and to be an artist in a neighborhood where daily sustenance is the main concern for many of its residents remain the purpose and motivation behind Aviles's monumental stance. It is by inhabiting these multiple positions and insisting on the possibility of intersubjective intimacy or *convivencia diaria* from within these recognized differences that Aviles insists community may develop and the feeling of being at home can arise.

Irreverent Performances: Popular Entertainment and Queer World-making

Thus far I have been discussing the contexts out of which Aviles has developed his dance practice and the strategies of homemaking he has incorporated into his participatory dance projects. I would now like to turn to his choreography to further explore the ways in which his dance performs home in the South Bronx. Few scholars have engaged Arthur Aviles's choreographic oeuvre.[56] Literary scholar Lawrence La Fountain-Stokes has offered the most sustained engagement with his work to date, including a chapter in his book-length study of queer Puerto Rican cultural production, which offers a close reading of *Arturella,* a piece I discuss below.[57] La Fountain-Stokes makes a compelling argument for the ways cultural adaptation serves as the foundation for Aviles's representation of "Nuyorico," which he defines as a "space of liberation, tolerance, and social justice, or at the very least, one marked by queer visibility and fulfillment."[58] I agree with La Fountain-Stokes's identification of the utopian impulse or Nuyorico that governs Aviles's choreography. In fact his critique supports my argument for understanding Aviles as a Latina/o queer homemaker. However, my approach to Aviles's work differs in significant ways. First, instead of a textual reading of the dramatic action on stage I offer a reading that is grounded on performance as a social event where the contexts of circulation and reception are critical and where the embodied actions of dancers on stage matter. In this way, I combine my critical decoding of the theatrical representations with an assessment of the collective responses of others who constituted, along with me, part of the counterpublic of the performance event. The spatiality La Fountain-Stokes identifies and theorizes as representation is for me also a lived and experienced materiality. Second, while La Fountain-Stokes positions Aviles's work within a specifically Puerto Rican critique, I understand it within the rubric of latinidad. In doing so I seek to establish politico-economic interconnections between representational traditions not necessarily addressed to Puerto Ricans but invested in the (mis)representation of latinidad internationally.

To understand the significance of Aviles's counterpublicity it is important to account for his complex relationship to commercial media and other hegemonic cultural sources. If we return to the two narratives about Hunts Point that have historically dominated public perception about the neighborhood—the corporate development and the sex and drug markets stories especially—we notice that they gain their representational weight from their distribution through media networks. Whether it is printed, radio, or television news coverage and commentary about Hunts Point; the fictional representations of the South Bronx in film, popular literature, and music; or the exploitative HBO films by Owens, the image of Hunts Point in the public sphere seems overdetermined by corporate media.

In developing a counterpublic discourse about Hunts Point, Aviles does not necessarily shun media. Rather, he appropriates them irreverently for local interests. Here one can apply Don Adams and Arlene Goldbard's approach to community cultural development:

> There is no indication that globalization will somehow bring about the reversal of its own destructive effects or even the amelioration of those effects. Rather, it demands responses that can exert powerful countervailing pressure. Community cultural development efforts constitute one such response, making democratic counterforces of some of the same arts and media tools previously used to promote global saturation and media culture.[59]

Fully aware of the dominance as well as the potential of media technologies for the work of cultural development, Adams and Goldbard observe that although media often produces antisocial modes of entertainment geared toward passive consumption, it may at times offer progressive sites of interaction and even collective imaginaries. Aviles is an expert at media appropriation and has built much of his fame as a cultural practitioner on the *latinization* and queering of popular cultural gems such as Disney's *Cinderella* (1939), MGM's *The Wizard of Oz* (1950), and other fairy tales such as *The Ugly Duckling*. As dance scholar Ann Daly has observed, for Aviles "the issue of originality is moot. He has taken the post-modern principle of appropriation to its extreme: he openly copies, everything from Disney movies to whole dances by Martha Graham, José Limón and even Mr. Jones."[60] Aviles's performances superimpose a Latina/o queer aesthetic or story onto the classical mythologies of American popular culture, and sometimes even onto works of "high art" dance traditions such as the choreographies of Graham and Limón. Through these acts of appropriation Aviles engages the narratives of mass media from the perspective of Latina/o queer experience and translates those experiences to the larger community in the Bronx. He recurs to the very mechanisms that have ensured the popularity of these representations. By doing this, Aviles extends the community-building effort of the intimate Latina/o queer site into the broader realm of Latina/o performance. This invites queer participation within publics that remain, for the most part, uncommitted or resistant to queer experience. Aviles attracts his audiences with the mass appeal of the entertainment classics and master narratives. This strategy is situated in pleasure as the unifying experience for all members of the audience and the production. Audience members are generally familiar with the stories and films that Aviles restages and are likely to come to the performance space with the expectation of enjoying a theater adaptation that embodies a similar aesthetic investment in showmanship and spectacle. That is, people come to the theater motivated to see *Cinderella*, *The Wizard of Oz*, and *The Ugly Duckling* assuming that the dance will closely resemble the experience of the original. Aviles satisfies this desire by constructing a carnivalesque staging that seeks to match the fantasy world of the originals, but does so through the incorporation of Latina/o vernacular languages of performance. For example, his choreography blends modern dance, a movement vocabulary with little circulation among many of his spectators, with the more easily recognized Latina/o social dance vocabularies such as salsa and merengue. Through a hybrid movement repertoire, Aviles translates the mass-mediated entertainments into local articulations of popular performance.

Interestingly, much of the work that Aviles so irreverently poaches to develop his work offers narrative structures based on displacement and the desire to return home or belong to a particular social unit. For example, in works like *El Pato Feo* (2000) and *Super Maeva de Oz* (1997) Aviles adapts the classic Hans Christian Anderson coming-of-age tale *The Ugly*

Duckling and the 1950 MGM film *The Wizard of OZ* respectively, into New York Rican queer fantasies.[61] In *El Pato Feo*, the ugly duckling is a young Latino transsexual who is mocked by his peers for not fitting into traditional gender roles. After much struggle attempting to assimilate to the standards of Latino homeboy masculinity, he finds the strength to accept his path into gender nonconformity and emerges gloriously as the swan/queen that he has been struggling all along to suppress. In *Maeva de Oz,* Dorotea, a young Latina lesbian, finds herself lost in the closet as she explores a fantastical world of queer characters who educate her to accept her sexuality and eventually to come out of the closet empowered by her newly assumed identity. The narrative structures of these fairy tales—the protagonists' journey through a path of rejection or distancing from the community, their fantastical experiences through a world of utopian possibilities, and their final emergence as newly realized subjects—serve as the basis for an exploration of Latina/o queers' own relationship to their community in the South Bronx. Aviles devises approaches to cultural material generally assumed as "mainstream" or "universal" that open up the possibilities for local identification and community transformation. He explains,

> I take these models [i.e., the fairy tale] because I think they are good classic models. I picked them because they provide a good structure. And my question is, where do we [Latinos and queers] live inside of that structure? Also, what can we change about that structure so that it speaks to us? Because there is something there that doesn't speak to us, but it is still a vibrant structure. So it's not a negation of the structure, it's a reworking of it so that we feel that we are involved. You know these fairy tales when they are given to communities, we don't feel involved, they are about white people who are living their lives in fantastical ways, and the ways the pictures are drawn and what they are saying are particular to that community. What we are saying is OK, we get it, but these are universal themes and we will show you how universal they really are.[62]

Through claims to the universality of forms, Aviles appropriates hegemonic cultural artifacts that generally exclude Latina/o and queer identities, and turns them into vibrant articulations of the very subjectivities these representations marginalize. In restaging dominant models as expressions of fantastical marginality, Aviles demonstrates the critical role of the imagination in the survival strategies of Latina/o queers who seek to find themselves and community in the midst of a heteronormative and xenophobic public sphere (remember that Latinas/os and African-Americans make their way to Hunts Point as displaced undesirables for the development of Manhattan). Cultural critic Ramona Fernandez has observed this very strategy in alternative navigations of Disney culture. In her discussion of Epcot Center, one of Disney World's most visited parks, she concludes that when the narrative construction of popular entertainment forms, such as Disney, alienates specific communities, there remain strategies for agency and intervention. She explains, "Those who are excluded for any reason must regularly draw alternative maps, rewrite narratives to move from a place of invisibility to imaginative inclusion. This is precisely what they do everyday [sic]: live lives of complex negotiation within a simulated and distorted landscape."[63] Aviles's own use of appropriation remakes structures of dominance into productive sites for Latina/o queer perspectives. However, his interventions in performance are not simple acts of mistranslation; instead, they present an explicit critique by pointing to the very structures of exclusion that popular culture representations circulate. Furthermore, Aviles performs this critique while maintaining the currency of pleasure that characterizes these forms.

In *Arturella* (1996),[64] for example, Aviles retells the story of Cinderella, popularized in the United States by the animated Disney film. In this dance-drama version of the story, Aviles follows the original plot closely but with a twist: he relocates the romance to the relationship between two young Puerto Rican men in the Bronx. Arturella, played by Aviles, is a young Latino queer man who lives in the company of his loud homophobic stepmother—performed by Elizabeth Marrero, who also appears as Maeva the narrator, the King, and the fairy godmother—and two stepsisters who only communicate through gesture. The prince (Principeso), performed by well-known Teatro Pregones co-artistic director and performer Jorge Merced,[65] is about to celebrate his *quinceañero,* a traditional fifteenth-birthday celebration where Latin American girls are introduced to society as women.[66] Frustrated by his son's sadness and depression over not finding true love, the King decides to take advantage of the public celebration and announces that there will be an official search for Principeso's love partner.

Aviles models different pathways to enter and experience the *Cin-*

Fig. 7. *Arturella* (1996). Arthur Aviles Typical Theater at Hostos Community College, New York. Dancers from left to right: Melina Mackall, Layla Childs, Elizabeth Marrero, Benn Quinones, Arthur Aviles, Jorge B. Merced, and Keila Cordova. Photo by Tom Brazil.

derella story from a queer Latina/o perspective. These alternative maps to the narratives of alienation, marginalization, and integration within the fairy tale further situate Aviles's work as a practice of counterpublic imagination. Disney's own celluloid "Latinizations" of Latin Americans and Latinas/os in the United States are of special importance to Aviles's seemingly simple translations. They also demonstrate the ways in which latinidad as a social imaginary increasingly holds significant explanatory power for Aviles's work even though it has thus far been understood as a primarily Puerto Rican diasporic project.

Beginning in the 1930s, the Good Neighbor policy of President Franklin Delano Roosevelt sought to defuse the onset of socialist national revolutions throughout Latin America by promoting the capitalist models of consumer culture of the United States.[67] Along with economic and military interventions, popular culture, especially film, became a major vehicle for the promotion of American lifestyles to the neighboring nations to the south. All major studios developed Spanish dubbing units and at times even shot Hollywood features with underpaid Spanish-speaking actors on third-shift schedules while the English-speaking cast slept the night away.[68] Walt Disney Studios, along with other film organizations and notables that included Orson Welles, were brought in on the governmental strategy to produce films that would befriend Latin America. The approach was to avoid stereotypical representations to which governments had continuously objected, and to simultaneously lure these populations into a more amenable relationship with the United States. The film career of Brazilian actor-singer Carmen Miranda, for example, emerges during this period as an image of U.S. / Latin American relations that attempts to expand the cultural and economic dominance of the United States throughout the hemisphere, but fails to escape the stereotypical constructions of racist discourse.[69]

In its massive distribution campaigns into Latin America and production of films such as *The Three Caballeros* (1945), Disney became a partner in the curtailing of Latin American revolutionary internationalism through the introduction of U.S.-based consumerist regionalism. The export of U.S. culture to Latin America went hand in hand with economic restructuring policies advocated by the United States. These attempts at selling the USAmerican way to the neighbors to the south led to failed experiments in economic and political "modernization" that motivated the arrival of many Latin American immigrants in the United States to begin with. These projects relied on the playfulness and supposed innocence of family-friendly entertainment. Cultural critic Henry Giroux unveils the way in which Disney representations prescribe dominant ideologies of community, culture, and nation:

> Capitalizing on its inroads into popular culture, Disney generates representations that secure image, desires, and identifications through which audiences come to produce themselves and negotiate their relationship to others. By ordering and structuring such representations, Disney mobilizes a notion of popular culture that parades under the longing for childlike innocence, wholesome adventure, and frontier courage.[70]

Disney played a central role in the integration of Latin American countries into the globalizing projects of American economic and political development through the distribution of seductive representations that modeled the United States as a fantastical utopia that matched the exotic worlds of the animated features. These were the images of hope and progress circulated (just as aggressively) in the island colony of Puerto Rico; and it was these representations of the U.S. courtship of Latin America from the 1930s to the 1950s that Puerto Rican migrants encountered on their arrival to New York City. In this sense the Puerto Rican diasporic imagination is always already interrelated to the broader networks of Latin American economies and cultures as imagined through the eyes of USAmerican imperialism. The interconnections of Puerto Ricanness with, and as, latinidad during the Good Neighbor period include historically proximate experiences with U.S.-originated economic and political policies and the shared circulation of U.S.-sponsored media. The insistence of these media in advancing a friendly wholesome image of the United States to Latin America masked a history of not-so-friendly interventions throughout the hemisphere.

Arturella overhauls Disney's sanitized version of the story by adapting it into an adult and queer public. Performances like *Arturella* critique the historical imposition of U.S. cultural forms and moral codes as part of an imperialist agenda and attitude toward the rest of the hemisphere. In this performance, Aviles disrupts the fantasy of innocence behind U.S. cultural imperialism by pointing toward the marginalized conditions of the Puerto Rican diaspora. Aviles uses the narrative structure and aesthetic conventions of the Disney film to showcase the very inequities of contemporary life with which the corporation and its representations are partially complicit.

Arturella was originally performed at the Eugenio Maria de Hostos Community College, a City University of New York campus that serves a primarily African-American, Latino, and economically disadvantaged student body two miles south of Hunts Point.[71] The theater is a state-of-the-art 367-seat proscenium stage located within the Center for the Arts complex in the Grand Concourse neighborhood of the Bronx. The institution has been characterized by its interest in offering educational opportunities that are specific to the needs of the South Bronx. Through season planning that reflects the interests and tastes of the community, Hostos Community College has managed to create a vibrant, well-attended performance season in the neighborhood. The seasonal offerings in the performing arts focus overwhelmingly on the presentation of Latino traditional arts, especially folk dance and music genres. The

Hostos season has also included more experimental performance genres such as the dance works of Merian Soto's Pepatián, a dance company dedicated to the blend of salsa and modern dance that often addresses issues of race and gender in performance. The works generally performed in the space are often progressive in their representation of and engagement with Latino communities in the Bronx, but relatively conservative in their handling of sexuality. The performances of *Arturella* were advertised as family events, and the lure of the Disney entertainment was crucial in convincing many residents of the South Bronx to attend a theatrical performance. The staging of *Arturella* was, and still remains, the most challenging performance event hosted at the institution, as it brought queer sexuality center stage in ways that some conservative members of the community found to be outside the definition of acceptable family-oriented latinidad.

Arturella is not quite a musical, which would seem the most appropriate genre for the adaptation of the Disney film. It is instead a hybrid performance piece that merges scripted spoken dialogue with stylized movement sequences that are at times fully representational and at others abstract displays of choreographic patterns that move the characters from scene to scene. In keeping with the expectations of the Disney film, *Arturella* adopts a dreamy, playful aesthetic with a purposefully marked sense of simplicity. The performance makes no use of scenic extravagance, favoring simple light cues and, as in "A Community That Dances Together," enacting the entire piece on a bare stage. The costuming does not attempt to re-create the film. Instead, Liz Prinze's costume design takes a more minimalist approach, dressing the mice, for example, with single-tailed gray tuxedo suits instead of the full-body costumes popularized in performances such as the Broadway production of *Beauty and the Beast* or the traveling productions of *Disney on Ice,* which, following the tradition of Disneyworld and Disneyland, present exact, oversized replicas of the animated characters. Aviles's barebones design for the performance is in part the result of the budgetary limitations of producing art in the South Bronx. Nonetheless, this simple approach to performance transforms the feel of the Disney film by grounding the story further on the performing bodies and thus presenting their actions, both aurally and kinesthetically, as the focal point of the performance.

Arturella opens with over-the-top Puerto Rican ghetto mother Maeva—a stock character of the Arthur Aviles Typical Theater repertoire performed by Elizabeth Marrero—welcoming audiences to the performance and spinning out the prototypical fairy-tale introduction to a fantastical and faraway land.[72] She is barefoot and dressed in an elegant purple gown that exposes her shoulders and contrasts her overall butch aesthetic and attitude. She flirtatiously addresses the audience, speaking with a powerful, deep voice, grand gesticulation of her arms, and an explosive repertoire of head rolls and exaggerated facial expressions that showcase Puerto Rican corporeality in comic proportions. With the opening line, "Once upon a time in a faraway land there was a tiny ghetto, peaceful, you know, with the occasional crime and the *gangas* and knives *pero* peaceful all the same," she historically situates the Bronx outside the mythical world of the original story. She continues to talk about the ghetto with an endearing sense of pride. Throughout her opening speech she builds up the fantasy world of the performance with inspired references to the kingdom where Principeso, the Prince, resides. These welcoming remarks announce the particular geographical boundaries where Aviles locates the performance. While the move situates the story locally in the Bronx, it also speaks to the extreme isolation from Manhattan that might enable such a characterization of mysterious distance to be believable.[73]

Appropriating the generic reference to distant and fantastical places positions the ghetto as the dialectical partner to the idealized geography of the fairy tale. The strategy of this appropriation is twofold. First, it elevates the ghetto to the status of communitarian idealism, contextualizing the difficult material conditions that characterize the Bronx with a more balanced representation that accounts for the "romance and tradition" that Maeva affectively invokes as she continues her speech. Maeva presents the Puerto Rican ghetto as a fantasy world, and although she acknowledges the presence of poverty and violence, she insists on the positive possibilities of this setting. Second, this relocation marks and makes visible the exclusions present in the sanitized versions of the fairy tale by pointing beyond the mere beauty of the scene to acknowledge that even love encounters difficulties, mounting a critique of the luxuriously unreal idealization of the fairy tale's mythical geography. Moreover, by breaking the spell of affluence in the Disney film, *Arturella* localizes the story in the Puerto Rican queer diasporic context and presents it as an appropriate milieu for a love story.

Arturella presents such demystifying signposts throughout the performance, reminding the audience of both the limitations of the original story and the power of the transgressive variation being staged. As the fairy godmother, played by Marrero as well, enters the stage ready to make Arturella's attendance to the *quinceañero* possible, the transformation scene of the play presents another pointed commentary on the illusionary idealism and material wealth that enable the Disney version of the story. After the evil stepmother manages to destroy his dress, Arturella stands naked center stage sobbing in lamentation. The fairy godmother, a working-class, bouncy lady with a biting sense of humor, enters and says, "Esta bien nene porque yo te voy a hookear!"[74] The fairy godmother is easily identified as an indigenous character of the Puerto Rican community using the vernacular Spanglish of *hookear* to provoke laughter in an audience that would have probably expected the more restrained family oriented propriety of the Disney character. The use of the word may also resonate within the broader webs of meaning that might confuse *hookear* with "hooking" and thus further enhance the sexual force of the performance and its disruption of Disney propriety, aligned as it is with a conservative obsession with family values. It also flirts irreverently with Hunts Point's image as a center of the sex market.

The scene continues as the fairy godmother prepares to magically produce Arturella's ball gown. She swings her arm back and forth and points to Arturella as the audience anticipates the magical moment of the dress's appearance that will cover his naked body. Arturella whirls in place as the mice circle around him in a swell of movement that sets up the transformation. Arturella pauses ecstatically in midturn and faces the audience, expecting to appear in beautiful regalia for the event. Instead, he finds himself still naked. He looks at his godmother in disappointment. She addresses the audience, "Qué tu te crees, that this is a big Broadway production?" and rushes offstage to get the dress.[75] In the middle of this comedy the audience is reminded of the material limitations of theater production in this community and at the same time validated by the "can do" approach by which this performance manages to create an engaging fantastical world with such scarcity of resources. "Qué tu te crees?" or "Who do you think you are?" offers a challenge to the audience to think beyond the fairy tale by marking the distance from a Broadway public. Maeva's interruption of the fantasy signals the counterpublic force of the performance event.

The queering of the fairy tale and of the Latina/o context in which the production is situated is achieved through strategies of intertextual appropriations. Once Arturella is costumed in a white midriff unitard with a connecting mesh skirt exposing the white briefs underneath it, his fairy godmother looks at him proudly and asks: "So how do you feel now, Arturella?" Arturella responds in calm delivery: "I feel pretty, oh so pretty. I feel pretty and witty and *gay!*" The "gay" in this sentence is delivered in an affirmative falsetto voice as Arturella goes on to sing the rest of the *West Side Story* song and moves about the stage in a carnivalesque celebration with his mice friends. This moment of queer affirmation is enacted through the linguistic pun of the "gay" adjective as an indicator of joy and gayness at the same time. The stereotypical performance of "Latinization" in the Broadway musical is here transformed into a pleasurable indulgence of Latina/o queer avowal that mobilizes latinidad in the making of an act of agency.

The gender incongruities of the performance—*Arturella* is a young man but wears dresses, and Elizabeth Marrero's multicharacter performance centers the production on a butch lesbian physicality—and the shift of the story into a same-sex romance further position the piece in a Latina/o queer context. These queering strategies are made more significant by the focus on the performer that the scarcity of scenic spectacle allows. In *Arturella,* the playfulness of gender is articulated without recourse to an exclusive fetishization of drag. Instead, *Arturella* showcases gender fluidity in all its diversity, presenting the strategies of queer identification across a broad spectrum of possible approaches. This maneuver is most eloquently achieved in Marrero's versatile portrayal of her characters. She models, through performance, the shifting sites of gender identification by expertly traversing the different bodily attitudes and vocal nuances of Maeva, the King, the evil stepmother, and the fairy godmother. Furthermore, Marrero becomes a representative figure for the multiple positions and desires found in the community, from the King's loving acceptance of Principeso's sexuality, to the fairy godmother's maternal support of Arturella's desires, and the homophobic irrationality of the stepmother. Through Marrero's embodiment of these multiple positions within the community, *Arturella* manages at once to stage the unspoken conflicts of homophobia and to model more queer-friendly behaviors based on the loving and supportive practices already known by an audience familiar with the Disney narrative.

The strategy becomes more complex as it draws the overwhelmingly Latina/o audience into a familiar geography in the Latina/o appropriation of the Disney classic and simultaneously seeks to challenge the assumed heteronormativity of the Hostos Community College Theater that originally housed the production. And it was precisely this disjunction, between the shared pleasure of watching the Disney story through performative codes specific to Latina/o entertainment and the affirmative showcase of queer sexuality that caused a conflict between the production crew, the local administration at the performing arts center, and the press.

The controversy over *Arturella* revolved around Aviles's use of nudity in the piece. He initially appears nude in the opening scene. As the morning sun rises, Arturella wakes up and is greeted by all the friendly creatures—birds, mice, cats, and dogs. He undresses from his nightgown, mimes the act of bathing, and changes into his house dress. Later on, in his argument with the stepmother described above, he is left naked once more center stage as his stepmother and stepsisters rip through his first ensemble, hand-made specifically to attend Principeso's *quinceañero*. The use of nudity in these two instances is not gratuitous and, as La Fountain-Stokes has aptly observed, offers important nuance to the constructedness of character and identity performed throughout the piece. He explains, "In *Arturella*, nakedness can be read as a symbol of social defiance, of the individual stripped of or placed outside social hierarchies and conventions; it is a sign of punishment, but also serves as an affirmation of identity."[76] This was not, to say the least, Hostos Community College's interpretation of nudity onstage. Although Aviles had made the theater aware of this convention during the rehearsal process, the administration at the college did not announce its opposition or ask Aviles to edit the piece until the opening day of the run. Aviles went against the advice of the administration and performed the piece as initially conceived, nudity included.

While the audience seemed comfortable with these conventions and expressed no particular objections to the presentation of nudity in the piece, conservative critics went on to attack the production based on an inflammatory interpretation of Aviles's naked body as unnecessary display. Most interestingly, *Bronx Times Reporter* critic Ricardo Trancoso implied that Aviles's work overstepped the standards of propriety of the theater, generally defined through its appeal to family-oriented traditional performance genres. He further opined, "Hostos is a public institution and has the right to dictate standards of appropriateness for performers on its stage. Aviles, as a guest on that stage, is obligated to observe those standards."[77] Hostos Center director Wallace Edgecombe went on to question the appropriateness of Aviles's aesthetics through a negative association of his work to the experimental work of P.S. 122,

one of downtown Manhattan's most active alternative performance facilities that frequently produces and presents queer performance. Aviles,
who publicly commented on the controversy during the curtain call at
the end of every performance, observed that much of the objection did
not seem to come from the use of nudity, a practice used in previous
performances by Merián Soto's dance troupe, but by the fact that this
production contained nudity in a queer context. The controversy over
the performance of *Arturella* showcased further the complicated negotiations at stake in the development of a Latina/o queer public in places
like the Bronx. *Arturella* insists on the presence and dignity of queer lives
in the Latina/o ghetto and goes onto unapologetically position them at
the center of the performance, even as a result of conflicts like the Hostos
incident.

Much like its presentation of the Latina/o ghetto, the staging of queer
sexuality in *Arturella* moves beyond simple pleasure or affirmation to
offer a materialist critique of homophobia in the community. In the Disney film, Cinderella, who has danced flirtatiously with the now swooned
prince, rushes out of the ball right before the stroke of midnight. This
dramatic encounter and abrupt separation turns the rest of the film
into a search for the lost damsel and future princess. In *Arturella,* the
prince, equally affected by the sudden disappearance of his dance partner, goes about the kingdom in search of his beloved. He manages to
find Arturella after a comic scene where both stepsisters desperately attempt to force themselves into the ankle ribbon left behind at the dance
(no shoes can be used since all dances are performed barefoot). As the
prince properly affixes the ribbon onto Arturella's ankle and embraces
him in a passionate kiss, the evil stepmother, the stepsisters, and a host
of other characters appear on the stage to express their disgust at the
same-sex couple and approach them in what seems to be an incident
of gay-bashing. While the audience sees the escalating antihomosexual
violence, Maeva, the narrator and commentator throughout the piece,
interrupts and says, "No, no, no. This is my house and what I say goes!"
On the matriarch storyteller's command, the scene is suspended and restaged with the idealized tableau of a wedding scene. The double ending
of *Arturella* denounces the prevalence of homophobia in Latina/o communities and presents an affirmative queer presence as authoritative, or
at least a legitimate alternative.

Aviles's staging of the fairy tale manages to dream the local possibilities of queer latinidad through the structures of dominant representations

constitutive of the public sphere. *Arturella* manages to create Latina/o queer alternative stories that challenge the heteronormative impulse of the Disney original. These appropriations and negotiations through performance manage to queerly rearticulate the mediatized moral codes of Disney representations and produce alternative counterpublics for the Latina/o queer community. Behind the mask of pleasurable playfulness lies the serious work of emancipatory imaginings instantiated in the present of performance. In *Arturella,* Aviles dares to imagine home through unapologetic appropriation of the Disney narrative. But most importantly, he dares to assemble a counterpublic in the "stranger relationality" of the performance space as a home for queer latinidad.

Home Is Where the Heart Is: On Loving Queerly and Publicly

In Aviles's work, dance serves as the cultural mediator through which participants may become a counterpublic. As I explained above, this relationship to the process of performance may be construed as introducing queer modes of sociality that invest in less fixed and hegemonic notions of what constitutes community or home. The performances of *Arturella* at Hostos Community College further demonstrate how Aviles's work is invested in the counterpublicity of queer sexuality within the home of latinidad. In another dance piece, *This Pleasant and Grateful Asylum* (1999),[78] Arthur Aviles performs a love duet to J. S. Bach's Italian Concerto II that allows us to understand further the relationship between the *convivencia diaria* occasioned by performance, counterpublics, and homebuilding. The piece, a short four-minute dance choreographed and performed with Aviles's then real-life partner, Charles Rice-González, presents "a couple in love surrounded by society's sexual repression" who "break through and explore sexuality and its relational impact on being together."[79]

On a bare stage, the two dancers open the performance moving slowly within a light-blue fabric tensed just enough to show the sensual intertwining of their bodies. The fabric both displays and restricts their range of motion as they lie horizontally side by side and proceed to alternately roll on top of each other in a progression toward the front of the performance space. The dancers sit facing each other, knees bent and legs touching, as they stretch the fabric with a slow but firm extension of the arms that rips through the material to expose the heads, then the torsos, and finally the full nude bodies of the performers. Once they break free from the material that restrains them—a reference to societal obstacles—they pull out a pair of oversized plastic water guns and point them at each other.

At this instance, the dancers's gender is exposed, transforming the preceding performance of stylized sensual exchange into a homosexual act. This moment, although performed with great solemnity, incites laughter on the part of the predominantly Latina/o and queer audience.[80] There are multiple possibile ways of reading this reaction. First of all, the laughter could be a recognition of the stereotype of Latina/o hypermasculinity. As the dancers emerge from their enclosure, point the toy guns and glance defiantly at each other, they measure each other up, not in a literal reference to their bodies, but through detailed attention to the object in each other's hands.[81] The guns, with their bright colors and rounded edges, are exaggerated in a way that makes the characterization of a macho standoff absurd, even comic, both in its literal reference to gun violence and its metaphorical allusions to phallic identification. This masculine fronting is in stark contrast to the naked bodies of the performers—emerging out of what we may understand as a sexual encounter. This contradiction reconfigures hypermasculine exchange as a homoerotic one. It also comments on the self-punishing denial of homosocial encounters through violent disavowal.

Second, the laughter from the audience may also represent a nervous reaction to the public staging of homoeroticism in a community where being out represents a serious departure from conceptions of normality, and where public display of queerness still represents a serious risk.[82] This performance, however, takes place within the safe environment of an explicitly marked Latina/o queer space. Audiences entering events at this location venture, in an act of affirmation, down the lonely, dark street where BAAD's building stands, marked by the gay liberation flag hanging from its front wall. And third, another possible and more complex reading of the audience's reaction to the performance lies in the recognition of the irony from an expert position. This response is capable of holding in tension the comedy and the fear that characterizes the readings above with a more critical and informed stance that addresses the harsh realities of being Latina/o and queer in the South Bronx. It also revels pleasurably in the playful display of eroticism in the piece.

After the opening sequence and the laughter it provokes from the audience, the piece turns quickly into an affirmation of homosexual desire.

Fig. 8. *This Pleasant and Grateful Asylum* (1999). Charles Rice-Gonzalez and Arthur Aviles. Performed at the Bronx Academy of Arts and Dance BAAD. Photo by Richard Shpuntoff.

The dancers put the guns away, as if dismissing both the restraint of the fabric enclosure and the hypermasculine stereotype of the gun, come together in a passionate embrace, and kiss. What follows is a series of balances, tender embraces with rocking motions, and slow sensual turns where the dancers shift their body weight back and forth onto each other without ever breaking the lock of their lips. It is indeed this staging of the kiss and the embrace between two men, known within the community of spectators as a real-life couple, that most successfully turns the performance into an act of Latina/o queer affirmation. Their theory in practice depends on their public performance of their personal life story, their own homemaking in Hunts Point.

Aviles stages his own life for the audience as a generous act of community formation. The audience inside BAAD constitutes, in large part, a community of spectators or a public. They "know" the couple onstage as the couple offstage and in charge of the BAAD operation. As audiences enter the performance space, both Aviles and Rice-González walk about,

Fig. 9. *This Pleasant and Grateful Asylum* (1999). Charles Rice-Gonzalez and Arthur Aviles. Performed at the Bronx Academy of Arts and Dance BAAD. Photo by Richard Shpuntoff.

welcoming everyone to the evening's event. There is no fixed boundary or distinction between the formal arrangement of a performance event and the social realm in which it is housed. At the curtain speech, Aviles formally welcomes the audience and explains how he came about developing both the space and his work as part of his personal desire to find a community where he could be Latina/o and gay in the South Bronx. His life is put on stage as coextensive with the performance. His exposure in the nudity of the dance is one of many public enactments through which his life takes a stand for Latina/o queer communities in the Hunts Point neighborhood.

Staging the performer's personal life allows the public enactment of community, not just through a simple identification with the subject matter addressed by the performance, but through the self-examination evoked in the audience members by the public staging of queer pleasure and fear in pieces such as *This Pleasant and Grateful Asylum*. Arthur Aviles's staging of his life story as a New York Rican gay man negotiating the local geographies of the South Bronx in search of community attempts to elicit similar self-reflexive responses from his spectators. Based on these responses and the identification of points of contact between the struggles, needs, and desires of his audience, Aviles attempts to create community, home.

The blurring of the boundaries between the social situation and the representational formality of performance illustrates dance scholar Ann Cooper Albright's understanding of danced autobiography as an "act of community." She explains, "Although on the surface this may seem like a contradiction in terms, in fact, autobiography has long served as an act of community. Giving testimony and bearing witness by recounting one's life experiences has helped marginalized communities hold onto the experience of their own bodies while reclaiming their history."[83] Aviles's staging of his own life story and his articulate discussion of his search for community allow audience members to identify with his journey and to perhaps embark on a search of their own. Yet home, as the performance playfully points out, is not necessarily an ideal space without frictions and contradictions. Aviles's queerness marked him as an outsider within the traditional Latina/o community of the area. As he explains,

> As a gay man it was difficult, coming back, first of all, to such a macho culture and a macho area. You know, the Bronx is known for its kind of male force and strength and power, a hardcore homeboy front with a great reputation. It just felt challenging for me to come to the Bronx and say, "I'm gay and I'm a man and I'm Latino" and for me to hold my ground in a community that I have an affinity for. And the affinity is really purely because I grew up in the culture.[84]

Aviles's stance as a gay man doubles the domestic battlefield of his upbringing. His negotiation with Latina/o culture—at the level of language, community, and history—complicates his fierce embrace of queer sexuality. He starts out from his affinity for the Puerto Rican community without ever losing touch with the specificity of his queer experience. Much like the insistence on his two geographical and cultural locations in his "New York Rican" identification, Aviles asks and helps his audience to grapple with the complexities of being both Latina/o and queer.

The performance work of Arthur Aviles opens the realm of the imagination for his audiences of Latinas/os and queers in Hunts Point to envision a world of Latina/o queer possibilities. By staging his erotic dance in the South Bronx, Aviles insists on the viability of queer identities, affects, and practices within a Latina/o locale. He exposes himself and his partner in their nakedness as examples of the unspoken desires of many residents in the area still enduring the repression of living their lives in a homophobic culture. *This Pleasant and Grateful Asylum* honors the Latina/o queer community by making a public stance out of the display of the most intimate of scenes. This public performance of queer desire allows residents of Hunts Point who would normally shy away from engaging in queer publics to recognize their membership to a wider community of strangers. This public shares not only the time-space of performance, but a collective investment in loving queerly. Aviles's engagement with the counterpublicity of queer latinidad goes further, attempting an expansion of the viable routes to homemaking in Hunts Point by insisting on the inclusion of queer and Latina/o perspectives within the neighborhood's public life. His investment in the articulation of such a position is a fundamental step in the development and organization of more explicit collective actions.

The outcomes of Latina/o queer counterpublicity need not always result in explicitly political programs. Aviles's unapologetic showcase of queer sexuality is matched by his enthusiastic intent to introduce the vocabulary of experimental performance to a community that is not necessarily proficient in postmodern forms or accustomed to attending performance events to begin with. Aviles sees performance as a practice that opens and mobilizes the possibilities for new experiences and definitions of community and art experiences to emerge. In this sense, the aesthetic pedagogy of postmodern dance may result in practices of what performance theorist Shannon Jackson describes as the "social work" of artistic practice. Understanding the sharing that aesthetic production entails, Jackson recognizes the infrastructures of performance making as materially consequential investments of resources, labor, and energy that, even when focused on aesthetic innovation alone, result in deep social formations. If we understand Jackson's "social works" as "publics," we can identify the potential import that learning a new aesthetic vocabulary through engaged spectatorship and practice, *convivencia diaria,* allows. Through these exchanges in and through Aviles's performance, queer Latinas/os in Hunts Point constitute a new intimate counterpublic.[85]

Latina/o Queer Homes

This Pleasant and Grateful Asylum represented a significant transition for Arthur Aviles and his work. In 1999, after three years of working at the Point, Arthur Aviles decided to relocate his operations to the American Bank Note Building on Baretto Street, just blocks from the Point in the Bronx. While most of the work I discuss in this chapter took place at cultural institutions not necessarily identified as queer (the Point, Hostos Community College), *This Pleasant and Grateful Asylum* was developed and premiered at the Bronx Academy of Arts and Dance. As I discussed above, BAAD!, as a location with an intentional focus on claiming the performance space as Latina/o and queer, further advanced the circulation of queer identities within the Latina/o neighborhood by literally creating a new public space for queer assembly or asylum. But the very situation of this performance space in the American Bank Note Building brings us back in touch with the politico-economic histories of Latina/o experience that have so shaped Hunts Point as a neighborhood and that frame any contemporary attempts by Aviles and other cultural workers to create home within it. The building opened its doors in 1911 and served as a currency press for Latin American economies until it went out of business in the 1980s. The production of money became the building's primary identity despite the rampant poverty and decay of the neighborhood. As Aviles observes, "People around here still remember it as the currency building. They call it the Penny Factory. The area here is called like that."[86]

The association of the building with global capital accentuates the state of alienation of the surrounding neighborhood, reminding people of a circuitry of exchange in which they do not participate. After the Bank Note Building closed its business, Gail and Max Browner and Associates purchased the building and turned it into an apparel center. Aviles is well aware of the complexities and significance of these histories.[87] As we walked through his studio inside the building during a check-in visit in 2003, he commented:

> The room we are sitting in right now had hundreds of sewing machines. It was basically a sweatshop, and there were many, many Latin American women sitting here every day, sweating and making garments for other people to wear. And you know it just would

not work. The Bronx was burning in the seventies and was still getting over it in the eighties. The reputation of the area was sinking lower and lower, so it was difficult for this building to make its claim.[88]

Aviles and his partner Rice-González approached the owners to rent the space for their dance company. The owners volunteered the space free of charge for a two-year period with the understanding that Aviles would spread the word to other artists about the availability of affordable studio space. The portion of the building Aviles occupies was subdivided into a 2,500-square-foot dance studio and a series of 600-square-foot artist studios. Artists have populated the building since (twelve of them down the hallway from Aviles's studio). The hallway was eventually turned into a gallery and often features the work of Latina/o queer artists in the neighborhood and beyond.

In taking stock of his accomplishments since arriving in the Bronx in search of home in 1996, Aviles acknowledges the abject conditions of the neighborhood and proudly narrates the transformation the arts have ushered in:

> You have to understand where you are; you are in one of the armpits of the world, the Hunts Point section of the South Bronx. This area is known worldwide for that kind of activity. This whole street right here was inundated with unfortunate situations of prostitution and drug gangs. And we came here and we said to her [the owner], "This is what we want to do, change things for my community," and it was a deal.[89]

Aviles's passionate account of the neighborhood's ability to rise up, phoenix-like, from the ashes of historical marginalization is not the naive fairy-tale narrative of Disney optimism. It is not a narrative of completed arrival either. Instead, Aviles's hopeful vision of community is a commitment to labor, in spite of the overwhelming odds. He has thus far succeeded in creating what David Román has described as "a rare safe haven in a neighborhood not known for its support of either queer Latinos or the performing arts, let alone both."[90] And it is here, where the practice of performance, the effort put into transforming cold, abandoned structures into sanctuaries of beauty and love, that Aviles's theory in practice is the most eloquent, hopeful. In his own words:

I'm here because I can be here, I'm here because I have an affinity
for my culture and I'm here to stand strong to be who it is that I
am here to be. I know that there is a contingent of people who are
like-minded and agree in what we have to give to the world.[91]

These affirmations, so eloquently showcased in Aviles's choreographic work, are the necessary building blocks for a thriving and viable
Latina/o queer future. But as the next chapter will demonstrate, they are
also the strategies of survival activated at moments when the very possibility of queer latinidad comes under assault. Aviles models a practice
of Latina/o queer homemaking grounded on the recognition of historical marginalization, on the acknowledgment of the incredible amount of
effort required to put together resources to create spaces and instances
of performance, and most importantly, on the desire for the pleasures
that participating in such hopeful collective ventures might provide. He
demonstrates for us the multiple influences and the barriers that shape
the production of Latina/o queer counterpublicity. He also enacts the
imaginative dexterity that producing such critically embedded performance entails. Queer latinidad thrives in this playful and frictive realm,
assessing with careful and invested scrutiny the state of our environs to
imagine and instantiate alternatives that most appropriately allow us to
feel and be at home.

3

MOVEMENTS OF HOPE

Performance and Activism

¡Todos somos Esperanza! (We are all hope!)
—Campaign slogan for the Esperanza Center Campaign

In order to resist oppression, we need to remember what our
elders, *nuestras antepasados,* taught us. They gave us values and
traditions of being good people, of community, of sharing, of
respecting, and caring, of *cariño, y compasión, y ternura y digni-
dad* [of love, and compassion, and tenderness and dignity]. From
these values we get our strength.
—Graciela I. Sánchez, executive director,
Esperanza Peace and Justice Center[1]

In this chapter we traverse along the downtown district of the city of San
Antonio, Texas. We will focus on the Esperanza Peace and Justice Center.
Esperanza is a queer Latina/o cultural organization dedicated to the use
of traditional and contemporary Mexican and Latin/o American arts to
advance progressive causes ranging from women's and LGBTQ rights to
the preservation of significant historic sites for the working-class Mexican community in the city. More specifically, we will attend to the Todos
Somos Esperanza campaign, a grassroots organizing effort launched in
1997 in response to the city council's decision to cut funding to the organization following a successful crusade by conservative groups. During
the three years of activity that this chapter documents, Esperanza Center
art activists took to the streets and used performance tactics to garner
widespread support for their legal battle against the city. San Antonio
is a city organized around the simultaneous display of a mythologized
USAmerican triumphalism over the "defeat" of Mexicans at the Battle
of the Alamo and the festive commoditization of Mexican folklore. In
their campaign, Esperanza activists created eloquent performances that

sought to rescue the dignity and pride of the historic Mexican community while advocating for the acknowledgment and embrace of contemporary figurations of queer latinidad. Performance offered the site and mode of communication that bridged Latina/o and queer communities at this moment of crisis.

While the previous chapter focused on the negotiations and labor involved in the development of queer Latina/o public space or home, this one is concerned with the maintenance and defense of those spaces when they come under attack. I analyze performances in the form of street theater, candlelight vigils, press conferences, and mock trials—all of which the Todos Somos Esperanza campaign put together between 1997 and 2000. I evidence how performance enabled strategic engagements with the emotional economy of San Antonio and its history of animosity and bad feelings between Anglos and Mexicans in order to create alternative experiences of collectivism that bridged queer Latinas/os to a broader community in the city and beyond. I work through documentation of the Todos Somos Esperanza efforts in the form of video and material culture, on-site observations of public performances and community meetings, and formal and informal interviews with participants to develop what queer theorist Ann Cvetkovich has termed as "an archive of feelings."[2]

I contend that Esperanza activists counteracted the homophobic anger of their detractors with the circulation of hope, an investment in political optimism. Of primary interest to my query here is how the physical movement of hope into the streets of the city through performance created experiences of political promise that demonstrate the crucial role of affect as a precondition for mobilization. In the pages that follow I examine the cultural and political climate leading up to Esperanza's defunding by the city council in 1997, as well as the strategies deployed and affects circulated by right-wing protesters to promote this defunding. However, the main focus of this chapter is on the strategies employed by Todos Somos Esperanza activists and supporters in promoting the continuation of funding for their queer Latina/o performance and exhibition space. I demonstrate how hope constitutes a theory in practice of queer latinidad.

The local debates over Esperanza Center's role within the broader public culture of San Antonio offer further evidence as to the complicated relationship between the increased presence of Latinas/os and queers in the nation's public sphere and the conservative pushback that accompanied it during the 1990s and early 2000s. By the mid-1990s the San Antonio economy felt the strain of shrinking federal support to industries including the region's military bases and a rise in the cost of maintaining basic city infrastructure and services. Like New York, San Antonio sought to make adjustments in budgetary investments and municipal policy with the goal of attracting additional economic activity. Central to this strategy was an effort to expand the city's substantial tourist sector, which already constituted one of the largest sources of income for the city. The case of the Esperanza Center demonstrates how a neoliberal logic of economic adjustments often involves both the commoditization and policing of identities. The defunding was variously justified as an economic argument that sought to secure the branding of the city for the tourist industry and a matter of public morale that framed queer sexuality as pornographic.

As the first epigraph to this chapter suggests, Esperanza's response insisted on queer Latina/o ownership of the cultural and political legacy of latinidad and advocated for its central role in figuring queer lives and communities. In claiming tradition, Esperanza also queered it. The gender is mismatched in "nuestras antepasados," or "our forebears" above. "Ours" in Spanish is feminine, "nuestras," while "antepasados," or forebears, masculine. I argue that this subtle misgendering of Latina/o tradition taps into "values and traditions" as a source of strength but also renders the affective repertoire of latinidad open to feminist and queer appropriation. Esperanza Center artists and activists worked within this paradigm of cultural heritage and also insisted in diversifying the pantheon of heroes and traditions by highlighting the contributions of women and queers to the social, cultural, and political well-being of the Latina/o community. Key to this practice was a commitment to remain connected to and active within the Latina/o community of the city. To do so, they deployed performance to create experiences where members of the community, queer and straight, could realize that they were all *esperanza*. I would like to turn to an ethnographic account of one such community performance.

Ceremonies of Hope

On the afternoon of Sunday, August 20, 2000, a diverse group of citizens gathers in front of the San Antonio Federal Courthouse in a candlelight vigil. It is the eve of the opening hearings for the Esperanza Peace and Justice Center's discrimination case against the City of San Antonio. After an exhausting year of legal strategizing and campaigning, the Esperanza Center staff and activists have taken to the streets in a final protest of the city council decision to defund the Center in 1997. The event is also a celebration of the community and those who have stood with the Center up to this climactic moment. Esperanza supporters—Latinas/os, African-Americans, white men and women, young and old, queer and straight, artists, politicians, manual laborers, white-collar workers, and academics alike—arrive at the courthouse steps at the corner of North Alamo and East Houston streets to demand justice. Approaching the courthouse, many walk by the Alamo, the iconic eighteenth-century Spanish mission, at the heart of the city and the epicenter of its tourist district. Across the way from what is now a national monument to the mythologized "Texas martyrs" who succumbed to Mexican troops in 1836, a group of young women dressed in embroidered Mexican cotton *trajes*/dresses sit in a circle plucking petals off flowers. In a ritual ceremony, the petals are offerings meant to honor the strength and indefatigable resilience of the gathering community. The ritual ceremonially and emotionally prepares the community for the difficult days ahead. In the morning, the arts organization will present its arguments before Judge Orlando L. García and fend off attacks from conservative activists and media outfits in the city. Organizers walk about the space, setting up a large quilt embroidered with traditional Mexican *milagros,* colorful utopian portraits, stitched by women in the community who wish for a resolution in favor of the Center. The event is both an intimate community ritual and a media spectacle. Television cameras move about the space, and news reporters solicit commentary from rally organizers and Esperanza supporters.

As daylight begins to fade, the fifty or so participants in this rally seem physically exhausted but strong in spirit and conviction. Many of them have worked tirelessly over the past weeks preparing the legal arguments for the case, ensuring proper coverage by the media, and courting public support for the Center's fight against the discriminatory elimination of its funds. This is the final hour before the official legal proceedings take over the yearlong advocacy campaign. The ceremony opens with a Native American–inspired invocation acknowledging a spiritual cosmology that asks all participants to salute in unison the four cardinal points. The young women release the flower petals in observance of higher powers and mark the liminal space of performance to ritualistically usher in their political intervention. Welcoming remarks to honor community elders, a prayer, and ceremonial lighting of candles invite the audience to participate in the ritual. One by one, a dozen or so participants take to the podium with words of encouragement and hope, much as in the general intercessions of the Prayer of the Faithful in the Catholic mass. Speakers, like Chicano scholar and San Antonio native Tomás Ybarra-Frausto, address the audience with inspiring messages. They narrate stories of the struggle and survival of working-class Mexican communities in Texas historically dispossessed of their lands, accounts of their long fight to be acknowledged and respected, and honorific speeches about the warriors who so bravely carry the torch in contemporary times. Other participants offer ritual blessings and expressions of optimism that the outcome of this legal battle will benefit Esperanza.

Spectacles of religiosity are not uncommon in San Antonio's public spaces, where thousands of tourists descend annually upon the city to witness Mexican folk celebrations of the Christian Nativity and tour in pilgrimage to the four Spanish missions.[3] However, the vigil's location in front of the courthouse and the cast of characters engaged in this public display of spirituality signal a radically different deployment of ritual practice for a city marketed under the rubric of tradition. The ceremony is not in keeping with the Catholic calendar or folkloric displays to entertain tourists. Instead, it appropriates the structures of religious performance and deploys them in the context of political activism. The simultaneity of a hopeful invocation of spiritual forces in aid of the community, emblematized by the acts of prayer performed by participants, and the very public outcry against marginalization and oppression in the city, showcases the strategic dramaturgies of latinidad. This ritual performance is optimistic while maintaining a critical grounding in the materiality of historical and contemporary experience.

At the end of the ceremony, the attorneys and staff will return to Esperanza's headquarters on San Pedro Street and continue to work throughout the night for what will turn out to be fifteen hours of grueling testimony by, and cross-examinations of, twenty-three witnesses over two days. After a two-hour ceremony, the participants' final offerings on the courthouse steps are bouquets of flowers with small wishnotes delicately attached with colorful ribbons. As darkness descends upon the crowd on this warm summer evening, the light of the candles persists in demonstration of the community's unity and hope, *esperanza*.

Fig. 10. Candlelight vigil, Esperanza Center. Photo courtesy of the
Good People of Esperanza.

As I explained above, I am concerned here with the circulation of
hope as a political praxis of queer *latinidad*. Among its many purposes,
the ritual before the courthouse also constitutes a queer performance.
The events are explicit interventions in favor of the funding rights of a
progressive Latina/o queer organization. The San Antonio City Council defunded the Esperanza Center because of its support and presentation of Latina/o queer arts and social activism. Homophobic objectors
to Esperanza characterized their artistic and cultural work as pornographic and were successful in convincing city officials to retire previously awarded public funding. In turn, Esperanza and their allies filed
and won a viewpoint discrimination federal lawsuit against the City of
San Antonio. I do not focus on Esperanza's legal strategies in court, an
aspect of the case that has been sufficiently addressed by other scholars.[4]
Instead, I focus on the extraordinarily creative campaign they launched
for the hearts of their fellow citizens. The performances of traditional
Mexican spirituality—by queers and queer sympathizers of all genders,

colors, and creeds—achieved the public and purposeful integration of progressive sexual politics to an ethnic and cultural identity largely shaped by Catholic morality. The ritual performances of hope at the courthouse steps were sincere displays of faith and clear articulations of how the assumed inflexibility of the structures of religious tradition can be transformed through public performance of the affirmation of queer lives. Participants inhabit the format of Mexican traditional spirituality to come together as a community to demand justice for queer Latinas/os. Here, the signs of the *milagros* and the votive candles ritualistically position queer sexuality as part and parcel of the *mexicana/o* community in San Antonio.

A Politics of Hope

We have begun our journey at the end. The ethnographic vignette above marks the last of the public performances that preceded the court sessions for the Esperanza Center viewpoint discrimination case against the City of San Antonio. I offer it as a beginning because my interest throughout this chapter is in pursuing the strategies that led to its accomplishment. Esperanza Center activists employed performance to make queer issues matter to the broader Latina/ community. Hope was key to their success. In Spanish, *esperanza* translates as hope. The word is most often invoked in reference to religious expectation, where it is intimately related to *fé*, faith. Esperanza is also a common name for women in Latin American and U.S. Latina/o communities. It is a familiar and powerful word in the United States, where it frequently names religious and secular organizations, mutual aid societies, and activist Latina/o spaces. It is at once a noun that evokes tradition—the Catholicism of the Spanish conquest—and futurity—the utopian realm of hope, of imagining a better world. At the Esperanza Peace and Justice Center both notions are fully in play.

Esperanza was founded in 1987 by a group of San Antonio women and activists concerned with the conservative turn in domestic policy and the international political bullying of the Ronald Reagan presidency. During the 1980s, President Reagan led the U.S. federal government in carrying out a neoliberal politics that increasingly favored multinational corporations over citizens. His administration increased corporate tax loopholes and legislative freedoms while reducing protections and entitlements for working-class and poor communities. Along with the unbalanced economic restructuring of the country came an appalling disregard for a host of critical issues including the developing AIDS pandemic, especially as it affected the gay community, pressures to revert protections of women's reproductive rights, and racial profiling of communities of color under Reagan's War on Drugs campaign. Reagan's presidency was not simply limited to Reaganomics. It was an ideological and political machinery that relied on the public revival of a US-American imperialist identity. He reactivated the ideologies of "Manifest Destiny" by deploying a playful cowboy aesthetic to launch a violently conservative agenda of "morality" and "values." Hollywood's idealization of the wild frontier and the cowboy hero as its friendly but forceful tamer shaped Reagan's affective vocabularies as confident, joyful, and patriotic. This glossy veneer over the arrogance of his politics also restaged Protestant religiosity—the language of duty, compassion, and freedom—to advance his doctrine.

The women of Esperanza sought a meeting place to express their disaffection and mobilize against policies and political attitudes that they saw as threatening the critical gains that resulted from progressive activism of the 1960s and 1970s. With the institution of Esperanza as a center for hope, they also meant to promote alternatives to the objectionable and depressing political present of the 1980s. The life experiences of working-class women of color, especially Mexican-Americans, and queers grounded the political imagination of Esperanza. Chicana activist and Esperanza cofounder Susana M. Guerra explains how the temporal duality between past and present experience shaped Esperanza's imagination of a better, even miraculous, future:

> I believe in miracles. I believe in Esperanza. Miracles have their roots in empty hands and a heart filled with hope. A sculpted body from memory and dreams. Critical thinking braided with the winged spirit of sharing. During 1986, on the front porches of San Antonio neighborhoods, semillas del milagro [seeds of the miracle], The Esperanza Peace and Justice Center, arose with these intangibles.[5]

The cultural center emerged from memories of past experiences of oppression. Hope fueled Guerra and her collaborators. In her vision, hope resides in memory as much as in dreams. The political ambitions of hope are founded in historical experience but open-ended in their conceptualization of futurity. Instead of installing a rigid political program a priori, the notion of hope aspired to by Guerra invests in the "winged spirit of sharing," a commitment to time spent together, as the seed of the miracle. Hope is thus described less in terms of an investment in the singularity of individual desire than as a trust in the intangibles of the social. It is in the intimate realm of balcony conversations and other modes of social exchange carried on in neighborhoods throughout the city where the shared feelings of hurt, dissatisfaction, emptiness, and, of course, hope animated the creative and political labor of Esperanza.

In pursuing the politics of emotions as they emerged and circulated in the Todos Somos Esperanza public relations campaign, I argue that the Center's art activism enacted a praxis of hope for both queer Latinas/os and the community at large. As philosopher Hannah Arendt proposes, praxis, as that most significant aspect of the human condition, comes into being through communicative exchanges.[6] In this way the power of an idea or a politics gains and maintains its force in the intimacy of a social collectivity. At its most basic level, it is the mutuality resulting from these exchanges that activates, and often constitutes, praxis. Esperanza's cultural and political work in San Antonio functioned as a praxis of hope that relied on the arts, especially performance, as the constitutive sharing, *convivencia diaria*, from which political affects emerged.[7] The circulation of hope as a political affect in turn yielded actionable politics.

Hope figures prominently in the political and quotidian discourse of marginalized communities that express their wishes or anticipation for better things to come. In recent history, hope as a political concept is most readily recognized in U.S. electoral politics, especially in President Barrack Obama's 2008 presidential campaign. Hope, as featured in Obama's 2004 Democratic Convention keynote address, his book *The Audacity of Hope,* and in his campaign slogan "Hope You Can Believe In," served as a mobilizing concept and affect that positioned him as a viable national leader.[8] The title for his address and book was inspired by a 1990 sermon delivered by pastor Jeremiah Wright at the Trinity United Church of Christ in Chicago. Wright's sermon was in turn motivated by a 1980s sermon by well-known Detroit orator Reverend Frederick G. Sampson at Virginia Union University about an 1885 oil painting by Victorian English artist George Frederic Watts. Hope travels across these various texts and contexts as an optimism to be embraced despite the difficult circumstances of the present.

In the nineteenth-century painting by Watts, hope appears in the image of a barefoot woman dressed in rags sitting atop a globe. She embraces a rundown harp. Her eyes are blinded by a bandage that signals past trauma, and perhaps even enduring pain. Wright, who recalls the painting during his witnessing of Sampson's sermon, describes this image "with her clothes in rags, her body scarred and bruised and bleeding, her harp all but destroyed and with only one string left" and celebrates her "audacity to make music and praise God."[9] For Wright, hope is a courageous undertaking that goes beyond the explanatory power of the blind leap of faith Christian dogma requires. Faith in a higher being motivates Hope's insistence on making music. However, faith does not stand alone in Wright's allegory. It is born of an embodied experience of trauma. As such, it is fueled by a drive to survive that is materially grounded and palpable on the scarred, bruised, and bleeding skin's surface.

In his address and book, Obama extends Wright's allegory of hope to the nation. Doing so, he rehearses the American dream and its exceptionalist promise of individual achievement in order to chart an imagined political future. Paralleling Wright's sermon, Obama introduces a horizon of possibilities made more prescient by references to historical and contemporary inequities. He identifies historical injustices (e.g., slavery) and contemporary disparities (e.g., economic, educational), making them the primary collectivizing narratives of his campaign. Frustration with the current state of being and the historical inequities that have led to it become the background rhetoric and affect that substantiate the emergence of hope. The emotional journey from discontent to hope gained sufficient force over the course of the electoral process to inspire a history-making movement for the election of the first African-American president of the United States.

The efficacy of hope in the Watts-Wright-Obama genealogy above does not rest exclusively or primarily in its representational or rhetorical force. In each of these instances hope is most compelling when practiced.[10] In Watts's painting, it is the resilience of playing music that exalts the sitter from the condition of misery. In Wright's sermon, it is the embodiment of hope in speech, along with the attendant emotive responses of the temple's congregants, that makes hope a felt experience. Lastly, it was the on-the-ground participation—especially the Internet-based social networks, parties, and musical concerts where hope became a doing rather than an ideal—that transformed the younger electorate into a mobilized community and a driving force in the 2008 election. In the case of Esperanza, hope does not figure as an uncritical or innocent utopianism. It owes much of its emergent force to a shared historical experience of marginalization that solidifies a disposition toward the world. Below, we will return to the historical legacy of this economy of dispossession as generative of dispositions. However, it is important at this point to recognize that this shared experience is accompanied by a repertoire of attendant emotions with long-established historical roots that shape contemporary practice. Much as in the Obama case, Esperanza's hope is primarily sustained in collective actions that actualize affect as political.

Artists, activists, and community members at the Esperanza Center utilized performances such as the candle vigil ritual at the courthouse steps in order to collectively experience hope. Hope as an acted upon materiality was Esperanza's most salient theory in practice. My account of the ritual ceremony demonstrates how, in their experience of hope, participants simultaneously engaged memory and futurity. They reanimated their connection to ancestral spirituality and historical trauma. At the same time, they identified present obstacles and future possibilities. Guerra, quoted above, beautifully conveys the emotional complexities of these engagements as "miracles" born of difficult "intangibles." Her invocation of embodied experience as the foundation for a politics of hope is attuned to Cherríe Moraga's conceptualization of a "theory in the flesh." Moraga defines theory in the flesh as "one where the physical realities of our lives—our skin color, the land or concrete we grew up on, our sexual longings—all fuse to create a politic born out of necessity."[11] In Moraga's description, a politics emerges from the critical standpoint achieved from experienced materiality. In advancing theories in practice, I acknowledge the historical weight of experience in the constitution of both theoretical and political orientations to the world. However, in doing so I also invest in performance's ability to instantiate new experiences in the present, to translate the movements of history into mobilization. As I have argued thus far throughout this book, it is in the shared time-space of performance, as an embodied practice, where I locate the critical becomings of a queer latinidad. Furthermore, performance functions in these movements of politics, creativity, and emotion as a site and a grammar of exchange where Latina/o queer publics and counterpublics emerge.

Much like the Point and the Bronx Academy of Arts and Dance (BAAD!) in New York, the Esperanza Center is chartered on the belief that the arts are appropriate sites and practices to address social inequities and to mobilize communities into action. The community center hosts a vast array of cultural and political events ranging from arts and crafts training to activist organizing around environmental issues. As historian and community activist Antonia Castañeda explains, Esperanza's programming "respects and nurtures the diverse cultures and arts of communities historically excluded from mainstream cultural institutions: women, people of color, lesbians and gay men and working class peoples, especially the youth."[12] If San Antonio's official public sphere is dominated by the mythologies of white masculinity and the Nation, Esperanza's counterpublic is constituted at its margins.

Circulating Fear, Defunding Hope

To understand the praxis of hope as Esperanza's theory in practice it is imperative that we first understand how the events that led to their defunding depended on a politics equally centered on affect, bad affect to be exact. On September 1997, the San Antonio City Council, in consultation with its mayor, Howard Peak, and without a required public hearing, reversed the recommendations of the city's Department of Arts and Cultural Affairs and defunded Esperanza.[13] The decision to remove support for the Center culminated a monthlong highly organized campaign by conservative activists, including radio talk-show host Adam McManus,[14] against what they labeled "the homosexual agenda of the Esperanza Center."[15] The pressure by conservatives in the city, who rallied primarily against the Out at the Movies Lesbian and Gay Film Festival, was successful in creating a state of panic among city council members who had continuously supported the funding of the Esperanza Center in previous years.

While the political positions from which Esperanza's defunding was advocated may be qualified as conservative and reactionary, the strategies employed by the Right in advancing these ideas were innovative. In fact, San Antonio's right-wing activists boasted an arsenal of approaches that modeled some of the best in cutting-edge corporate media campaigning and political organizing at the time. Affects, especially those associated with idealized motherhood, were central to their approach. The circulation of specifically targeted affective ties to a fragile, often-times infantile, imaginary community evidences the strategic invocation of the emotional expectations of motherhood in right-wing politics. Activist cultural critic Linda Kintz terms this investment a "sacred intimacy," or the emotional and political investment in "the belief that the fundamental definition of a woman is her identity as a nurturant mother."[16] The campaign against Esperanza was initiated by Martha Breeden, executive director of the Christian Pro-Life Foundation, an antiabortion crisis center in San Antonio whose messages against abortion precisely deployed the nurturing feelings of motherhood as a marketing strategy. She organized a mass mailing of flyers cleverly portraying the Center as a lesbian and gay organization advocating queer lifestyles and indoctrinating vulnerable youth throughout the community.[17] The Bexar County Christian Coalition, San Antonio Right To Life, and the Association of Spirit-Filled Pastors soon joined Breeden in calling for a massive campaign addressed at the city council. Networks of fundamentalist churches and conservative talk radio mobilized to recruit volunteers to execute telephone campaigns and public actions, in this way accessing institutionally sanctioned public forums. Right-wing activists wisely circulated an inflammatory rhetoric through a wide variety of channels: mass mail and e-mail, telephone marathons, radio and print media, and live interventions at public hearings, religious and social meetings, and private appointments with political representatives at the council and beyond. Their message was loud and clear: Esperanza's cultural and artistic work was a threat to the moral fabric of the community because of its homosexual propaganda.[18]

The visibility of the conservative opposition against the Esperanza Center prompted some drastic reactions from the city council. At the time of implementing budget revisions—primarily based on the limited availability of city funds due to reduced revenues from the property tax base—the council decided to cut public funds to arts organizations by 15 percent across the board. However, the entire budgetary contributions to the Esperanza Center and its affiliates were eliminated.[19] The decision by the city council countered the Department of Arts and Cultural Affair's peer review process, which positioned Esperanza at the top of the ranks in key categories of evaluation, including artistic excellence, audience development, and administrative capacity.[20]

The defunding was certainly suspect. Although it was never publicly acknowledged that it was due to Esperanza's queer programming, the political nature of the organization's work was alluded to by multiple officials discussing the case. Among the political figures who referred to Esperanza in this manner was Mayor Howard Peak, who in a 1997 interview with the *New York Times* declared: "They [Esperanza Center] seem to go way beyond what people want their money spent on. That group flaunts what it does—it is an in-your-face organization. They are doing this to themselves."[21] Through statements similar to Mayor Peak's comment, critics characterized Esperanza's work to be fundamentally queer and too political on matters of little concern to the local San Antonio community. Arguments for regarding the arts as an exclusively aesthetic experience devoid of political insight were also circulated to justify the Center's defunding.[22] Taking into account the controversy, Councilman Robert Marbut proposed the development of a new criterion for funding: grant decisions should focus on the ability of arts institutions to attract tourist dollars. Anti-Esperanza activists and city council members used his unofficial criterion to justify refusal of funding. Although Marbut's proposal garnered limited support from other council members, $100,000 was set aside for special applications from arts organizations that supported tourism.[23]

The moves and countermoves that characterized the initial attacks on Esperanza, the defunding decision by the council, the lawsuit against the city, and the debates that ensued along the way relied heavily on manipulations of public feelings. The strategic engagement with the complicated emotional economy of the city by anti- and pro-Esperanza activists alike, through public performance, offers a unique opportunity to investigate the entanglements between affect and activism. Anti-Esperanza activists recurred to anger and fear to rally emotional forces in their fight against the center. Esperanza mobilized hope. In accessing the emotional force of performance activism we will turn to an "archive of feelings." Ann Cvetkovich describes cultural texts "as repositories of feelings and emotions, which are encoded not only in the content of the texts but in the practices that surround their production and reception."[24] The court transcripts, television interviews, theatrical performances, street demonstrations, speeches, and testimonies circulated to protest or defend the Esperanza defunding not only offer a snapshot of the competing interests invested in managing queer latinidad in the public sphere but evidence the pivotal role emotion played in the organization of San Antonio public lives during the three years of this crisis and more generally in the history of intergroup relations in the city.

For example, the transcripts from the September 11, 1997, public hearings at the San Antonio City Council archive the Right's strategic use of fear. Conservative San Antonio residents addressed the council members in an alarmist tone that characterized queer media as a threat to traditional conceptions of the heterosexual family. For example, an African-American man approached the podium during the preliminary budget hearings and proceeded to argue in an aggressively raised voice,

> I think it's unhealthy. I think that any person even if you are not of a religious background or of a normal American moral background or make-up [sic]. You can see how some of these things are now weaving themselves into the fabric of our society and breaking them down terribly. And I would encourage you to eliminate them, not reduce, but eliminate those things. What they call progressive thinking now, Mayor Peak, was perversion years ago. And I would encourage you, you are able to take a couple of steps back and imagine what it must have been like to grow up teaching your children normal, sound things. And I just say let's just make this job easy, remove the moneys from where they are targeted.[25]

This and many other speeches framed Esperanza as a danger to the traditions of a "community" in fear of the undoing of a "normal American" past or tradition. They appropriated the language of austerity circulated in Mayor Peak's "back to basics" approach to advocate a "back to basics" conservative morality. They called for a return to the utopian world of "normalcy" where homosexuality is properly classified and contained as "perversion." The fear of rupturing of fragile moral communities through homosexual perversion is here further intensified through an association of homosexuality with disease. A white woman in her forties stood at the microphone and commented in a slightly trembling voice: "As a parent of four children I am concerned about the money and how it is spent. And the money that is being requested for Esperanza Center for a gay and lesbian film festival. The behaviour that is promoted and encouraged by these films is unhealthy and in some cases deadly."[26] Clearly, homosexuality in this testimony is problematically associated with moral disease and the AIDS epidemic.

The carefully crafted speeches by anti-Esperanza activists at the public hearing articulate the rhetorical mantra of right-wing homophobic discourse. It also showcases the ugly feelings that such a rhetoric, skillfully performed in the public forum of the city council, circulates. At this public forum, conservative activists successfully performed a fear of homosexuality with the intention of creating a moral panic among the city council and the San Antonio community at large. This strategy sought to successfully block the funding of Esperanza and work toward the desired purging of homosexuality from public life. The performances at the budget hearings were part of a complex model of activism employed by the Right in its struggle against the cultural and political work of Esperanza.

References to the language of moral disease and the risk of contagion were abundant in the public commentaries of the Right against the Esperanza Center. Homosexuality would spread quickly, many commented, if allowed to appear unchallenged. The comments registered a broad spectrum of discourses from religious morality to legal statutes. One right-wing activist expressed his belief that the Center was part of an organized conspiracy of gay agendas. He stated to the city council, "You are allowing our City tax dollars to go to various items of the homosexual agenda. I for one don't like that. Well, the homosexual agenda permeates through the Esperanza Peace and Justice Center and has done so for years."[27] Another anti-Esperanza critic referred to legal discourse as his rationale, stating, "What I think we are saying is: 'It is not the business of the city to use tax dollars to fund an organization that has such [gay and lesbian] film festivals.' An organization that promotes a lifestyle that is in essence a violation of the law in Texas. For sodomy is still against the law.[28] And these were the issues."[29]

Queer scholar Gilbert Herdt defines "moral shock" as "a socially significant incident or threat that galvanizes public outrage."[30] The public performances of fear against Esperanza resemble this phenomenon. For Herdt, moral shocks are localized expressions of collective sentiment against particular groups and practices deemed threatening to the imagined cohesiveness of the normative social realm. Moral shocks may escalate into the "large social events" that are moral panics.[31] Herdt understands sexual panics to be a subset of moral panics whereby the motivating anxiety or perceived threat is focused on queer or nonnormative sexuality. The case against the Esperanza Center prompted a moral shock wave that quickly spread throughout San Antonio's public sphere and upscaled into a sexual panic. Sexual panics, as Herdt explains, operate as affective engines that produce fear and anger in excessive mobilizing amounts. In creating a fearful public image of the work done and showcased at the Esperanza Center, antihomosexual activists in San Antonio positioned homosexuality in terms of pornography. They presented it as an aberration from the legal, moral, and religious codes of proper citizenship. Furthermore, conservative activists cited already well-known discourses of fear that exhibited homosexuality and/or AIDS as objects of panic; the discourses of AIDS and homosexual panic often refer to homosexuality as interchangeable with AIDS and vice versa.[32] The conflation of AIDS and homosexuality was evident during the Esperanza controversy, where references to AIDS were frequently advanced as strategies for increasing the perceived threat of homosexuality. Adam McManus consistently made this connection in his radio show. In one of his comments aired on his show and proudly displayed on his website, he claimed:

> I've been accused of being "homophobic." But I'm not afraid of homosexuals, I'm afraid for homosexuals. The average age of death for a homosexual male with AIDS is 39. And the average age of death for a homosexual male without AIDS is only 42. It seems like the compassionate approach would be to challenge the person to stop participating in unnatural deviant behaviors that lead to his own premature death.[33]

The deployment of the language of compassion, famously popularized in George W. Bush's 2000 election campaign, masks the homophobic position as a public health, or even a humanitarian, concern. The right-wing invocation of epidemics and panics reactivated the threat of contagion paradoxically attributed to the queer body to which their compassion was allegedly directed.[34] The broad circulation of fear using inventive media technologies and morally inflected logics of "proper" behavior saturated San Antonio with divisive anti-Esperanza rhetoric.

A Brief History of Bad Feelings

Attending to queer latinidad as a praxis of hope in this particular case study requires attention to the layers and the folds of conflict. Public feelings, after all, have histories. San Antonio is shaped by the multiple traumas of the shifts in the U.S.-Mexico border and the layered histories of colonial and national conflict that have produced them. From the disruption of indigenous communities by the arrival of Spanish conquerors in the seventeenth century to the succession of nationalist struggles that scarred the territory under the flags of Mexico, the Texas Republic, and the United States in the nineteenth century, the city's history is one built on shifting allegiances and hurt feelings. Originally known as Yanaguana by the indigenous inhabitants of the region, San Antonio was named in honor of Saint Anthony of Padua in 1691 to commemorate the day in the Catholic calendar Spanish explorers and missionaries "encountered" the Native American community adjacent to what we know today as the San Antonio River. The San Antonio de Valero mission, presently the Alamo, was founded early in the eighteenth Century to convert indigenous communities to Catholicism and protect Spanish possessions from the adjacent Louisiana Territory, which was under the French Crown. Over the course of one hundred years San Antonio grew into the largest Spanish, then Mexican, settlement in Tejas. By the 1830s, when settled communities from the young United States began to organize with dissaffected locals around the idea of governmental autonomy under a Texas republic, tensions between Anglos and Mexicans (many of them descendants of the Spanish settlers but also of mestizo and indigenous extraction) were already on the rise. In December 1835 the Texian Army, as the republican troops were known, successfully took control of San Antonio. The struggle between Texas republicans and Mexican troops peaked in the now mythic Battle of the Alamo, which began in February 1836 when the Mexican forces attempted the recovery of San Antonio and the iconic Alamo. The Republic of Texas lasted a decade until annexation to the United States in 1846. Annexation to the United States intiated a new journey for Mexican-Americans, shaped by the historical legacy of prior conflict and crossed by a political border that sought, unsuccessfully, to forget or misremember history.

While the realignments prompted by the various political conflicts outlined above ushered radical shifts in the lives of San Antonio residents across generations, they do not tell the entire story. In his landmark study *Anglos and Mexicans in the Making of Texas, 1836–1986,* historian David Montejano suggests a much more complex set of dynamics in his documentation of the social exchanges between Anglos and Mexicans in the region. He argues for the necessity of a sociological and economic view of history that can account for the complex relationships between Anglos and Mexicans as textured by ideologies of race and ethnicity in daily life. He is especially concerned with the social and economic exchanges lost to an account of history focused exclusively on Anglo-Mexican conflict. He opines that "drama, the easiest virtue to fashion for southwestern history, has long taken the place of explanation and interpretation."[35] By "drama" Montejano means the realm of popular discourse he describes as a "romanticized awareness" of Texas history grounded on the triumphalism of Anglo Texan victory and Mexican defeat.

Montejano is correct to pursue the up to then much ignored sociological complexities of racial and ethnic relations in Texas. His methodology uncovers critical points of contact, especially through labor, between Anglos and Mexicans that revise the all too simplistic assumption of Anglo supremacy and Mexican subordination. For example, he reminds us that under closer historical scrutiny Anglo cowboys during the late nineteenth century emerge as wage laborers in an old model of the hacienda economy developed during the Spanish colonial period and inherited by the landowning Mexican elite.[36] However, his all too sudden dismissal of popular discourse as "drama" at the opening of his book obviates the structuring force of the "legendary aspects" of this history. Anthropologist Richard Flores has observed how the enduring influence of these romantic representations of Texas history, what they tell as well as what they silence, "mark the contours and bring into relief appropriate moral and ideational values that constitute both the social terrain and one's location in it."[37] I dwell precisely on the "drama" of history and the ways in which its circulation or performance in public spaces structures particular affective narratives that "construct the cultural and social map through which social agents find their way to themselves and their place in the world."[38] Although the emotional aspects of these relationships are not Montejano's main concern, hate, distrust, jealousy, aggravation, resentment, and other "ill feelings" figure among the conflicted sentiments cited in the testimonial and historical accounts of his study and endure in the rhetoric of the Right, as I demonstrated above. The prevalence of a recurrence to the language of affect demonstrates what Sianne Ngai has discussed as the significance of "ugly feelings" in the aesthetics of social and political ecologies.[39] The resonances of this emotional journey continue to shape contemporary relations in the region. These resonances are much more than surface aesthetic tendencies. They govern much of the public space, and arguably the public sphere, of downtown San Antonio.

Despite Montejano's implicit antitheatricality, his call for substantial attention to the politico-economic contexts out of which group relations in Texas have emerged is critical. In the case of San Antonio, especially in the tourist district, the very arrangement of public space, labor management, and governmental policy is dictated by the "drama" of Anglo-Mexican conflict. Contemporary downtown San Antonio is literally built as a stage for the highly edited and commodified experience of this history. Simply put, the city's economy depends upon the theatricalized rendering of historical conflict. But the history mapped out in downtown San Antonio's spatial arrangements runs much deeper than the artificially constructed riverbed of the Riverwalk. San Antonio Mexicans who comprised the majority of the landowning class became destitute after the takeover of Mexican territory by the Texian Army and the annexation of Texas to the United States. At the end of the nineteenth century, the city became a hub of activity under Anglo control, and new construction of public buildings, private housing, and businesses began to push Mexican residents away from the central district to make way for the new urban elite.[40] This historic shift in the urbanization and demographic distribution of the city has been described by Raquel R. Marquéz, Louis Mendoza, and Steve Blanchard as resulting from the "growing imbalance in the distribution of power between Anglos and Mexicans."[41] Marquéz, Mendoza, and Blanchard, parsing Raul H. Villa, characterize the pressures that displaced Mexican communities from downtown as "barrioizing" effects or practices of economic, social, cultural and political marginalization that resulted in the development of barrios or ghettos like the Mexican west side of San Antonio during the first six decades of the twentieth century.[42]

The development of a tourism industry in the city during the second half of the twentieth century contributed significantly to the "barrioizing" pressures that displaced the Mexican community from the urban core. The initial push resulted from San Antonio's participation in federally supported urban renewal projects that funded the relocation of Mexican and African-American communities from downtown and into public housing developments on the north central west side of the city.[43] Cultural geographer Miguel de Oliver observes that the development of tourism accelerated with the celebration of a world fair in commemoration of the 250th anniversary of the founding of the city in 1968. The HemisFair, as it was called, displaced "manufacturing plants, shops, stores, warehouses, two schools, two parks, and four churches" to develop its grounds and other related accommodations.[44] It also prompted the expansion and transformation of the historic Mexican settlement of La Villita south of the Alamo into an ethnic tourism showcase. As the city core continued to look outward in orientation of its economy, it continued to develop an infrastructure that further marginalized the historic Mexican, as well as working-class Irish and German, settlements

of the city center. During the 1960s, the construction of the freeway in-
terchanges around the urban core to facilitate traffic in and out of the city
further isolated downtown from its neighboring communities. Among
the most dramatic effects was the separation of the Mexican Mercado,
a historic public market, from the Mexican community by the freeway
overpass. During the 1970s and 1980s the expansion of the tourist district assumed residential properties under eminent domain laws to build
hotels, parking lots, retail centers, and other service industry-related
businesses. As San Antonio transformed into an international tourist
destination dependent on the image of Mexican history, it reconfigured
its urban core to avoid the presence of poor or unscripted Mexicans. All
the while it depended on the image and low-wage labor of Latinas/os to
make the fantasy of the festive Riverwalk possible.

The Alamo is single-handedly the center piece around which the rest
of the tourist economy in San Antonio has been built. It is also the em-
blematic example of the weight of history and the contradictory feelings
it engenders. The multiple uses of this single structure—once a mission,
then a military fort, and now a national monument—begs our accounting for the tridimensionality that animates the flat tourist postcard. At
this site, Mexican defeat of the Texas republican troops has been transformed into a national allegory for the United States. Mexicans, who
figure as the very enemies upon which the nation is built according to
the site's narrative of American exceptionalism, welcome visitors to the
Alamo memorial site who venture into the Riverwalk district to lunch on
burritos and chimichangas to the backdrop of colorful paper cut orna-
ments and smiling mariachis.

Since the 1950s and up to the time of writing, tourism has represented
one of the largest sources of revenue for the city of San Antonio. Mexico
and Mexican folklore sustain the public image of the city. Catholic religious imagery, festivals, and celebrations are notable elements of *mexicano* culture on display for the tourist. Mexican culture (crafts, mariachi,
conjunto and *ballet folklórico*) circulates as a commodity for the pleasurable consumption by visitors who rarely venture beyond the Riverwalk
district. Located only steps from the Alamo, San Antonio's Riverwalk is
the center of tourism in the city. The canal that shapes the Riverwalk was
built initially as a protection against overflooding of the San Antonio
River. In the 1930s architect Robert H. H. Hugman supervised the development and beautification project. The Riverwalk has since seen multiple expansions. As I discussed above, the adjoining La Villita turned into

a series of galleries and restaurants in one such development. Throughout the second half of the twentieth century and into the twenty-first the Riverwalk has remained one of the most visited tourist destinations in Texas and the nation. Early developers of the site for tourism include Disney Corporation affiliates Marco Engineering Company of California, which originally suggested an early Texas-Mexican fantasy theme park. While the proposal was ultimately voted down, some of the suggested features in the original plan, including the focus on showcasing Mexican folklore through frequent festivals and celebrations at the site, were implemented. El Paseo de Rio, a pedestrian walkway along the canal, was completed in the 1960s as part of the HemisFair. By the mid-1990s San Antonio's Riverwalk boasted a wide variety of restaurants, nightclubs, hotels, and retail establishments. It has become an island of entertainment isolated from its less affluent surroundings. Tourists in the area can and often do experience San Antonio, including a visit to the Alamo, without ever leaving the Riverwalk.[45]

Public showcases of Mexican folklore in the district evidence the historical positioning of Mexico at a geographic and temporal distance from dominant USAmerican realms. As Richard Flores has observed of spectators of the *pastorela,* the annual staging of the Mexican nativity play in San Antonio, "Tourists attend to experience the 'local color' [*sic*] that is promised, void of the social interactions and obligations of human activity from which it is produced."[46] Mexican presence is key to the thriving tourist economy of the city. Mexican labor is a critical component of the local and regional service sector. Indeed, even the display of Mexican folklore for the tourist transfigures tradition into a performance of commodity.[47] The happy Mexicans on the Riverwalk are but a glossy veneer over a history written in blood. The idyllic heterosexual world of handsome *caballeros* and beautiful *señoritas* showcased for tourists displaces the stark realities of a majority Mexican-American city with disproportionately high levels of economic, educational, and health disparities. In the space of the Alamo and the Riverwalk district, Mexican otherness secures the story USAmerica. That is, images of Mexico and Mexicans become constitutive of the Other that defines San Antonio as the "somewhere else" of the tourist destination.[48] But as de Oliver observes, "Despite the Latino culture being centrally positioned in the promotion of the city, and despite the advancement of this population being a stated objective (amongst others) of ethnic tourism, these urban environments tend to promote anxiety and consternation (real and imagined) among the mainstream mass market."[49] To be a politically active feminist queer Mexican in this landscape is to provoke a confrontation with the monumentality of San Antonio in national history and its concomitant placement of Mexicans as villains or happy entertainers. It is to risk awakening bad feelings.

Hopeful Anger

The campaign against Esperanza operated under the fear that the Center's pornographically queer and dangerously unhappy *mexicano* politics threatened the moral and economic traditions of conservative San Antonio. Against the well-funded campaigns of fear by the Right, Esperanza activists took to the streets with fierce performances of hope. Their strategy included community meetings, radio and television interviews, street theater, and the distribution of colorful yard signs and bumper stickers with their slogan Todos Somos Esperanza. It centered on spreading hope or *esperanza* everywhere. However, Esperanza's engagements with hope should not be confused with a naive form of optimism or escapist utopia. Their activist strategies in performance were carefully aware of the Right's strategy and publicly upset with the historical and material contingencies that made conservative complaint so appealing to the city council. Esperanza's hope is an angry hope.

In a dialogue with cultural theorist Lisa Duggan, performance studies scholar José Esteban Muñoz passionately advocates for the central role hope plays in contemporary politics. He proposes an understanding of hope—an affect oriented toward the future—that maintains a critical connection to hopelessness—an affect that critiques past and present inequities.[50] He introduces "educated hope" as an alternative political affect that embraces futurity without venturing into an uncritical escapism. Muñoz explains,

> Invoking this notion of an educated hope may sound like it is participating in both the ladling out of accusations of false consciousness and the prescribing of what our futures ought to be. Here I risk setting up a rather strangling binary between good hope and bad hope. That is not my intention. Instead, after [Ernst] Bloch and in a certain tradition of both idealist and materialist thought, I am making a distinction between a mode of hope that simply

Fig. 11. Todos Somos Esperanza sign, Esperanza Center. Photo by the author.

keeps one in place within an emotional situation predicated on control, and, instead, a certain practice of hope that helps escape from a script in which human existence is reduced.

Esperanza's angry hope is an educated hope. The Center approaches hope from a minoritarian perspective grounded in the historical and material experiences of queer latinidad. Events such as the candlelight vigil at the steps of the federal courthouse historicize injustices committed against the Center and its constituencies. They assume this shared standpoint as the "theory in the flesh" that brings the community together into the praxis of hope as imagined, even wishful, critical alternatives. Muñoz's theorization of hope illuminates the hopeful anger that characterizes Esperanza's theory in practice. For it is in doing and laboring hope as/in performance, the site of *convivencia diaria,* where Esperanza activists and supporters become a social collective.

The economy of performance is key to how angry hope operates. Esperanza activists could not count on networks of mass distribution available to their detractors. How could the Center respond to the widely circulated campaign of the Right? How to intervene in an emotional ecology so successfully overtaken by the broadcasted fear of sex panic? For disenfranchised groups, financial limitations represent their primary disadvantage from right-wing activist organizations. In the struggle for public opinion, live performance emerges as a significant venue that is affordable and accessible to those at the margins of media culture. It is precisely at the site of live performance where Esperanza activists focused their interventions.

Unable to access or purchase airtime in local television and radio networks, Esperanza Center activists had to maximize the impact of any available opportunity to transmit their message to the San Antonio community. A central piece in this plan was to carefully stage Esperanza executive director Graciela Sánchez in her interviews with local media networks. Throughout the anti-Esperanza campaign, right-wing activists focused a great deal of time on defamatory characterizations of Sánchez as an in-your-face communist lesbian.[51] Sánchez became the focal figure in the public attacks against the Center. In the antagonistic rhetoric of right-wing activists, Sánchez's performed passion in defense of the Center was read as unfeminine. It signaled homosexual conduct devoid of decorum. These larger-than-life characterizations were in stark contrast to more sympathetic portrayals by other sources, including journalist Barbara Renáud-González, who described her as "an unlikely person to be the center of so much contention. A petite woman who seems almost shy in personal conversation, she can be blunt when speaking about her convictions and passion for social justice."[52]

Sánchez offered a series of interviews to various local media the day prior to the hearing. She met network representatives at the Center's gallery space. Dressed in a white cotton shirt with colorful Guatemalan embroidery, she posed against the backdrop of equally colorful ceramic figurines and other traditional Mexican crafts created by the women in the MujerArte program run by the Center. In contrast to the angry lesbian stereotype pinned on her by the right wing, she spoke with a paused and gentle demeanor. Her performance was decidedly not the "happy Mexican" of the tourist imaginary. She managed to maintain a cool seriousness when addressing the issue of the defunding while invoking the language of hope, strategically pointing to the religious figurines and images of the arts-and-crafts display. While Sánchez discussed the gross injustices imposed on the Esperanza Center due to its commitment to gender and sexual diversity, the visual backdrop consciously challenged the references to the pornographic popularized by the opposition. The staging of folklore made claims to Latina/o authenticity, offering audiences a more complex view of Esperanza. Sánchez directed the cameras toward the artwork in order to explain the variety of programs (the youth media project, MujerArte, and the Annual Peace Market) being cut.[53] The framing of the Center's director within a stage of Latina/o "authenticity" claimed *mexicanidad* queerly.

Sánchez did not avoid addressing any of the questions regarding the queer work developed and presented at the Center. Instead, she insisted on contextualizing the Center's educational and cultural agenda. Through the public interviews, successfully distributed through the television networks, Esperanza announced that it could be simultaneously queer and Latina/o. The maneuver relocated folklore from the tourism-oriented models of institutionalized display to folklore as a living vehicle of cultural affirmation.[54] Esperanza Center deployed the performance of folklore for the local interests of their own politics and in doing so rebelled against the market-oriented circulation of these forms within a tourist economy.

Performance in/as Translation

While staging Graciela Sánchez's media appearances was a key strategic intervention into the public discourse about the case, the vast majority of the efforts organized by Esperanza activists focused on participatory modes of communication intent in relaying the case to the broader San Antonio citizenry. They opted for live performance events that stressed interaction with the community. Performance enabled a public pedagogy that was efficient without being excessively didactic. Before moving into a discussion of the street performances organized by the Esperanza Center throughout San Antonio I want to dwell briefly on the idea of translation as a critical motivation and tactic for the Todos Somos Esperanza campaign. No aspect of the campaign was more illustrative of the investment in reciprocal communication and in making the campaign accessible than the mock trial event just two days before the court hearings. This event models the communication strategies but also the emotional space created in Esperanza's praxis of hope.

On August 19, 2000, Esperanza staff, lawyers, activists, and other

Fig. 12. Graciela Sánchez, Esperanza Center. Photo courtesy of the
Good People of Esperanza.

community members gathered at the Center for a mock trial. Journalist
Bárbara Renaud-González reported,

> The judge in Rudy's black graduation robe winked at me from
> the homemade pine platform. The pretty gringa lawyer wore cut-
> off shorts with her pearls. The witnesses, especially la Gertrude,
> could have won an Oscar testifyin' on the makeshift stand. The
> bailiff was about seventeen years old. Sporadically, the courtroom,
> packed with dedicated gente, erupted into laughter, then wild
> clapping. At lunchtime, they happily shared a feast of last night's
> pollo con mole.[55]

At this widely advertised open meeting, the legal team presented its case
to the Esperanza community. Lead attorney Amy Keastely opened the
session, asking the audience to take extensive notes and stay for discussion. She encouraged all participants to ask any questions they had
concerning the case or the legal terminology used. In such relaxed and
welcoming fashion, the legal team "rehearsed" its opening statements,

interviewed lead witnesses, and performed counterarguments in preparation for the upcoming "real" trial.

When the time came for cross-examination of the witnesses, Esperanza Center lawyers played devil's advocate, performing for the audience
what they expected would be the strategies of city lawyers. Witnesses
were challenged to respond to these performances of conservatism and,
at times, homophobia. Members of the audience hissed in disapproval of
the "city lawyer's" questions and comments. They also applauded come-
backs by witnesses or Esperanza lawyers. Esperanza activists imperson-
ated leaders of their opposition such as Martha Breeden, executive director of the Christian Pro-Life Foundation. After six hours of serious play,
Keastely presented her closing statements to the audience and opened
the floor for discussion.

In this public rehearsal, Esperanza activists and community members engaged ludically with the serious legal discourse of the trial and
"mocked" the flawed logic of their detractors' arguments. In addition,
in the postperformance discussion, audience members inquired about
particularities of the law, pointed to omissions in the lawyer's strategy,
and openly discussed their feelings of anxiety, doubt, confidence, and
hope about the upcoming trial. Publicly voicing personal opinions or
feelings about the trial helped collectivize the experience, especially for
those unaccustomed or afraid to engage or challenge the city's authority.

Anyone, even anti-Esperanza activists and lawyers, could attend the
open meeting. When I asked Sánchez whether she worried the defense
lawyers would drop in on this rehearsal, she responded, "The arguments
still stand; it's the community's argument."[56] In this sense, Esperanza's
mock trial functioned as a rehearsal of democracy. As such, the public
act of the mock trial on the eve of the federal court case contrasted with
the hidden backroom meetings held by the city council on the eve of the
defunding. Above all, the commitment to share discourse about the trial,
to engage in a practice of *convivencia diaria* where emotional reactions
such as the commendation of the applause or the condemnation of the
hiss circulated freely, constituted a theory in practice. Here in the public
intimacy of the mock trial, Esperanza activists embodied hope, not as a
detached, faraway possibility, but as a palpable collective experience that
required focus, effort, and endurance.

Audience members who had never been to a courthouse or were
unfamiliar with the legal issues surrounding the case realized how the
courts work. Their fear of the law was demystified in the process. In

Fig. 13. Mock trial, Esperanza Center. Photo courtesy of the Good People of Esperanza.

learning how to maneuver the courthouse, the community arrived at the empowering discovery that the wealthy, the historically privileged, and even the city itself should never enjoy blind or unchecked authority. Formulating ways to speak back to power within the context of the flirtatious and joyful event, Esperanza lawyers, community activists, and audience members performed acts of translation: performance interventions invested in enabling the agency of disenfranchised communities by sharing the language and the tools to determine collectively their own futures. Playwright and performance artist Virginia Grise, then a staff member at Esperanza, illustrates this need for translation.[57] She states:

> I am not someone that could understand the courts. So I would shy back from the kind of more formal legal conversation. But once I came back [to San Antonio], I became much more familiar with it through the Todos Somos Esperanza meetings. Translation was crucial. People were taught how to make the connections between what was going on at Esperanza and other issues that affected their everyday lives, like institutional racism or the economic alienation of our communities, even corporate tourism. What I have always found interesting about Esperanza is that the person with the third-grade education sits in these meetings with the PhD professor of history. And it's like they are together in determining what this lawsuit looks like. And that's something that I didn't understand before. What I saw at those meetings was a lot of different people coming together and what shaped the direction of the lawsuit.[58]

What is most telling about Grise's statement is not the much-rehearsed edict "knowledge equals power," but the egalitarianism with which that knowledge was attained through performance collaboration. The model of public pedagogy performance in/as translation advances does not rely on the assumption of an educated elite imparting its wisdom to the less fortunate. Instead, it empowers all participants as agents in a process-based cohabitation at the site of performance. These grounded, embodied, affectively charged *convivencias* are laboratories where knowledge not only circulates but is also created. Most saliently, the self-awareness arrived at by the community, the realization of its ability to act, and the emotional charge achieved by the consolidation of the group in the ritual performance of the mock trial, actualized the campaign slogan, *todos somos esperanza* (we are all hope), into a lived, experienced reality.

Hope in the Streets

Todos Somos Esperanza was both a collaborative practice for the Latina/o community and a campaign to consolidate support from the public at large. Key to this strategy was the need to engage citizens, many of them *mexicanas/os,* unaware of Esperanza or resistant to supporting the much-maligned queer work of the organization. In order to counteract the widespread negative discourses and feelings of the Right, Esperanza activists took to the streets, performing hope at plazas and parking lots, community centers and public celebrations all over San Antonio. Telling the story of the defunding entailed both captivating an audience in the public spaces of the city and communicating a message in a clear and direct manner. Esperanza's praxis of hope went further. It aspired to a more profound engagement, one that went beyond logical rationalizations and straight into the hearts of San Antonio residents. The Center's politics was a politics of affect, an engagement with the public emotions of a city scarred by a history of conflicted feelings and tainted by the ugliness of the Right's fearful tactics. In doing so, Esperanza activists sought to share the energy and enthusiasm for their cause. Their efforts respond to performance scholar D. Soyini Madison's equally hopeful proposition: "Might the whirling energy and vitality of a common cause to survive under certain conditions (for ourselves and others) capture us—the (e)motions of this too grand a moment—and invoke emergent performances?"[59]

Esperanza's street theater troupe, Teatro Callejero, became one of the most memorable efforts in the campaign. Much like the candle vigil and the mock trial, it modeled performance strategies born of the plight and emotional force of the community. The idea for Teatro Callejero emerged out of a series of brainstorming meetings hosted at the Center to devise creative ways to circulate its message. Many in attendance cited the role of *teatro*/theater in previous Chicana/o organizing efforts, including the farmworkers' struggle in California. They saw groups like El Teatro Campesino as an inspiration and a model for their own actions.[60] In order to pursue this idea, the Center scheduled a series of workshops with

Cristal Rojas, a San Antonio–based theater practitioner with a history of involvement in political and street theater. In the 1970s and 1980s, Rojas performed with Mexican street theater troupe Teatro Mascarones and collaborated with Teatro Campesino.[61] Her history with two legendary political theater organizations framed for many the idea of *teatro* as an engagement with history and tradition. Anthropologist and troupe participant Peter Haney observes, "I think there is a desire to connect with a history of political struggle involving theater and people doing theater who are committed to the political struggle."[62] Interest in approximating and embodying this history motivated many to join the troupe. *Teatro* as a genre, and its subgenre the *acto,* facilitated this process. It provided an aesthetic framework and a *movimiento* Chicana/o cultural script easily recognizable by audiences.[63]

In his definitive study of Chicana/o theater, scholar Jorge Huerta discusses how the *acto* was effective in bridging amateur performers to audiences of farmworkers with little experience spectating formal theater. He explains,

> The acto was the perfect form for those teatro members who were not experienced in performance techniques. The actos can be characterized as brief, collectively created sketches based on a commedia dell'arte model of slapstick, exaggeration, stereotypes and allegories poking satiric jabs at any given enemy of issue(s). The targets of the actos ranged from institutions to individuals, elected officials or organizations such as a Police Department; targets that were easily recognizable to the delighted audience members.[64]

Teatro Callejero played with these conventions fully. Following the model of troupes like Teatro Campesino, Rojas developed an engaging workshop format that centered on improvisation techniques, development of stock characters, and collective devising of short, comedic, and accessible skits. The collaborative process was framed as a conversation between the contemporary concerns of the participants and the historical weight of performance within a tradition of Chicana/o activism. This dialogue was enhanced further by the diversity of the workshop participants, their life stories, and perspectives. Bearing witness to this experience, Virginia Grise remarks,

I had never done any teatro before. [There were] kids twelve to thirteen years old, and the oldest person who worked with us, who never performed with us, was I think . . . over sixty years old. I had done student organizing in Austin, on campus, and did organizing in the schools as a teacher, but I had never seen anything like what was happening here. I had never seen so many people coming together—such different people and they were connected as artists, community members, professors.

Teatro could be productively understood here as folklore.[65] It carries forth an institutionalized authority drawn from its iconic place in the *mexicana/o* political imaginary of Texas. In this sense, its status as a traditional *mexicana/o* art practice represents a secular version of the religious ritual traditions that so shape Mexican public life and identity in San Antonio. However, this is neither the institutionalized folklore of the tourist industry nor the inflexible archival theater of the genre purist. Grise's account speaks of *teatro* as a breathing, malleable phenomenon. The interactive social context of performance enlivens it.

Teatro allowed participants and spectators alike to identify with *mexicanidad* in performance. They cited tradition in acts of recovery that rehearsed a language of performance associated with the struggles of the community. At the same time, Esperanza insisted on drawing parallels between the shared experiences of *mexicanidad,* and its attendant histories of discrimination, and homophobia. Thus, the Center's defunding was contextualized within a broader history of marginalization and oppression in the community. Esperanza was most successful at persuading San Antonio residents of its position when these connections across identitarian locations were translated into the engaged and affective language of *teatro.* The acts of translation performed by the *teatro* members literally put hope on the streets. Esperanza activists scouted public venues where they could reach potential supporters. On the Sunday before the trial, *teatro* volunteers gathered outside San Antonio's San Fernando Cathedral to perform their intervention. Parishioners exited mass in their Sunday best and were greeted by performance artist Maria Elena Gaitán playing classical music on the cello. Curious spectators, still caught in the solemnity and exaltation of the religious ceremony, extended their time to parade about the plaza, seemingly pleased by the musical accompaniment. Volunteers announced their theater performance and encouraged the quickly dispersing crowd of hundreds to attend: the performance is about to commence.

Gaitán marks the beginning of the *acto* with the Mexican folk classic, "La Cucaracha."[66] Additional audience members approach, enticed by the familiarity of the song. Some laugh and remark on the contradiction of listening to such lighthearted music emerging from an instrument perceived as formal, even stuffy. As the song ends, Haney appears dressed in a two-piece gray suit and addresses the audience enthusiastically, microphone in hand, "Good afternoon, ladies and gentlemen! Welcome to another installment of 'Who Wants to Be a City-Funded Organization?' My name is Regis Philbin and I will be your host this morning." With his introduction, Haney as Regis parodies the successful ABC game show *Who Want to Be a Millionaire?*[67] Some audience members applaud. Haney continues, "That's right folks, you are watching the show where we distribute arts funding for the City of San Antonio, before a live studio audience!" He solicits audience members' involvement by asking them to demonstrate how "live" and how "ready" they are to see the show. More members of the audience, now fully engaged with the dynamics of the performance, respond with a loud and encouraging applause. Regis answers, "All right. You may remember that last week we gave the majority of our moneys to the established organizations, so this week we scatter the crumbs to organizations headed by women and people of color!"

The audience applauds again, with even more gusto, as Regis introduces the first two contestants. They represent the Girl Scouts of America and the Quilting Circle of Texas respectively. Both actors, *mexicana* activists, perform in stereotypically naive midwestern Anglo personas in speech and demeanor. When it comes to introducing the Esperanza Center, Regis struggles, comically, to pronounce the name. Victoria, performed by Grise, abruptly takes the microphone from Regis and states assertively, "My name is Victoria Con Safos from the Esperanza Center for Peace and Justice. We do artistic and political work to promote the expression by communities that have been traditionally misrepresented by the mainstream." Before she goes any further, Regis pulls the microphone and looks at her with disdain. By this point in the *acto*, the emotional dynamics of the performance are clearly established. Representatives from the Girl Scouts and the Quilting Circle perform with an arrogant demeanor that places them at a distance from the rest of the group. Victoria performs a hopeful anger that mixes an abundant energy with direct political commentary. Philbin begins as the friendly entertainer and turns in the sudden transformation of his facial expression into a discriminating bigot who performs fear, disgust, and anger. The audience becomes a collective through its participation within the television entertainment format and its reactions to Philbin and the rest of the performers. Soon the upbeat mood of the clapping and cheering will mix with the serious politics of Esperanza's defunding.

The "show" progresses when Regis asks the first contestant,

> Suppose that a mainstream city-funded arts organization has its funding cut in a sudden manner. What would be the decibel level of the squeal that would ensue from its elite clientele? Would it be (*a*) 10 decibels, (*b*) 100 decibels, (*c*) 1,000 decibels, or (*d*) 10,000 decibels?

The representative from the Girl Scouts of America answers without hesitance and with a big smile on her face, "10,000 decibels!" "Correct!" responds Regis as he hands over a small bag of pennies.

Regis asks the second contestant, representing the Quilting Circle,

> Suppose that an ordinary, decent, moral, outstanding, and, above all, normal citizen of San Antonio were to encounter a performance event that seemed to promote a gay agenda. What would be the distance that this perfectly moral citizen would run to get away from such a scene? Would it be (*a*) one city block, (*b*) the distance it would take to get to the nearest bus stop, (*c*) the distance that it would take to reach the Marriage and Family Institute of San Antonio, or (*d*) the distance that it would take to get to the San Antonio Airport to get out of this town?

Miss Susan Underhill, as the character is named, thinks nervously about her answer and in a burst of energy says, "The distance it would take to get to the San Antonio International Airport!" Regis delays his response as the audience giggles. "Is that your final answer?" he asks, citing the iconic phrase of the television show. "Yes, it's my final answer," Ms. Underhill responds. "Well, you are right! And here is your bag of pennies!"

As the turn for Victoria Con Safos approaches, Regis tenses up and approaches her hesitantly. He says,

Fig. 14. Teatro Callejero, Esperanza Center. Photo courtesy of the Good People of Esperanza.

Suppose that you are involved with a city arts organization that has its funding cut because some members of the community object to programming that appeals to the subversive-queer-feminazi-Mexican element. What would be your logical response? Would you (*a*) run away, (*b*) hunker down, (*c*) stand tall, or (*d*) knuckle under?

"What kind of question is that?" asks Victoria defiantly while facing the audience. Regis replies, "That is the question you need to answer if you want to be a city-funded arts organization." Victoria, now visibly angered, questions the standards of evaluation. She asks the audience, how is it that she is being put in such a situation after Esperanza ranked so high in all the peer evaluations. Regis, irked with her political speech, hurries Victoria for a response. Flustered by his impatience, she requests that her options be presented to her once more. Regis consents and repeats Victoria's options with an exaggerated condescendence that collapses the persona of the entertainer into the realm of a perverse children's show. Victoria pauses, right hand at her chin as she contemplates her options, and chooses to "stand tall." The audience breaks into applause in support of her decision but is quickly interrupted by Regis who kicks her out of the game in protest. Regis returns to the jovial television host persona and attempts the traditional sign-off for *Millionaire.* At this point, all three contestants walk toward him holding Todos Somos Esperanza signs and interrupt his grand finale. The women turn the friendly television show into a protest performance. They exclaim, "If we all stand tall together, this kind of abuse will no longer happen!" Immediately after performing this short skit, the actors break character and address the audience to explain the legal case of the Esperanza Center and pass flyers for the upcoming vigil at the courthouse steps with which I initiated my journey into this chapter.

The *Millionaire* skit models an effective practice in political communication: it clearly delineates a political or moral problem, it identifies its viewpoint, and it advances its argument in an engaging manner. What is more, the skit showcases an impressive ability by Esperanza activists to develop affective communication. In the scene above, most audience members approached the performance immediately after the communal experience of the Catholic mass. They could be assumed to constitute an extension of the congregation in the plaza. But they were soon asked to realign their membership from one oriented toward the church to that of the television audience. This transition was achieved in the participatory format of the exchanges. The shared laughter and applause, as well as the collective suspense and investment in answering the questions presented to the "contestants," opened the performance to audience collaboration. What could have turned into the didactic confrontation of political speech became a playful engagement with the emotional complexities of Latina/o queer activism. The closing scene of the *acto,* when all the characters turn against Philbin and become Esperanza supporters, prepares spectators for the postperformance engagement. Here, for a final moment in the public intervention, the audience is once more activated as a determining component of the experience. Those watching can choose to join in and remain for the discussion or simply walk away.

Esperanza's praxis of hope functioned as a mode of engagement and a medium of communication. In her discussion of the ritual function of community-based performance, Jan Cohen Cruz explains: "On the ritual end of community-based art is a tradition of performance created *with* a community to serve a social or spiritual function."[68] I find Esperanza's work, especially its engagement with religious practices and diverse communities, to constitute one such ritual where artists and activists create *with* the community. In the final pronouncement of the *Millionaire acto*, the "if" clause "If we stand tall together" calls the collective into being as a conditional futurity dependent on coordinated action. This is, in part, the *"with"* in Cohen-Cruz's understanding of performance as ritual. It is also the practiced futurity where hope resides. However, hope, as I have been discussing it throughout this chapter, is grounded in a critique felt in the flesh of history. Only hope as a practiced commitment to the collective can ensure that "this kind of abuse will no longer happen." The main clause in the statement speaks of a future produced by and in the practice of hope. This future is the avoidance of a past or present experience of "abuse." Esperanza's "educated hope" or "hopeful anger" circulated in performances that assumed the political to rest on the *convivencia diaria* that would ensure that *todo somos esperanza*.

From 1997 until the court decision in favor of Esperanza was released in 2001, the Esperanza Center modeled practices of translation that made its position in the midst of the defunding scandal both relevant and intelligible to the broader community. In doing so, Esperanza activists relied on the traditions of Chicana/o and *mexicano* religiosity and activism along with their respective affective charges. Over the course of the Todos Somos Esperanza campaign, they cultivated a critical approach to political performance and public actions that was complex and multivalent. As an organization located at the center of one of the most contested sites of public memorialization in the United States, the Alamo, the Esperanza Center developed a discourse around history, memory, and public performance that sought to awaken deep emotional connections to contemporary struggles. As Virginia Grise and Marissa Ramírez explain in their report on the Teatro Callejero:

> Beyond theater, performance in general plays a vital role in cultures of resistance. For example, in Mexico, marches that fill the streets in waves are also participating in rituals of dance, music and art. As we claim a voice from our heart, art becomes a central part of feeding the soul.[69]

In their beautiful essay about their performance activism, Grise and Ramírez call forth connections between political performance practices and emotions. The goals of performance as activism rest as much in the ability to formulate "resistance" as in the necessity to "feed the soul."[70]

Esperanza's praxis of hope seeks to intervene against the reductive rhetoric and ugly feelings of sex panic. Esperanza exercises a politics of coalition by promoting the future conditional of the collective good as a doing that is critical, educated, angry, and hopeful.

In embarking on a campaign to perform angry hope across the city, Esperanza activists also challenged the social choreographies of public space dictated by the history of Anglo-Mexican conflict and the tourist economy. I explained earlier that the downtown district has been configured across the years to exclude the presence of some Latinas/os while at the same time depending on a highly scripted version of Latina/o visibility to market the city as a tourist destination. If, as American studies scholar Jane C. Desmond has observed, the "live presence of the performers" is "crucial to this economy of pleasure" as "a guarantee of authenticity on which such commodification rests," then the refusal to remain in place or assume the command performance of happy Mexicans constitutes an affront to the very foundation of San Antonio's manufactured and marketed image of itself.[71] Taking hope to the streets, performing a political optimism that queer latinidad might thrive within the Mexican Catholic backdrop of the urban landscape and its idealization in the tourist industry, entails an orientation toward political participation that puts the body on the line.

The assemblage of Latina/o queer bodies assuming public space in the urban environment during the Todos Somos Esperanza campaign required a coordination that Susan Leigh Foster understands as the "choreographies of protest." But the occupation of space in and through Latina/o queer performance also introduced another way of being in the city and allowed other queer Latinas/os to rehearse these new routes within the relative safety of the group protest. In this sense, the political movements of the Todos Somos Esperanza campaign instructed partakers, especially other Latina/o queers, on how to move assertively through what might be otherwise perceived as unwelcoming public space. However, I do not mean to give the impression that the pedagogy of this practice was in any way prescriptive. Very much as in the case of the mock trial discussed above, the model of participation required the development of technical proficiencies but did not impose a fixed model. That is, involvement was solicited but not scripted. In discussing the learned embodied techniques of ACT UP protestors, Foster observes that "over the time that they are practiced, they acquire increasing influence over corporeal and also individual identity. Not a script that the protestor learns to execute, these are, rather, actions that both require and provide strong commitment and, once practiced, slowly change the world in which they occur."[72] Similarly, insisting on the value of embodied cohabitation, Esperanza Center activists activated and shared with each other repertoires of Latina/o queer publicity that became over the two-year period of the campaign not so much scripts of communication but social realities. Queer latinidad was mobilized in the public movements of Esperanza activists. These mobilizations in turn emerged from the emotionally moving experiences of being and performing together. In the next chapter we move from the streets to the club as I turn to the choreographic displays of Latina/o queer social dancers that practice similar modes of being and becoming in the public enactments of performance.

4

QUOTIDIAN UTOPIAS

Latina/o Queer Choreographies

Dancing in the club is my chance to have space of my own.
—Néstor, Rochester, New York

. . . when I dance and the Latin music or just drumming comes
on in another song, that's when the *puertorriqueña* comes out.
—Clara, Austin, Texas

This chapter (and the next) mark a turn in this book from the public interventions organized at Latina/o queer arts organizations to the quotidian aesthetics of Latina/o queer performance. I offer here a tour of Latina/o queer dance floors at various clubs in the states of New York and Texas. In looking at examples in the cities of New York, Rochester, San Antonio, and Austin from 1998 to 2003 I pursue the cultural trends and social contingencies that shaped Latina/o queer nightlife in the late 1990s and into the early 2000s. I approach the club as a site where queer latinidad was practiced in critical and consequential ways during this period. I turn to the experiences of queer Latinas/os who, like me, have come of age within the realm of the club. I refer to five years of observation at eight different clubs across the four cities I visited, including detailed descriptions of choreography, formal and informal interviews with social dancers, and recorded and published sound archives from the musicians and DJs I discuss to offer a portrait of queer latinidad in motion.[1] Through the voices and choreographic approaches of my informants I argue for the formative and utopian potential that dancing in a club engenders. At the heart of this project is an attempt to approach the feelings of community and agency produced in the acts of club dancing. Dance in the club, as an improvisational social practice, is both immediate materiality (getting ready, traveling to the club, interacting with others) and utopian futurity (the emergence of community, the world of possibilities and strategies, the promise of pleasure). Yet the utopian realm of the club (i.e., community and pleasure) must always be negotiated, sometimes even fought for, in its live material context. In the space of the dance floor, pleasurable exchanges are complicated by social hierarchies enforced inside and outside the club. In this constantly evolving social environment I identify and look critically at the place of utopia in Latina/o queer club dancing. I suggest that it is in the improvisational bodily articulations of the dancers, their theories in practice, and in the transactions that unravel from these actions, where utopia, in its connotations both as liberation from oppression and the constitution of community, resides.

As I have been stressing throughout this book, the period from the mid-1990s to the early 2000s saw the rise of commodified Latina/o and queer identities into the national public sphere. It also saw invigorated conservative homophobic and xenophobic discourses about and actions against these communities. The politico-economic backdrop to these negotiations of identity was dominated by rapid shifts in the global economic models and local adjustments meant to integrate municipalities into these models. As the previous two chapters demonstrate, cities and neighborhoods were significantly reconfigured to build up housing, tourism, and other infrastructure and services intended to welcome new corporate investment and economic growth. We have already seen how New York City transformed Manhattan by pushing against other locales like Hunts Point to carry the burden of the elite's financial stability. In the case of San Antonio we have observed how a turn to tourism as an economic development strategy imposed expectations about the built environment, the circulation of bodies, and the policing of expressive culture in the city core. In both instances, Latinas/os were pushed out of residential enclaves, marginalized from services and opportunities, and largely (mis)represented as marginal to the story of urban renewal and growth, even when standing in as the marketed aesthetic of the festive tourist destination.

The other two cities I visit in this chapter experienced similar economic stresses and reconfigurations. Austin, Texas, was one of the protagonists of the dot.com business boom during the 1990s, following its rise as a center of high-tech industries in the 1980s. Ushered in by the incredible success of the computer maker Dell and further supported by city and state, Austin found itself in the midst of rapid growth over the course of my fieldwork. Its ascendancy as a center for the "new economy" was so remarkable that the city figured as one of Richard L. Florida's centers of the "creative class."[2] Especially significant to the concerns of this study were the pressures gentrification presented to both downtown and near downtown businesses and historic working-class Mexican and African-American communities south and east of the city's core as Austin built up its skyline in aspirations of attracting even further economic activity.

While buildings were going up in Austin, they were going down in Rochester. The western New York city had seen its economic glory as a center of technology-driven industries in an earlier period. Throughout the late nineteenth century and the first half of the twentieth century, industrial giants such as Eastman Kodak, Xerox, and Bausch & Lomb developed and manufactured top products in the areas of imaging and optical technologies for photography, film, document reproduction, and vision.[3] The city also counted with a garment industry that dominated the national market in the early twentieth century and whose remaining activity motivated a substantial portion of the Puerto Rican migration of the 1960s. However, by the 1980s most of the garment district had disappeared and the corporate giants had begun to downsize manufacturing operations and raze old industrial complexes in the region to save costs. They shrunk further as digital technologies took hold of the world economy and other players, both national and international, introduced competing alternatives into the market. The Latina/o population in the city suffered significantly from this collapse, most especially the urban residential district of Clinton Avenue, which saw its infrastructure and availability of basic services quickly deteriorate as the city encountered drastic shortages in revenue.[4]

In light of the diverse and at times divergent economic pictures presented by the four urban locations I visit in this chapter, the increased marginalization and displacement of Latina/o communities represent a significant convergence of Latina/o experience. For queer Latinas/os in particular, the stresses of either deteriorating or gentrifying Latina/o neighborhoods meant increased difficulty in locating, building, and/ or experiencing sites of Latina/o queer leisure and conviviality. I have argued already that arts organizations provided important alternatives. In this chapter I introduce the dance club as a cultural geography that was just as significant to the figurations of queer latinidad during the period of this study. I understand performance here as a practice motivated partly by what Jill Dolan has identified as a "desire . . . to reach for something better, for new ideas about how to be and how to be with each other."[5] The epigraphs to this chapter offer testimony from the dance floor by two Latina/o queer dancers whose stories I engage in the pages that follow. In their declarations that dancing enacts for them a space of their own where they may come out into their own ethnicity, and also their sexuality, they position the small-scale environs of the club as significant interventions into the rest of their experience, dictated as it is by the macroeconomics and politics outlined throughout this book. The performances in the dance club serve as rehearsals for choreographies of the everyday that extend well beyond the few hours of music, movement, sweat, and desire that characterize the more frivolous description of queer nightlife. In proposing utopia as a theory in practice of queer latinidad I propose these choreographies as practices of resistance.

Walking in the Hood

I begin my engagement with the club with an autoethnographic account of my own embodied experience traveling to one such establishment. I offer this narrative to demonstrate how social relations outside the club govern the motivations and dynamics within it. Of central importance to my account are the emotional and choreographic adjustments of moving queerly in public space. I also showcase how identitarian affiliation is much less narratively scripted than performatively achieved in social contexts.

It is a sunny summer afternoon in 1999 as I leave my Williamsburg, Brooklyn, apartment, a block from Avenida Puerto Rico, en route to the train station. I walk down Lorimer Street and listen to the homeboys' chatter outside the corner bodega fronting to each other about who will dare talk to the young woman who approaches, baby in arms, to buy diapers or perhaps even a cold beer to quench the unbearable thirst. They are all Latino men in their late teens or early twenties, most of them Puerto Rican and Dominican. These young men are indeed a permanent fixture of my street's human landscape. They gather every afternoon in a group that ranges from six to ten. They gossip, drink their beer or soft drinks wrapped in a paper bag, smoke cigarrettes or weed, and simply hang out between the bodega and the barbershop late into the night. Most of them have come to know me as part of our neighborhood too, as

I frequent the bodega to buy last-minute cooking ingredients or simply pass by it daily on the way to or from my apartment four doors down.

These young men always greet me and I reply politely. They "know" or assume my sexuality. My effeminate straddle or my postpunk hairstyling and fashion give me up. I do not match the masculine swagger and hip-hop aesthetic that characterizes "our side" of the neighborhood: a corner of a Latina/o enclave quickly being pushed out by the skyrocketing cost of housing brought forth by the hipster gentrification of Bedford Avenue just a few blocks away.

I am relatively comfortable in this environment. I enjoy some privileges as a light-skinned Puerto Rican, *a blanquito*, with a private university education. I am also aware of my own marginal status as queer. This is especially so when the young men at the corner bodega whistle at me as I approach the store or address me with effeminizing comments. "Vaya mami. ¿Cómo estás?" and "I see you doing good, *mami*," are frequent comments that playfully flirt with my supposed queerness while asserting my neighbors' masculine superiority over me by publicly addressing me as a feminine. My neighbors often perform these *piropos*[6] or spoken flirtations with tilts of the head to the side, backs slanted with concave chests, forward thrusts of the hips, and slow but firm rocking of the torso with arm extensions to the side. Their approach characterizes a combination of laidback coolness and seductive aggressiveness common in quotidian hip-hop choreography.[7] The image performs a simultaneous distancing from me—pulling away of the head and torso—and an approximation—the extended arms of a suggested embrace and the sexual suggestiveness of the hip thrust.

The young mother and I are in some ways equals in these exchanges. We are both available to the young crew as objects of seduction; as others in relation to whom they may perform the gender scripts of their Latino hypermasculinity. I have never seen them address other Latino males or white or African-American patrons of the store the same way. I assume their daring approach to be a sign of intimacy and recognition. They have seen me and the young mother in the neighborhood and they know us both to be Puerto Ricans from the block (although I have lived here less than a year). To the extent that we are "one of them," as Latinas/os we are addressable, approachable. We are both used to these quotidian exchanges since we recognize them as part of "our community" as well. We smile, flirt cautiously to tease them back, or simply ignore them depending on the mood. Sometimes the young mother and I chat inside the store and poke fun at their overtures by cracking jokes about their need to be so vocal with their showing off of macho supremacy. She oftens describes them to me with a mix of frustration and delightful familiarity, "perro chiquito con complejo de Rottweiler" (little dog with a Rottweiler complex). Other times my responses are corporeal. I may exaggerate my effeminate walk and gestures, articulating my buttocks as an ironic flaunting, or I may simply neutralize my gestures to avoid engagement on a particularly stressful day. Despite our casual handling of their *piropos* and gestural advances, their address to us is clear evidence of the patriarchal and homophobic context shaping many social exchanges in our neighborhood.

I am much more guarded when passing by other groups of men further down the street, aware that they might not be as comfortable with my presence as my neighbors at the bodega. I often accelerate my walk and avoid eye contact when addressed with an effeminizing greeting or when I am simply called a faggot or *maricón* in the middle of the street. I know at times these scare tactics are performed upon me based on a perception of me as white and thus out of place in the neighborhood. "Gringo!" often accompanies the homophobic slur when that is the case. When this happens, I try to understand the behavior as a survival mechanism meant to draw the boundaries of the Latina/o barrio and guard against rapid gentrification. But I am troubled by the homophobic formulation entailed in such an attempt to mark ethnic territory by recurring to an aggressive hypermasculinity that assumes whiteness as threatening faggotry. Sometimes, I muster enough energy and courage to answer back. Most of the time, I simply act as if did not hear a thing and keep on walking.

I continue my walk down Lorimer Street and approach the train station; the neighborhood's human landscape begins to shift from primarily brown and black to almost exclusively white. Once I cross the boundaries between my Latina/o neighborhood and the borders of gentrification, I change my attitude. My walk is less directed. I meander down the street at a slow, relaxed pace. Queerness abounds here. Not just in terms of visible same-sex couples walking about hand in hand, but also the overall attitude toward masculinity. A hipster aesthetic becomes the primary visual and performance code of this part of the street. Men demonstrate a purposeful abandon in their funky asymmetrical haircuts and five o'clock shadows. They dress in tighter-than-tight jeans and T-shirts short enough to intimate the presence of a belly button and contrasting the baggy clothes and baseball caps through which my neighbors tend to hide their bodies. The bodily stance and attitude are markedly different as well, accentuating a certain softness in gesture that I can only relate to the East Village scene out of which many of these arrivals have come.

A simplistic reading of this stroll down my neighborhood might reinforce binary associations positioning latinidad as inherently homophobic and queerness as inherently white. I do not wish to circulate such notions. I want to articulate the varied topographies Latina/o queers traverse in their daily lives. If we think of queer latinidad in relation to my neighborhood streets, we can identify some of the day-to-day negotiations at the heart of such lived experience. This does not mean that Latina/o neighborhoods are always or entirely homophobic. In fact, the flirtatious address from my neighborhood's young men shows ways in which familiarity with my presence, *convivencia diaria* as Ricourt and Danta would term it, leads to a certain comfort zone where these differences coexist and interact.[8] This is not the language of tolerance either. I truly believe I had established meaningful acquaintances with the men at the bodega by the sheer experience of living in proximity to them, and even though they often asserted it as a double entendre, I knew they always "had my back." They were aware, and I think proud, that I was a graduate student and that I taught at a city college. I often received visitors—rarely one of the bodega boys, but often their younger brothers and sisters—asking for advice in preparation for college admissions or help with their school assignments. I also requested their assistance when bringing heavy items into the house or when I needed recommendations on local merchants and community institutions. Our relationship was reciprocal despite its shaky foundations in homophobic and classed distance.

Further down the street, things were not as clear-cut either. I frequented establishments down Bedford Avenue with other queer friends, many of them white, who lived in that section of the neighborhood. They loved to savor the flavors of a Mexican *elote con crema, queso, y chile* (corn on the cob with cream, cheese, and hot pepper) at a hip establishment on their street but were hesitant to walk over to the taco stand or the Puerto Rican restaurant at my end of the neighborhood. Their dismissal was not about safety over a perceived homophobia; they clearly knew I lived contentedly in my block, but more of a class distinction between what they deemed as the hipster neighborhood and the hood. My Puerto Ricanness was apparent. It was frequently remarked upon in comments about my accent or even my demeanor. Nonetheless, the aesthetics of my self-presentation were congruent with my scenester friends, facilitating my navigation of these hipster environs. I knew that had I chosen to participate in the hip-hop fashion codes of my Latina/o side of the neighborhood, I would have stuck out like a sore thumb in this context.

Queer latinidad can only be approximated by accounting for the full range of experiences demonstrated by these encounters and many other intersections in travel. That is, queer latinidad is not a site with clearly defined boundaries but a busy street with lots of foot traffic. This generates both intimacies and frictions for the traveler who walks along its path. I thoroughly enjoyed the experience of living in a Latina/o neighborhood with access to Puerto Rican and other Latina/o goods and services. I felt at home in proximity to other Latinas/os. The *boleros* blasting from my neighbor's apartment on Sunday mornings while she cleaned the house with Fabuloso soap, the aroma emanating from the *fritura* (fritter) stands on Bushwick Avenue, and the Sunday dress of Mexican immigrants on the way to mass are just a few of the sights, sounds, and smells I will forever remember of my Brooklyn neighborhood. I clearly and affectionately recall my flirtations with the bodega crew despite being fully aware of their potentially injurious nature. But I also enjoyed the possibility of walking down a few blocks to join my friends in queer fellowship. My personal geography in my making of home was extended to include the other side of the neighborhood. I too liked eating at the hipster Mexican restaurant or sharing drinks at one of the local bars. Most importantly, I enjoyed being "comfortably queer" on that side of the street.[9]

Being Latina/o and queer in my Brooklyn neighborhood is not impossible. Nevertheless, it requires a dancerly strategy that pays attention to the nuances of moving from one place to another. I revel in the creative maps formed as a consequence of this movement and assume these travels as constitutive components of who I am or become through my action. The experience of traveling through my neighborhood, as Latino and queer, is one fueled by a search to satisfy multiple interests, desires, and identifications. It also requires strategic caution in order to avoid or manage risks and potential injury from crossing borders. These social borders demarcate one side of the street from the other with rigid notions of who and what belongs to a particular territory. They are crossed often by many who explicitly or tacitly challenge the logics of exclusion that structure racial and class difference in the city.

The trajectories available to queer latinidad cannot be ascribed to simple cultural differences either. Such an approach to the marked differences between the two sides of my neighborhood would run the risk of simply attributing my various experiences to cultural attitudes toward sexuality and would elide the critical role that other vectors of experience play in the exchanges I outline above. In addition, the scales of influence that shape such experiences require attention to global, national, regional, and local dynamics that have and continue to influence daily life on my city block. The territorial tension I experience when confronted with a homophobic slur coming out of the mouth of a Latina/o resident in my neighborhood requires further contextualization. Residents in my neighborhood experience the economic stress created by contemporary gentrification by primarily hipster whites with what might be interpreted as queer aesthetic codes. The prices for rental apartment units, property taxes, and even basic goods have increased dramatically as landlords and business folk identify opportunities to profit from the arriving population. In turn, the community of hipsters settling in the neighborhood, many of them artists from the East Village, have experienced similar pressures at their respective neighborhoods as formerly rundown residential districts in Lower Manhattan were also transformed by gentrification.

The competition for space and resources is not new to the neighborhood. Previously an industrial and manufacturing district, Williamsburg attracted a large number of Puerto Ricans seeking to live close to work opportunities during the 1960s. Once the neighborhood was established as a Puerto Rican enclave, waves of other Latina/o immigrants, primarily Dominicans, followed during the 1980s. But while the Latina/o population was in the upswing, manufacturing jobs in the neighborhood, which were estimated at close to 93,000 in the 1960s, declined dramatically to under 12,000 by the 1990s.[10] Latinas/os, primarily Puerto Ricans, have also been historically marginalized from public housing opportunities near the Hasidic sections of the neighborhood. Most recently, gentrification has brought shifting discourses about who properly belongs. This poses a particularly heavy burden on Latina/o youth, who have become both the symbolic enemy against which gentrifiers narrate their "clean up" strategies and the scapegoats of antigentrification activists who often characterize them as the culprits in the neighborhood decline and vulnerability. In my walking, I step through the material and emotional traces of past encounters and leave my own footprints as I make my way home.

Even as I narrate my skillful navigation through my neighborhood's geography in strategically queer and Latina/o ways, I am cautious to call forth queer latinidad as a valued or even presenced component of the street's public sphere on either side. There are no public spaces here where queer Latinas/os interested in encountering each other can do so openly or within a particularly Latina/o cultural context. Aside from private gatherings at other folks' homes or a walk to the "white" side of the neighborhood, there are few options to encounter others occupying similar identitarian coordinates. Likewise, when I venture into the hip queer-friendly side of my neighborhood, my latinidad is at times suspect. I could hang with the other queer boys, but the terms of engagement, aside from the food, remain primarily white from the specificities of colloquial language to the overall content of our conversations.

Instead, I take the L train into Manhattan and switch to the blue line northbound to Port Authority in search of such a rare intersection of my cultural, emotional, and sexual desires. I exit the train station and walk to Escuelita nightclub, a temple of Latina/o queer nightlife where Latinas/os much like myself travel in search of possibilities, pleasures, and encounters not yet available in our own neighborhoods.

Utopian Moves

As a migrant to the United States from Puerto Rico in the early 1990s I learned to articulate my sexuality and my political identity at the dance club. Within the erotic realm of clubs like Heaven, Carpe Diem, Escuelita, and Limelight, I learned to embody my position as a queer Latino.[11] The club offers me a space to experience what freedom from homophobia, and sometimes from racism, feels like. The club also provides me with spaces where experiences of discrimination can be addressed and exorcised in the company of others who, like me, understand the at times difficult and pleasurable path of being a queer of color. My experience in the club not only allows me to feel desire, love, and community, but gives me the confidence and the knowledge to step proudly into other, more dangerous venues, like portions of my own neighborhood described above, and seek, even demand, similar experiences from the world outside it. The club provides me with strategies of survival, but also with the comfort and pleasure of knowing that I can return to its realm and experience once more this utopian community of queers.

The argument for understanding the gay club as a utopian safe haven is a dominant narrative in gay cultural criticism.[12] Contemporary analysis of club dancing ranges from celebratory approaches to the liberating potential of clubs as sites of uncensored expression, to critical arguments that outline normative forces that dominate social relations in these spaces.[13] In his analysis of gay dances at Sydney's Mardi Gras celebrations performance scholar Jonathan Bollen discusses how the club is often characterized as "a safe place free from the violence of a homophobic world." The club appears here as a realm of possibility born of a constraining, even violent, materiality; a "utopian promise that literalizes a metaphor: the dance floor as ecstatic vision and grounded experience of gay and lesbian community."[14] Within a designated "safe place" imaginative self-presentation and communitarian affiliation can occur outside the pressures of a heteronormative society. If we think about my own trajectory from my apartment door to the train station en route to Escuelita in midtown Manhattan, we can conceive of the club to be a utopian destination. It offers an unabashedly queer and Latina/o social space. The celebration of Mardi Gras offers an event framework that is more publicly sanctioned by outside authoritative structures, in part because of its temporary nature. The gay club offers a similarly carnivalesque environment that allows for the free expression of queer sexuality within its "safe" structure.[15]

However, as the musicologist Walter Hughes argues, the assumptions of *communitas* or collective coherence in the gay dance club may be reframed by understanding the club as a disciplinary social space in itself.[16] Hughes argues that the club imposes expectations of behavior and standards for membership and participation that demand adjustments, choreographic as well as social, from its patrons. The rhythm of music is the clearest demonstration of these demands. Dancers literally move to the temporal schema introduced by the speed and arrangement of the music. Following Hughes's assumption that the beat of the music functions as a dominant sensual mechanism that imposes its rhythmic structure on those who experience it, Bollen adds an equally dramatic layer of disciplinary performance in the mimetic act of dancing with others and its relationship to hierarchies of movement and legitimacy. As Bollen explains, "The beat may register its disciplinary effects not through direct infliction, but through the way in which others dancing to the beat rhythmically textures [sic] the choreographic ensemble in which you dance."[17] We can think of the beat or rhythm more generally as the element that animates and structures social exchanges on the dance floor since it influences how bodies will move and thus under what conditions they will relate to each other. Dancers in the club negotiate not only the aural stimuli marked in the rhythm but the body and movement ideologies of those surrounding them.

The dance floor is, in this model, always involved in an economy of hierarchies that depend on the binary arrangements of majority-minority relationships in the ownership of queer public spaces.[18] Mainstream gay clubs, for example, are often invested in the construction of normative homosexuality, and in the context of the United States this normativity is generally regarded as white and male.[19] The complex nature of these exchanges is particularly significant when addressing minoritarian subjects who do not fit as easily into the dominant definitions and aspirations that shape the social realm of the club. Latina/o queer dancers in the United States enter the "safe place" of the club with a marked difference. Their pursuit of experiences of sexual freedom is often intersected by a similarly intense desire to acknowledge, embody, and act out their latinidad. Dance, as an act of self-presentation and community building, becomes one of the mechanisms through which Latina/o queers negotiate their place and membership within and outside the club. Envisioning utopia from the perspective of the dance floor is not as simple as dancing along with others, but the result of serious experiences in multiple communities and their intersections, sometimes in stark contrast to or in conflict with one another. The emergence of utopia for queer Latina/o dancers is both an individual act of survival and a communitarian experience of and yearning for freedom. Addressing utopia in this context requires an engagement not only with the cultures of pleasure that characterize the club, but with cultures of struggle that mark the multiple trajectories and negotiations undertaken by dancers on their way to and as a precondition for the utopian experiences of the dance floor.

As it will become evident from the discussion that follows, none of my informants recurred to utopia as a term to define or describe their practices in the club. While the previous chapters have defined specific theories in practice of queer latinidad with concepts articulated by the performers themselves—home and hope—this chapter focuses on embodied practices for which no easily identifiable word emerged during fieldwork. In part, the inability to identify a term has much to do with the multiple communities across a variety of locations that constitute my sample. However, I argue that this has mostly to do with the fact that in many of these encounters my informants spoke through the body in motion and not the voice. Nonetheless, the language my interlocutors used to explain their experience in the club was conceptually spatial and affectively hopeful.

Jill Dolan's theorization of utopia in performance allows for an engagement with club dancing that retains a material grounding in social exchange while approaching the world-making dynamics of the club.[20] Citing Lyman Tower Sargent's comments regarding utopia's opposition to contemporary conditions, Dolan defines utopia in performance as a phenomenon that "takes place now, in the interstices of present interactions, in glancing moments of possibly better ways to be together as human beings."[21] The utopian performative is deeply rooted in a materialist appraisal of the inadequacies of contemporary experience and addresses them in the moment, through enactments that produce alternative experiences and visions of how things could and should be. This positioning of utopia as critique redirects the analysis of the social relations of the club as interventions in the larger sociopolitical debate over queer sexualities beyond their local geography on the dance floor. That is, the performances in the club are interventions into dominant discourses of sexuality, gender, race, and ethnicity, among others, that construct the very geography of the dance floor as an alternative to structures of oppression and prohibition.

Furthermore, Dolan locates the utopian performative here and now. This focus on the effects of performance in the present tense positions practices like improvised social dance as activities that produce utopia in its affective and most immediate sense. This proposition is central to my understanding of the club, where the improvisational acts of dancers perform alternative modes of being in the extravagant and assertive display of their bodies in motion, as well as how to be with each other in their sharing of space, time, and kinesthetic resources with those around them. David Román has recently discussed this notion of performance's utopian construction in the present in his autobiographical essay on dance as liberation. Román comments, "Perhaps the reason that so many accounts of gay club culture read it as utopian has something to do with the idea that dance, as a kinetic experience, enables social configurations of same-sex bodies not imaginable elsewhere."[22] The act of dancing in itself constitutes the utopian "doing" of the club by materializing bodily exchanges that articulate, showcase, even flaunt queer sexuality publicly. I argue that for Latina/o queers these doings involve the articulation of latinidad and alternatives to it that incorporate queer attitudes to gender and sexuality.

Improvising the Social

The practice of dancing in clubs engages bodies in social dance and in the realm of improvisation. These physical exchanges are character- ized by dancers constructing their identities as subjects and community members in space, in an environment established for intimate social in- teraction. These interactions are made possible by the theatricality of the club environment. The visual and aural spectacles of lights, music, and clothing, the mind-altering effects of alcohol and drugs, and the sexu- ally charged interactions between dancers make clubs sites of pleasure. Within this hypersensorial medium improvisation is the central para- digm and possibility of club culture. How dancers react to the sensory stimuli of the club, the body in relation to its surroundings in the moment, constitutes a training of sorts; both in techniques of self-affirmation as dancers attempt to perform themselves in public, and in communitarian practice as they share the moment of cultural performance with oth- ers. Although structures of power constitute these social spaces and ex- changes, the live transactions that take place within them (re)define and at times challenge them through performance. Focusing on the kines- thetic rhetorics of the dancing body, and particularly local interventions by individual dancers, offers a radically different picture of the club expe- rience. A discourse focused on improvisation allows for the articulation of strategy within the (dis)orderly logic of the dance club. Here perhaps, within the context that showcases spontaneous social relations and the skills developed to thrive within them, lies the utopian potential of club dancing. This is where the presentness of performance—its ability to do something, and the versatility of improvisation, the possibility of trans- formation and change—becomes the driving force of dance club culture.

In her ethnography of club dancing, Fiona Buckland explores the world-making power of improvised social dance at gay, lesbian, and queer clubs primarily in New York City. She observes that improvised social dancing in the club is a playful practice that depends upon the agency of its performers, [which] produces queer club culture, not as a homogenous, transhistorical object, but as a process of counterpoint, contestation, and polyvocality. This more fluid model shifts agency away from culture and its structural forms, including dance, to participants who improvised movement in response to everyday experiences, which, in turn, influenced the experiences and understanding of everyday life.[23]

According to Buckland's argument, dancing serves as a creative forum in which to articulate as well as experience the quotidian. Through dancing, performers navigate the specific social realm of the club. Sexuality, race, gender, and class are negotiated among patrons who travel to these sites in search of both individual pleasure and community. These acts of affirmation and community performed in the club may in turn reshape the attitudes and approaches dancers take to their daily lives.[24] The dramaturgical processes brought into the theater of the dance club are especially significant to queer Latinas/os. They require improvisational skills as a strategy to inhabit and perform their multiple identities in and out of club environments. In such a way, they differently accommodate the exigencies of their own needs and desires. My opening autoethnographic account of walking in my neighborhood demonstrates the ways in which my adjustments to multiple encounters and constituencies that constitute my everyday demand specific choreographic strategies. Whether it is an adjustment in posture or pace, I respond to social situations bodily. My skills at moving through the public space of the street are enhanced by my experiences in the club. While the movement strategies I employ in the club and the street may be different, the general awareness and practiced attention to movement transfers from one location to the other. Improvisation in the form of code-switching (linguistic and otherwise) enables minority subjects like myself to perform in and out of multiple circumstances and contexts.

That said, I understand improvisation within the club as a practice that is not exclusive of skill, technique, and hierarchical ideologies of proper choreography, fashion, and even body types. However, and here I echo Buckland's focus on contestation and counterpoint, I advocate an approach to improvisation as a survival skill that is at once a participation in the structural realm of the club, including disciplinary performance, and a challenge to it. Positioning improvisation as the driving force of the utopian performative in the club allows me to address the polyvocality of approaches to the performance of queer latinidad as an emerging identity that is textured by the at times contradictory nature of both of its primary sites of identification.[25]

Latinidad takes new meaning at the club and the dance floor: it is not only an enactment of identity in movement but a social improvisation. In this sense, the improvisational exchanges among dancers may engage latinidad as an aesthetic or affect as much as an articulate self-knowledge. The encounters taking place in the club under an assumed latinidad are often as productive as they are frictive. Friction offers a much needed adjustment to the uncritically utopian assumptions of Latina/o cohesiveness and will be the primary focus of the next chapter. Latinidad offers a site for identification invested in the articulation of difference from a critical position where the marginality of Latina/o populations matters. It constitutes an intersection or home to a diverse community of millions who remain significantly disenfranchised from U.S. material, social, and cultural economies. For queer Latinas/os, latinidad gestures to the emergence of a sensibility, a shared feeling of placeness, and at times placelessness, in the dance club. This sensibility is in part the product of the circulation of Latina/o popular culture, especially music and dance, through media networks. The experiences of marginality outside the club texture the engagements with latinidad within it.

For queer Latinas/os, the experience of the club is further motivated by their search for sexual liberation and materialized fully on the dance floor. Queer Latinas/os struggle daily with their racial and ethnic marginalization in the United States and they encounter, with equal intensity, the homophobia within their own communities. Queer latinidad offers a respite by bringing together multiple migrant and border communities through common cultural traits and affects, as well as acknowledgment of similar histories of discrimination and sites of pleasurable investment. And it is within the realm of affect that I think club dancing manifests most profoundly the nature of the utopian performative.[26]

The dance floor may be one of the most vivid examples of the material conditions from which queer latinidad emerges. Within the club the improvised choreography of the dancers showcases modes of being that are both Latina/o and queer. The world envisioned and embodied in these performances strategically invests in both of these affective registers to produce a utopian third space. The performances of utopia in the club rehearse strategies of survival and interconnectedness that might enable the emergence of queer pan-Latina/o communities beyond it. Dancing in the club produces queer latinidad as a utopian performative that is the articulation of something new, an identity in motion that bridges both queerness and latinidad. It is also an intervention in the histories and struggles of these identities.

This possibility for community—enabled in the club by the physical interactions of improvisational dancing—is one of the most salient features of the utopian performative as defined by Dolan. She argues that the experience of performance may produce *communitas*.[27] "This, for me, is the beginning (and perhaps the substance) of the utopic performative: in the performer's grace, in the audience's generosity, in the lucid power of intersubjective understanding, however fleeting. These are the moments when we can believe in utopia. These are the moments theatre and performance make possible."[28] I similarly propose Latina/o queer dance practices as exercises in "intersubjective understanding" among Latina/o communities that differ greatly in their experiences of entry or forced incorporation into the United States, but who share similar experiences of racism, cultural marginalization, and homophobia. Dance clubs, I argue, provide *convivencia diaria* as sites for dwelling, temporarily limited but spatially vast homes, within which Latina/o queers perform the desires often prohibited outside these spaces. They must still address the structures of dominance that still seep into this "safe haven." In doing so, they rehearse strategies by which to survive collectively. These are the queer-world-making strategies Buckland attends to so passionately in her own ethnographic account. And it is precisely in the leap of faith from the experience of everyday life to the imagination of community, even across national, racial, and class borders, where latinidad suggests its most utopian performances.

In my ethnographic fieldwork in gay and lesbian clubs in Texas and New York I have encountered and experienced powerful performances of Latina/o queer utopia. I locate these glimpses into the possibility of Latina/o queer utopia within the choreographic strategies performed by dancers who negotiate the club as both hegemonic discipline and utopian promise. I would like to turn to some examples that illustrate the multilevel sense of negotiation that is required of minoritarian subjects entering the realm of the club.

Stepping into Utopia

For queer Latinas/os, the acts performed in social dancing and their location at the gay club bring together a whole series of intersecting identities, experiences, and desires that produce a truly hybrid and at times conflicted notion of place and being in the world. Entering the gay club is an act of affirmation for Latinas/os, many of whom reside in neighborhoods where traditional conceptions of Latina/o heteronormativity and homophobia prevail. Dressing up and making the trip to the very public space of the club requires immense courage and strength. Victor is a gay man in his late twenties and a recent migrant from Puerto Rico now living a few blocks from Krash, a Latina/o club in Queens. He explains, "A mi a veces me da un miedo porque mi familia no sabe. Yo salgo a escondidas. Tu sabes, perfumaito y todo . . . pero yo digo que voy a dar la vuelta y ya. Pero dar la vuelta es que camino dos cuadras por ahí pa' bajo y me meto en Krash!"[29] Like Victor, close to a third of the informants I interviewed spoke of sneaking out to the club scene.

Those who were out to their families still commented on the danger of getting to the clubs, especially when they are located in remote sites of the city. In New York City, for example, Nilda, a twenty-two-year-old lesbian of Dominican and Filipino descent, commented that she is often harassed on her three-block walk from Port Authority in Manhattan on her way to Escuelita. "I get off the train and me and my girlfriends are like 'Run, run, run!' 'Cause people be coming by, 'Hey baby what's up?' 'Cause there is a lot of hooking around here still," she says. Despite the stress sometimes involved in getting to the club, Latina/o queers venture passionately into this world. This is, after all, one of the few safe places where they can be queer, many of them argue.

In an interview Nestor, a forty-three-year-old Chicano gay man in Rochester, New York, explains, "Dancing in the club is my chance to have space of my own. Even if I am surrounded by a bunch of people, I make sure that my dance floor is my dance floor and nobody better mess with me. I am fierce when I take the stage, honey, and I has got to shine!" For Nestor, who works as a supervisor of seasonal farmworkers in Sodus, New York, and shares a small one-bedroom apartment with five other men who labor at the same camp, the club is truly a space of his own. During his weekend outings to Rochester he is able to assume, perform, and live his identity as a gay man, far from the homophobia prevalent in his household. The club offers him an experience of community, a chance to be in the company of those who identify with his interests and desires. This is the utopia of his experience.

However, the gay club is not without its own conflicts. Some interviewees referred to these experiences of alienation within mainstream gay clubs as the reason why they seek Latino queer spaces. However, many saw the same power relations in Latino clubs, pointing especially to the comparative prevalence of gay male culture at the expense of more inclusive involvement of lesbian patrons. All informants mentioned their continued patronage of these spaces, mainstream and Latino, and often said they continued to feel safe within them. Addressing this issue, Nilda says, "I know there is always going to be something that bothers people. I mean, we are not perfect, right? But when you are in there and you are dancing, everyone is about the same . . . just that some of us dance better than others, that's all."

Nestor also explains: "You know, people are generally nice, but you never know. I've seen a lot going on around here, some dude thought I was a *puto* [hustler] the other night! Man, you know, just 'cause I'm Latin and shit. And I'm not about to just fall for the first one that comes around. That's why, you know, you see me in my corner, you know. I like keeping to myself." "Well, what about relationships? Are you looking for relationships in the club?" I ask. "Well, I also want to meet someone, you see. I am nice and I flirt and all . . . I just don't want to be messed around with, you know. I got to test people out. You feel me?" These are the experiences shaping and being shaped by Nestor's performance in the dance club. He sees his time in the club as time for the free expression of his sexuality, but at the same time resents the risks he runs of racism and stereotyping. The mythology of the safe place and unbreakable community is shattered by the possibility of racism often prevalent in these spaces, demonstrating that despite the general free environment, the club's Anglo-dominated power structure remains to be negotiated.

Nestor's choreography on the dance floor engages fully with these contradictions. He takes to the dance floor alone. He is in a small, racially mixed gay club in Rochester. A version of "Rumba," the Latin house track recorded in 1993 by New York City–based Pirates of the Caribbean, plays through the speakers. In the song a heavy house bass blasts with layers of polyrhythm played out by congas, bongos, timbales, and electronic percussion. Nestor untangles the percussive line with stylized steps in a forward cutting motion across the floor. Nestor's improvised choreography explicitly demarcates space on the dance floor. His movements are characterized by a slight bending of the right knee and a rhythmic pause in which the right shoulder punctuates the beat traveling through his torso onto his hip. This movement is followed by pointing forward his left foot on the step. His movement sequence is adorned with a forward rotation of bent arms performed in Caribbean social dance genres such as salsa.

Nestor further accentuates his assertive use of space by intensely fixing his stare across the room during his cutting forward progression. He ends approximately ten feet of travel with a sudden pause, a coquettish smile, and a slow sway of the hips that ushers in a quick right turn, a sustained pose, a sharp bending of the knees, and a back drop to the floor. An almost immediate recovery to standing impresses onlookers before his return across the floor to the spot where his story began. His travel across the floor synchronizes the performance to the dominant sensory stimuli in the club: the beat. But his on-the-beat motion, matching the intensity of the music, is subverted by the softer feel of his pause-and-pose sequence. These flirtatious instances bookend his movement through space. Slowly shifting his hips to the sides, Nestor tilts his head in synch and smiles both before and after he drops and recovers from the floor. For the next few hours he remains on the dance floor, traveling back and forth on this kinesthetically constructed catwalk, adjusting his strut to the various rhythms of DJ Victor's mix and pausing only to drink water from a bottle strategically placed between the speakers and the go-go boy platform.[30]

Nestor's attract-and-repulse strategy to dance is echoed by Clara, a Puerto Rican lesbian in her midtwenties, who enters the dance floor with her partner at a primarily Anglo gay male club in Austin, Texas. Here a house mix of the Nuyorican actor and singer Jennifer López's "Let's Get Loud" is heard. Clara takes up very little space in her dancing, focusing on a tight kinesphere with her partner. She faces the crowd and positions her back toward her partner, who moves closely from behind with slow, rhythmic weight shifts. These shifts side to side at the knees are initiated with a forward isolation of the shoulder, marking the beat. Clara begins synchronizing her movements with her partner, who also marks the rhythm with her hands on Clara's hips. As the rhythmic line accelerates Clara breaks from her partner's movement and shifts her alignment, teasingly flaunting her behind at the crowd. She makes a quick transition from the slow, cool shift of weight from side to side to isolating the hips in a back-and-forth rocking motion on the beat. The lyrics in López's song invite the crowd to get loud, to take life on their own terms. Meanwhile Clara's feet remain motionless, although she articulates her hips playfully with the rhythm. She pauses counterpointally and then accelerates to a double-time articulation, only to return to the beat again. She repeats this sequence over and over until the song ends. At this point she smiles devilishly at her partner and leaves the floor for a break.

These two examples showcase two different choreographic practices performed by U.S. Latina/o queers in dance clubs in distinctly different places. Nestor's dance floor is located only forty-five minutes from the northern border of the United States, in a state where the Puerto Rican presence, although no longer demographically dominant, remains the primary referent for latinidad. Clara, on the other hand, dances in a city a few hours from the southern U.S. border with Mexico, where latinidad is currently defined by historical negation and suspicion of citizens of ethnic Mexican communities. In both examples, how the dancer moves and how he or she reacts to other people's movement is both a strategic negotiation of the realm of the gay club and an engagement with larger social issues and discourses. The movements performed by Clara and Nestor are in an immediate sense a matter of pleasure, an engagement with the sensory and sexual realm of the gay club. These actions also articulate hopeful performances of desire and agency that enable the possibility of community beyond restrictive notions of national or regional identity.

Sharing Movement

In the *convivencia diaria* of dancing along with others, witnessing bodies on display, displaying one's own, and cruising on and off the dance floor, one discovers that a sense of community emerges. Dancers move in relation to each other's movement. Those movements that are witnessed and rehearsed in relation to other dancers become an improvised repertoire of the present moment. The body becomes conditioned to move through those previous but still immediate experiences on the dance floor. As Jonathan Bollen argues:

> Whether the sharing of kinesthetic resources occurs in the present moment—"picking from the crowd"—or whether it is the

result of an accumulation or re-performance of past dance floor experiences—"a stock standard type of dancing"—the pleasures of the dance floor are often the pleasures of slotting into a choreographic ensemble, where "moving in a way that fits together" means "connecting" with other dancers.[31]

The exchange of "kinesthetic resources" is one of the many behaviors that dancers negotiate within the realm of the club. Through this exchange dancers also negotiate their identities and desires. Bollen presents a dance floor where dancers learn not only how to move, but how to be in communication with others. What this means for the analysis of dance is that no matter how extemporaneous the interactions between dancers, these interactions carry with them the stamp of prior and future relationships in movement. It is out of this sense of diachronicity that a feeling of community arises.

On the dance floor dancers perform the duality embodied in the club between the individual pursuit of pleasure and safety and the emergence of community out of the collective act of moving together.[32] Nestor's dance, for example, is both an invitation to watch and perhaps to engage, as well as a setting of boundaries. You can look, but be aware that you are not being allowed easy access. The spectator is at once lured and challenged. Nestor's cutting across the floor is deliberately about owning the floor for himself, and yet his attitude across the floor is ultimately imbued with irony as he works his upper body in counterpoint to the step progression and eases into the teasing sequences that frame it. His movement is not an emasculated stance; instead, it gains its strength from a directed and articulate performance of queer effeminacy. He fiercely combines a repertoire of "queenie attitude," much as in voguing, to accomplish the spectacular sense of groundedness he performs.

Clara, on the other hand, complains about the assumed entitlement of other dancers: "They just think they own the place, especially white boys. They'll just dance around bumping into everyone. That's rude, you know. I keep to myself and to my girlfriend. It's nobody's business how I dance." She continues to describe a series of movements on the dance floor that come close to describing Nestor's choreography in New York. She prefers contained polyrhythmic movements and sees the more open movement choice as intrusive. She explains that she doesn't want to deal with forced contact with other people on the dance floor: "I am tired of it. You grow up going out to straight clubs and all these guys be coming up and trying to get with you. I mean, even the street people are always talking about your ass out loud and shit. That's just wrong!" Clara articulates how frictions of gendered and racialized experience outside the club texture the affects and aesthetics of choreography within it. The violence played out on her buttocks by an unrelenting male gaze prompts her awareness and orientation to the world around her, a theory in the flesh, as Moraga would term it. She soon turns this into a theory in practice. Her movements in the club become her way of rehearsing her embodied discomfort otherwise.

Clara's choreography with her girlfriend, although allegedly in total isolation from her surroundings, is also invested in public display and community. While her dancing performs a difference from the crowd that she seemingly ignores, it also becomes a conduit for the communal experience of dance spectatorship in the club. Indeed, her strategy lies in the rhythmical articulation of the body, a strategy that Nestor also prioritizes in his own understanding of his dance choices. She maintains a closed space around her, but by flouting the hip isolation movement facing the audience she commands an attentive spectatorship. On the dance floor she reacts to her spectators on the street by rearticulating the racialized and often racist comments about the size of her glutes through the virtuoso contraction of her rear muscles. Shaking her ass on the dance floor is a way to address her everyday experience, to exorcise the racist fetishism of her onlookers, inside and outside the club. Both performers stress a rhythmic layering of their movement that challenges the more common on-the-beat choreographies characteristic of primarily Anglo clubs. Rhythm, specifically the upbeat sensuous articulation of Latin rhythm,[33] functions as the dominant aesthetic of these performances. Through the articulation of rhythmic proficiency as a shared "kinesthetic resource" and marker of latinidad, Clara participates in a community that involves other dancers, like Nestor, despite her keeping to herself. She performs actively as a member of the community even when critically articulating and resenting the tensions that arise inside and outside the club.

Embodying the Sounds of History

As Celeste Fraser Delgado and José Esteban Muñoz explain, "Dance vivifies the cultural memory of a common context of struggle that bolsters a cultural identity itself forged through struggle and dance."[34] One of the key struggles worked through the embodied practices of social dancing is the history of Latina/o sound. The relationship of identity and rhythm is historical in the case of Latin America, as it is throughout the Caribbean, where rhythm is explicitly connected to an African aesthetic and heritage.[35] Through the circuits of music publishing, promotion, and distribution—including live performance tours, radio, television, and film—Afro-Latin rhythms have become the international marker of latinidad. Ana M. López says regarding this transmission of Latina/o and Latin American musical practices through Hollywood films,

> Rhythm has been—and continues to be—used as a significant marker of national/ethnic difference: the cinema locates and placates Latino/as and Latin Americans rhythmically. But this placing has also served to provide a curiously unfettered space for ethnic and other nationals: a place for performers and a space of multiple identifications. Here we can perhaps begin to think about a different rhythmic cartography, not tied to borders to be crossed or transgressed, but where spaces become lived-in and dancing places in which the body—reclaimed from its subservience to work—can be a locus of resistance and desire and enjoyed on that basis.[36]

López reads the productive process of Latinas/os forming imagined communities under the influence of global mass media. It requires articulation of local interests through strategic engagement with globalization. In the case of the club, for example, the sexual economies of a commercially globalized Latina/o culture, generally assumed to be heterosexual, are queered at the site of the local, reconfigured under a different cultural economy. A localizing maneuver is performed at the gay club, not only bringing a specifically Latina/o sensibility to a typically urban Anglo-American social space, but queering latinidad in the process, rearticulating it for the circulation of queer pleasure.

The most obviously global element of contemporary club culture is music, which is published, publicized, and distributed on a global scale. As George Lipsitz has observed:

> It has a peculiar relationship to the poetics and politics of place. Recorded music travels from place to place, transcending physi-

cal and temporal barriers. It alters our understanding of the local and the immediate, making it possible for us to experience close contact with cultures from far away. Yet, precisely because music travels, it also augments our appreciation of place. Commercial popular music demonstrates and dramatizes contrast between places by calling attention to how people create culture in different ways.[37]

For Latina/o communities, music might be a site of historical recovery or, through translocal identification, a way of constituting a strategy based on relationships of affinity and affect to other Latinas/os and their respective cultural traditions. For example, salsa, a music and dance genre associated with the Spanish Caribbean diaspora in New York City, may provide a space of identification for Mexican migrants in Michigan who might revel on the performances of love, often the subject of the lyrics, performed in Spanish to the seductive rhythms of Afro-Caribbean musical traditions.[38] The act of dancing further allows this act of home-building through the embodied localization of the global representation.

In most of my interviews, dancers referred to their identification with Latin music without clear distinctions to national or regional origins of the performer or the sound. There were definitely regional variations in taste based on their own life trajectories and influences, such as *banda* and *norteñas* in the San Antonio clubs and salsa and merengue in New York City.[39] These distinctions, in the case of Nestor for example, were not fixed. He says, "I'm down with salsa . . . I mean, back in Texas I was already into it, you know. My mom was all salsa queen when she was young. But, I also like *quebraditas*, man. Those I do miss, 'cause you don't hear them much around here." Nestor expresses his knowledge and enjoyment of a great variety of musical genres. Love of music, as he explains, records relationships to people (his mother) and places (Texas). He is not only a master of this musical inheritance but rejoices in the translation of this precious archive into beautiful, and for him, deeply meaningful choreographies. He identifies salsa, merengue, Latin house, pop stars like JLo and Christina Aguilera as part of his Latina/o heritage; however, he retains an interest in Mexican regional sounds such a *quebraditas*.[40]

When asked further about the music he hears in the gay dance club, he answers, "Well, salsa and merengue you hear a little bit, but not like real salsa. Here it's more like American music with the salsa in it . . . like when you spice your macaroni and cheese with chile." Nestor identifies the trace of Latin rhythms in the club music he dances to as salsa. Afro-percussive music in its broad variations, and even in the synthetically developed rhythmic patterns that approximate them, are identified under the umbrella term of salsa, although not as "real salsa." His gastronomic metaphor expresses his affinity with Latina/o culture in the Rochester area. He is conscious of his outsider status as a Mexican-American in a primarily Puerto Rican territory. He is fully invested in making this world also his own. By "spicing things up" through his identification with salsa in the club, Nestor reclaims salsa as his own. Many dancers in San Antonio and Austin also attested to enjoying salsa and merengue. They sought clubs that played those particular musical genres despite their association with Caribbean cultures. They also found satisfaction in listening to Latina/o music when available in the Anglo dance club.[41]

The abundance of Caribbean musical traditions nationally can be traced to the integration of the Latino music markets in the United States. This is an industry largely owned or controlled by multinational corporations.[42] The centralization of the markets has consolidated the available platforms for circulating Latina/o music and significantly amalgamated musical tastes nationally. What were previously independent regional markets have been largely folded into a national, and increasingly global venture.[43] Latin musical genres have also made their way into the American popular soundscape. Here they have been generally characterized by the "exoticism" of Afro-diasporic percussion. Mexican musical styles, on the other hand, have a tendency to remain closer to their regional communities with the exception of crossover acts such as Selena in the early 1990s.[44] Selena's songs still appeared at all Latina/o clubs in this study between 1998 and 2004, at times with a layering of Afro-Caribbean and house beats.[45] Despite regional variations in taste, Afro-Caribbean rhythms remain the dominant sonorous characteristic of the Latin music market.[46] Contemporary club music, especially Latin House and Jungle, use Latin motifs as rhythmic overlays onto contemporary pop music. For example, just like in the case of Selena's club remixes, a recent Latin house version of Pink's "Get the Party Started" at Escuelita, a Latina/o gay club in midtown Manhattan, brought up the energy of the song with the cutting in of fast-paced percussion that looped after each repetition of the title phrase.[47] As such, Afro-Latin rhythm functions as a global text, mass produced and circulated around the globe as a marker of latinidad.

In the club, it is generally the DJ who performs the first act of localization by transforming recorded musical tracks into live displays of the local community's taste. As Brian Currid has explained in regard to house music, "This focus on local production and 'ownership' consciously breaks from the slick, universalistic packaging of generalized pop production, reclaiming popular music as local property."[48] The source material for the club's soundscape is formed out of a large pool of recorded tracks. The actual performance of the music is up to the expressive manipulation of the DJ, who will loop, mix, and cut tracks as desired to put out her signature sound. The same popular song will sound completely different depending on the DJ who plays (with) it and this allows for the characterization of club spaces based on their particular musical styles, even when the source materials are often the same across the board. The music is gathered from the realm of popular music and its global circulation, to be transformed by the DJ into a uniquely local soundscape.

The second move takes place on the body of the dancer, who assumes the task of performing through this doubled text, both local and global. A localization of a transnational musical heritage takes place on the dance floor as dancers embody styles of movement. Sarah Thornton has argued for the local nature of club culture: "Although club culture is a global phenomenon, it is at the same time firmly rooted in the local. Dance records and club clothes may be easily imported and exported, but dance crowds tend to be municipal, regional, and national. Dance styles, for example, which need to be *embodied* rather than just bought, are much less transnational than other aspects of culture."[49] As Thornton explains, dance practices in the club are local to the extent they depend on the improvised interactions of performers to share "kinesthetic resources," and these transactions occur only between bodies. This formulation is based on different scales of access to commodified culture. They favor the immediate live interaction at the club but do not deny the role of global systems of transference and their influence in the transmission of choreographic strategies. Primarily through the distribution of film and television, and now most importantly through music video, dancers acquire a kinesthetic repertoire inherently global in reach.[50] However, the performance of these media-transmitted knowledges depends on localizing practices very much like the ones the DJ performs in her manipulation of the music in the club. Here dance may be characterized as an intervening agency. It translates the global for the pleasurable engagement of local communities. Because live performance cannot guarantee exactitude in transference or execution—whether or not the source material is reached through live or mediatized transmission—the result is always articulated locally. It is the performer, individually and in relation to those around her, who ultimately emerges in the act of localization. And it is precisely in the critical act of rearticulating the dominance of globally distributed media from a Latina/o queer perspective, and the pleasure of doing so in communication with others, where Latina/o queer utopias may be felt.

Agency on the Move

Clara and Nestor experience rhythm with an active sense of agency, communicating relationships through the body that go beyond mere synchronization but that display their knowledge and ability to sustain it in their bodies. In the club, Nestor and Clara localize music through articulate movement. The showcasing of skill is paramount to these performances. In the display of rhythmical understanding, through flaunting that they get it, arises the assertive embodiment of queer latinidad. At this juncture, and through this act of identification with rhythm in movement, utopia is performed. In this realm of pleasure, politics is most pronounced on the body. Dancing in the club becomes a practice of what I term *choreographies of resistance,* embodied practices through which minoritarian subjects claim their space in social and cultural realms. The Latina/o queer body in motion, the ability to move to the Latin rhythm eloquently, shifts the power dynamics of the dance floor and the club, at least temporarily, to articulate the particularities of queer Latina/o experience. More specifically, although the sensorial stimulation of these safe places is often prepackaged as a product, even concept, its architecture is easily overruled by the live actions, performances, of the dancers. Similarly, club dancing for queer Latinas/os represents an engagement with commodified gay and lesbian popular culture, but one in which the dominant narratives of these cultural products are interpreted and rearticulated. This approach, I argue, exemplifies the performance of queer latinidad. In this dynamic, the sexual economies of commercially driven Latin culture, generally assumed and marketed as *heterosexual,* are queered at the site of the local. They are reconfigured under a different cultural economy. Likewise the often-unquestioned whiteness of the gay club is challenged by the virtuoso demands of the Latina/o dancer.

As mentioned above, this not only entails Latinizing the white gay club but also the queering of latinidad by introducing new sexual and gender possibilities into its heteronormative script.

Moving to or against the rhythmic patterns of Latin music or Latin-beat-layered-house allows the dancer to "own" the club, even if just momentarily. Wilbert, a twenty-one-year-old gay man of Guatemalan descent, demonstrates this approach in his dancing. I first saw him on the dance floor in 1998 at Krash, a Latina/o gay and lesbian club in Queens.[51] Dancing to a club version of Lou Vega's remix of Perez Prado's "Mambo #5," he assumes the upright position of the body with bent elbow and arms parallel to the floor and palms down characteristic of traditional mambo. He begins a series of short flat-footed forward steps led by a slight bend at the knees directly over the foot, maintaining his weight over heels. He presses on the floor, left foot first, and straightens his knee, bearing the full weight of his body on the left leg. As he frees his right foot, he performs the forward step with bent right knee and repeats the press down and leg-straightening sequence. He repeats this step fluidly over the 4/4 tempo of the original mambo used as the basic pattern for this musical remix. But this approach to the music does not focus exclusively on the more consistent percussion of the piece. Instead, Wilbert inserts variations to his upper-body movement that parallel the rhythmic patterns of his steps while alternately swinging his arms forward, accentuating the motion of the opposite leg. Then he breaks away into a fast shimmying of his shoulders. During these frenzied instances of polyrhythmic display Wilbert throws his head back in sheer enjoyment of the physical experience of dancing. When asked what he felt at these moments, he responds, "Just the rush of shaking like a *licuadora. Yo creo que ni escucho la música.* Just like an adrenalin rush, that's what they call it right? *Se mete la música por dentro*" ("Just the rush of shaking like a blender. I think that I don't even hear the music. Just like an adrenalin rush, that's what they call it, right? The music just comes inside me"). Wilbert mentions that the music comes inside him and simultaneously comments that he doesn't think he listens to it any longer. At this point he is all agency, riding the club's soundscape to experience the ecstatic experience of his dancing.

Wilbert's choreography is equally an articulation of the traditional framework from which the club dance track originates and an individual response to the act of dancing, as he becomes deeply involved in his own actions and the pleasure he derives from them. In this way the transaction is at once an identification with the broader category of latinidad, through the recognition of mambo, and an individualized articulation made possible by an engagement with club music in a queer context. Like Nestor, Wilbert works within the rhythmic structure of the music, marking it with his shoulders. He also works against it, through his commanding use of pose sequences that showcase him in flirtatious acts of self-assertion. In doing this he articulates how the realm of the club opens the possibilities for practices of identity formation and experience. Other dancers in the club, myself included, join this moment of ecstatic display and identify in it the potentiality of our own experiences, the possibility of our own pleasure or utopia. Wilbert's performance allows us to appreciate the beautiful and skillful performance of queer latinidad. He points to the critical sharing of this space, one grounded as much in the act of moving as in the intense and pleasurable act of contemplation that is queer spectatorship.

Critical Pleasure

The pleasure derived on the dance floor is also quite simply the pleasure of queering latinidad. This aspect of queer Latina/o dancing is equally invested in the circulation of particular affective approaches to dominant cultural practice. In the club this strategy requires a rearticulation of the generally heterosexual nature of Latin music. Popular musical genres such as salsa, often performed at queer Latina/o clubs in San Antonio and New York City, are more often than not about heterosexual courtship or conflict. The cultural critic Frances Aparicio has outlined a genealogy of salsa in Puerto Rico that departs from a patriarchal and heteronormative articulation of gendered relations. She further discusses how these characterizations were equally invested in a racial fetishization of African diasporic cultures.[52] However, Aparicio also discusses postmodern rearticulations of salsa, mostly in literary form, that reassign the orientation of desire within the seemingly heterosexual narrative. This queering may in part be facilitated by the performative excess of salsa. The over-the-top sexuality of the genre allows for the demystification of naturalized gendered or sexual positions. Through a playful reassignment of gendered categories these excesses undo the compulsive heterosexuality of the salsa script.[53]

One of the men I interviewed in New York City supports such an assumption. Josué, a young Puerto Rican man in his thirties who frequents primarily Latina/o gay and lesbian clubs, says, "Oh yes, I do listen to the lyrics . . . why not? Sometimes I dance like the man, you know, I sing the song to the other guy on the dance floor like he was the woman. I don't know how to say it . . . *tu sabes*, it's like you just feel it, *lo romántico* [the romance], and it's just sexy to dance like that to the music you grew up with."

"Does it matter that the song is about a man and a woman?" I ask.

"Not really. Why, you think it's a problem? I just play along with it. It's how you feel it that's the matter."

Josué outlines a strategy that is tactically playful. His identification is with the feel of the song. He revels in the romance being performed and mimics attitudes rather than narratives. In performing through the heterosexual lyrics of salsa Josué queers it for the distribution of queer pleasure.

Josué's comments are echoed in Clara's opinion about her own dancing: "You just learn to feel it without even caring who is singing to who, you know. The music is the most important thing. . . . I mean if you are at the club, most of the times you don't even listen to the words. It's just rhythm . . . the rest is regular club music. But when you are listening to Spanish music, you also remember the rhythm in the club and groove to it." Clara's statement enters further into the realm of affect. She admits to not paying attention to the lyrics and opts for "grooving" with the rhythm. She identifies the musical elements that mark latinidad for her and performs her sexuality to it. Talking about the Anglo gay club she frequents in Austin, she says, "You know, in the club we are already all queer . . . so when I dance and the Latin music or just drumming comes on in another song, that's when the *puertorriqueña* comes out. That's when I get down."

On a visit to the Electric Company, a primarily Latina/o gay bar in San Antonio, I encountered a majestic queering of latinidad. Lena and Gina, a lesbian couple, both Tejanas in their late twenties, perform an affective rearticulation of Latina/o popular music. They take to the dance floor to Marc Anthony's "La luna sobre nuestro amor." This romantic salsa song is a celebration of love and passionate sexual union between lovers:

You and me
caught in a spell
on the way to paradise

alone you and me . . .
lovers without remedy
you and me
and desire as always
betraying reason
and your eyes begging please
make love to me.

The couple face each other in traditional Latin social position.[54] Lena places her left hand over Gina's right shoulder and raises her left arm, elbows bent in a right angle to meet Gina's left hand. Gina wraps her right arm around Lena's waist and brings her close to her. As the music plays, the dancers follow the rhythmic structure of the song with short syncopated steps in unison. Gina pushes her partner slightly away from her and almost immediately pulls her back in with a sudden turn under her arm. At the end of this turn, the couple reverses the initial position of the arms and Lena assumes the lead. They continue to dance through the song, alternating between leading and following, expertly stepping through the cool insistent rhythm of the song and caressing each other gently as they fully enact the sensual narrative of the lyrics. As the song reaches its end Lena and Gina are locked in a kiss and walk away from the dance floor holding hands. In this short and simple sequence, Lena and Gina articulate their love for one another publicly, through redefinition of the choreographic logic of salsa, which usually requires one partner, gendered male, to lead throughout the full extent of the dance. Lena and Gina refuse the mixed parameters of this convention and share equally in the leading role in this affective exchange. Their public display of affection to the lyrics of a song, which circulated as an anthem to heterosexual love, further queers traditional Latin music for the emergence of queer pleasure. This exchange depends on the safety provided in the club and in the community of equally passionate dancers who surround them as they embrace each other publicly on the dance floor.

For Latinas/os in the United States, encountering models of gay and lesbian culture, *convivencia diaria,* offers opportunities for learning and sharing strategies of survival and performing queer latinidad as an alternative mode of being. Cultural critic Lisa Sánchez-González eloquently describes this two-level relationship between engagement with utopian aspirations and hopes, and the more local quotidian experience, as a "p'acá y p'allá" aesthetic, a "here and there" aesthetic. She uses salsa dancing as a metaphor for the social and cultural maneuvers of Puerto

Rican as well as other Latina/o communities in the United States. She explains, "As it glides between p'acá, the whole context of its immediate interaction—the dancing, improvisations, and joy we experience, as well as the racism, exploitation, and sorrow we encounter everyday—the p'allá, a geo-philosophical projection of past, present, and future possibilities, an audaciously hopeful realm that is just beyond reach but so close you can feel it coming."[55] The affective complexities of pleasures emergent out of historical oppression are beautifully worked through, never absolutely resolved, in the corporeal intelligence of the dancers. The demarcation of space through movement centers the body as agent in negotiating the proximities as well as the distances of social intimacy. This dual logic, here and there, is masterfully articulated in Nestor's and Clara's choreographies. As Nestor explains, "Anyone can come into the club and walk around, you know. I just think I do something special. I shake my can better. I don't know how to explain it. Like, it's a Latin thing, you know, you just got that rhythm inside you. I just let it loose." This dance between the immediate materiality of the club and the histories embodied, performed, and queered in the act of dancing by queer Latinas/os characterizes the choreographies on the dance floor as theories in practice.

Through these practices dancers assume ownership of and membership in the world of the club and develop strategies that might allow them to assume equally assertive stances outside it. Utopia in the club is thus a social doing, a sometimes fractious but pleasurable achievement of cohabitation in performance. In the *convivencia diaria* of the club and the choreographies of resistance performed within, utopia is a practiced here and now that makes the "there" of hope palpable on the flesh. *P'acá y p'allá*, here and there, anywhere, when there is one such character assuming her place on the dance floor, flowing majestically with the music, challenging its assumed rhythms and desires, making it pleasurable, grinding the hips in an act of identification, shaking that ass in a gesture of defiance, stepping in a fire of memory and pain, of struggle, of hope—this is where queer latinidad dances.

This chapter was driven by an enthusiasm to engage improvised social dance as practices of Latina/o queer world-making. My own investment in these practices of queer Latina/o sociality may indeed be regarded as utopian. However, throughout this chapter I have maintained a tension between the aspirational affects enabled and enacted in dancing and the social restraints—both historical and contemporary—that animate their very force. These restraints include the quotidian violence of walking as Latina/o and queer in public spaces unwelcoming to one or both of those identities, the politico-economic history of commodified Latina/o music, and the cultural normativities and social expectations that often govern club experience. These are the contexts that lead me to understand choreographies that are affirmative of the particularities of Latina/o queer experience as resistant. Nonetheless, as promising as choreographies of resistance are to the notion of utopia as a theory in practice, it is important to understand that the frictions encountered in queer latinidad are formative and often part and parcel of intragroup experience, or *convivencia diaria*. In the next chapter I focus exclusively on such frictions of intra-Latina/o class difference as a critical component of queer Latina/o club cultures and queer latinidad more broadly.

5

DANCING REGGAETÓN WITH COWBOY BOOTS

Frictive Encounters in Queer Latinidad

No fancy drinks, electronica or twinky go-go boys. At Club
Zarape, the standard swill is a can of Tecate beer with a lime
wedge and salt packet on top. . . . these men, and some leather-
booted women, are here to dance the night away to salsa and *rock
en español* and, of course, norteño, vaquero cowboy music. Big
belt buckle to big belt buckle.

—*Phoenix New Times*[1]

Where other LGBT establishments around the Valley proudly
fly the rainbow flag, Karamba lights it up with neon and adds
sparkle and swagger into its after-hours mix. . . . The expan-
sive dance floor is almost always packed with bodies, whether
it's boys dancing with boys, gals getting down with other gals,
and various other combinations. Although the crowd here is
Latino-heavy, it gets downright ethnically diverse during frenzied
weekend events, when folks of every race and sexual orientation
dance until dawn.

—*Phoenix New Times*[2]

In this chapter we travel to Phoenix, Arizona, the second fastest growing
metropolitan area in the United States next to Las Vegas, Nevada, during
the first decade of the twenty-first century. I focus on the Latina/o queer
club scene in the city between 2004 and 2007, a time of explosive economic transformation and growth in the metropolitan area. This was also
a period when the story of Latina/o ascendancy seemed to have taken
hold in Phoenix's mainstream public sphere despite the anti-immigrant
sentiments that characterized the state as a whole. I trace the narrative
of Latina/o middle-class arrival as it was negotiated in the specific queer
contexts of the club scene. However, I also position the club as a criti-

cal site of interclass exchanges that question and at times challenge the monolithic expectations of an aspirational middle-class identity as the goal of a Latina/o politics of mainstreaming. Lastly, I look at the introduction of reggaetón, a Puerto Rican popular music genre highly influenced by Jamaican dance hall and hip-hop, into the primarily Mexican Latina/o queer clubs of the city around 2005. I document how the arrival of this musical culture to the southwestern United States enabled sites of possibility for queer Latinas/os who found in this music an explicit playfulness with sexuality in the content of the lyrics and the choreographies that accompanied the heavy percussive line characteristic of the genre. In doing so, I attend to the ways in which Puerto Rican culture contradicted the expectations of class upheld in mainstreaming narratives of Latina/o queer culture. The intraethnic and interclass negotiations that queer latinidad entails are of primary concern to this chapter. The chapter identifies friction as a theory in practice of queer latinidad.

During the period covered in this chapter, the Phoenix metro region enjoyed a consistent population growth rate of near 25 percent from 2000 until the burst of the housing market bubble and the economic meltdown it prompted in 2007.[3] As the city grew, the aesthetics of a Mexican-influenced modern look, along with a similar appropriation of Native American culture and aesthetics, circulated as evidence of the growing "sophistication" of the southwestern metropolis. Nouvelle-Mexican cuisine menus, resort architecture, and the promotional rhetoric of the tourism industry showcased an emphasis in regional specificity while purportedly upgrading to metropolitan standards of luxury. This is also the time of reggaetón's rise. In 2004 Latina/o popular culture was entering what was then heralded as the music industry's second wave of the Latin Explosion. This new spin on Latina/o arrival into the national, a pattern that as I mentioned at the opening of this book has repeated with now expected frequency, was ushered by the rise of reggaetón and other hip-hop-influenced acts like Daddy Yankee and Calle 13 into the U.S. mainstream.[4] At a time when many questioned the success of the Latin music market following disappointing sophomore releases by the pantheon of stars of the 1999 popular culture phenomenon, reggaetón became a beacon of hope for music entrepreneurs intent on riding the wave of the explosion by announcing its second coming to the rhythmic base-line of hip-hop.[5] By 2005 reggaetón was heard everywhere in the Phoenix valley, including the Latina/o queer dance club.[6]

The rising influence of Latina/o culture in Phoenix's mainstream public sphere during the early 2000s, including reggaetón's arrival, stood in stark contrast to the spectacular animosity circulated in the events leading to the passage of SB 1070 in 2010. In large part the result of its rapid growth, Phoenix became the center of the immigration debate in the United States. By the late 1990s Arizona was the primary point of entry for northbound undocumented crossers of the U.S.-Mexico border. This occurred after the militarization of urbanized crossing points in Texas and California pushed traffic to the more dangerous desert regions. But this shift was further motivated by the boom in development of the Phoenix metro region, especially the new real estate industry and its demand for cheap construction labor.[7] Anti-immigrant sentiments and practices in Arizona were already under way by the 1990s but picked up pace in the early 2000s. For example, the primary architect of SB 1070 and Republican state legislator Russell Pearce had been at work on measures against undocumented immigrants almost a decade earlier. In 2004, legislation requiring government-issued identification for voter registration and ballot casting passed the state legislature without much fanfare.[8] Although the practices of humiliation of undocumented immigrants by Sheriff Joe Arpaio go as far back as the early 1990s, they became increasingly theatrical during the early 2000s.[9] The Minutemen Project, a conservative group of vigilantes intent in sealing the U.S.-Mexico border, was founded in 2005. The Arizona crisis garnered extensive media attention before 2005 but catapulted into the national scene with the coverage of 2006 marches for immigration across the United States in 2006. An estimated 3.5 to 5 million took to the streets in Phoenix, Chicago, Los Angeles, Houston, and many other places at the time to demand the protection of human rights and the dignity of undocumented immigrants.[10] This series of dramatic events, followed by the 2008 departure of Democrat Janet Napolitano from the governorship and conservative Republican Jane Brewer's assumption of the post, led to the passing of SB 1070 and to the further heating up of the immigration debate in the city.

Latinas/os were at once the base upon whose labor the housing industry and many other development ventures in the city were built, a sign of its cultural distinctiveness as a destination for business and pleasure, and the scapegoats of an extreme nativist movement that carried on the vile work of the 1990s anti-immigrant movement in California into the rapidly developing desert lands of Arizona. The Latina/o queer club scene reflected and reacted to this social turmoil. However, searching for signs of what would become of the Arizona immigration debate in 2009 and 2010 in the Latina/o queer dance clubs between 2004 and 2007 would simply prove impossible. The undercurrent of frictions that animated anti-immigrant sentiments were in circulation at the time and palpable in the social exchanges that I outline below, but nothing in the dance club could have predicted the precipitous escalation of the crisis. My ethnographic data does not offer sufficient evidence on this critical legal and policy issue. However, what my experience of the Latina/o queer club scene during the years prior to the SB 1070 does evidence are the creative survival practices and the internal community dynamics that would have served as the building blocks for a specifically Latina/o queer response to the deteriorating climate of the later 2000s. In part, the clubs served as temporary sites through which to escape the difficult climate of anti-immigrant aggression. They also required a confrontation with this hostility. Assembling in queer public space already entailed significant risks for Latina/o communities, which more often than not lived within heteropatriarchal and homophobic kinship structures. Doing so as Latinas/os at a time in Phoenix when public figures like Sheriff Joe Arpaio and conservative activists were scrutinizing and threatening all Latinas/os as suspect border crossers made the risk even more palpable. Interestingly, a rhetoric of tourism cast Latina/o social dance establishments and waterholes as faraway adventures for Latinas/os and other patrons in search of diversion from the stresses of daily life. However, as I demonstrated in the previous chapter, the escapist imagination of the club as utopian detachment is insufficient for explaining the cultural work that happens within its realm. In following reggaetón into the Mexican gay club scene in Phoenix, I am invested in continuing the analysis of home, hope, and utopia as central to the figuration of queer latinidad, even when xenophobic violence lurks at the door. Here, in a context where "coming out" into bodily pleasures as queer and as Latina/o has increasingly different, riskier connotations, I attend to reggaetón, and music more generally, as a practiced phenomenon.[11]

If the previous chapter explored the utopic engagements with the culture of the club, this one centers the tensions that arise out of the social encounters that occur within and around it. In doing so, I shift from the dancer's choreographies to chatter, verbal as well as written, about the clubs and their patrons. I look into an "archive of feelings" in published reviews, promotional materials, and everyday talk to map some of the cultural frictions that shape Latina/o queer club life in Phoenix.[12] I also draw evidence from field notes, formal and informal interviews, and material culture about these two clubs over the three years of my fieldwork and additional check-ins up to 2009.[13] Undisputedly, dance remains at the center of this inquiry. It is both the cultural context and the theoretical concept that governs the practices of queer latinidad I address here. And it is to dance that I would now like to turn to.

Choreographic Transitions: Latinidad on the Move

Two men in their early twenties walk onto the dance floor wearing tight jeans, Western plaid shirts, cowboy boots and hats, and large belt buckles advertising their home state in Mexico: Jalisco. They face each other in standard Latin ballroom position; one set of hands held together above shoulder. One holds the other firmly at the waist while the other places his free hand softly upon his partner's chest. A steady *cumbia* step marked with a smooth walked turn and slight knee-bend dips to the back dominate the choreography for most of the set. They flirt with each other. One caresses the other's face as they move in synch within their tight kinesphere. Suddenly the music shifts. The basic *cumbia* rhythm remains but speeds up slightly in the DJ's transition into a reggaetón set. The lead-in song in the mix is Calle 13's 2005 breakthrough hit "Atrévete-te-te."[14] The song—a mixture of Colombian *cumbia* with Puerto Rican hip-hop, and Jamaican dance hall stylization—became one of the anthems of reggaetón's ascendancy as the supposed "next wave" of the Latin music explosion in the United States.[15] At this Phoenix, primarily Mexican migrant, dance club, just a couple of hours from the U.S.-Mexico border, this Mexican vaquero (cowboy) gay couple shift their orientation to each other by coming closer, very tightly together, placing their hands on each other's buttocks. They grind their hips in rhythmical circular motion to the base of the song; their legs seductively entangled. The lyrics' invitation proceeds:

> *Atrévete, te, te, te*
> *Salte del closet, te*
> *Escápate, quítate el esmalte*
> *Deja de taparte que nadie va a retratarte*
> *Levántate, ponte hyper*
> *Préndete, sácale chispas al estárter*
> *Préndete en fuego como un lighter*

Sacúdete el sudor como si fueras un wiper
Que tu eres callejera, street fighter[16]

The dancing couple rides the affective waves of this freedom anthem. The song and its widely circulated music video invite women to break away from the expectations of middle-class Puerto Rican propriety. To a large extent it mocks the aspirational whiteness associated with this realm. It also encourages its audience to embrace their sexuality in explicit, freaky ways. The song addresses a *chica intelectual,* an intellectual chick, with a serious face, pop-rock Latina/o tastes, and modest demeanor. It asks her to let loose from her uptightness by simply indulging in the pleasures of dancing. Here the sexual "coming out" (*salte del closet*) works less as a narrative and more as an embodied performance of pleasurable movement, despite reggaetón's tendency to narrate the dancer's liberation while objectifying her performance.[17]

The song articulates the restrictions of middle-class pop taste as a "show" (*mira deja el show*) and asks its addressee to simply let go: "Que ahora vamo'a bailar por tó'a la jarda" (because now we will dance all over the hill). "Atrévete-te-te-te" establishes the contrasts between the affluent, white Puerto Rican suburbia of Guaynabo—where rock and punk-pop like Cold Play and Green Day are preferred—and the overwhelmingly working-class city of Bayamón—where rap and hip-hop abound. It destabilizes the coherent identity of the nation with class distinctions and aesthetic imports. It also moves to perform a Puerto Rican unity grounded in pursuing a shared investment in the pleasures of dancing reggaetón. Puerto Rican women from across the class and racial divide become a collective, moving, entity in the cultivation of "14 karat buttocks" and the sophisticated articulation of the abdominal area "que va a explotar" (as if it was to explode).[18]

The cultural frictions the song performs, particularly its engagement with class and racial differentiations, trouble in productive ways the assumptions of Puerto Rican ethno-national coherence.[19] The song also crosses gender and sexual boundaries by indulging in heterosexual erotic pleasure while camping up the queer playfulness of the closet metaphor. All of these clashes are ripe with possibilities for the critic invested in articulating significant tensions in contemporary Puerto Rican culture. But while the scholarship on reggaetón has offered rich engagements with these frictions, their imagined geography has remained significantly insular and the approach primarily textual. While reggaetón has become a legitimate object of study focusing on the narrative of identities, there has been little attention paid to how it is lived.[20] In looking at reggaetón I engage this popular music genre as live culture, an embodied practice of queer latinidad.

The couple on the dance floor performs, in their articulate shift from *cumbia* to reggaetón, a mapping of the moving geographies of queer latinidad. In this short dance sequence, a transition from one musical set to another within the specificity of the Latina/o (primarily Mexican) queer club, latinidad is articulated as a dynamic intersection. While on the surface, latinidad may give the impression of coherence in identitarian scripts, it more often than not challenges easy categorizations. The song enables the intimacy between these two dancers. But the presence of this Puerto Rican anthem to class impropriety in the Mexican queer dance club proposes a repositioning, a critical move if you will, that manages to dance along with its traveled reality. The dancers' engagement with reggaetón as a choreographic embodiment of inter-Latina/o and queer exchanges invites a reading of the musical genre that attends to the sociological versatility of club cultures. It asks us to move beyond expectations of fidelity to identity and pay attention instead to the adjustments—from one rhythm to another as much as from one context to another—and the frictions queer latinidad entails.

In accounting for how latinidad becomes manifest in the queer dance club, I follow this couple's strategy by dancing reggaetón with cowboy boots. That is, I trace the arrival of reggaetón to Phoenix's Latina/o queer clubs with special attention to the negotiations it occasioned, the affective and identitarian exchanges it made possible, and the transformations it endured. More specifically, I focus on the frictions around class that dancing to reggaetón in the queer Mexican club highlighted. I do so through an engagement with the social world and performance protocols of the dance club. Just like Calle 13's "Atrévete-te-te" I invite a coming out of the class closet into the reading of queer latinidad.

Class Matters: The Unspoken Frictions of Queer Latinidad

A survey of recent literature in the field of Latina/o studies shows little engagement with the role class might play in shaping social relations among queer Latinas/os in the United States. Latina/o queer scholars have tended to subsume all *latinidades* into one abstract class category relative to the more affluent whiteness that often serves as a marker of hegemony or cultural dominance. In fact, the ethno-racial orientation of the analytical model of Latina/o queer critique has relied heavily on the dichotomous positioning of Latina/o queer aesthetics—assumed as a primarily working-class aesthetics—as a challenge to the codes and conventions of a homonormative whiteness. This scholarly model seems to propose queerness as a leveling agent at the expense of more critical engagements with class or ethno-national Latina/o differences. My fieldwork in social dance clubs, especially in the southwest United States, showcases the increasingly significant role class especially plays as a crucial element in the day-to-day interactions among queer Latinas/os. My purpose in analyzing the role of class and its relationship to ethno-national identity in Latina/o queer exchanges is twofold. First, I want to offer an example of the ways distinctions of class—both *material* (those categories we most clearly occupy based on our placement within economic hierarchies) and *aspirational* (the positions we imagine or often perform ourselves as belonging to)—shape contemporary Latina/o queer public culture. Second, I want to document Latina/o queer dance clubs as significant interclass meeting places, organizational engines that activate social networks and affective crossings not always possible or accounted for in other contexts. In these terms, I see friction as a theory in practice invested in the encounters that constitute queer latinidad while insisting on its provisional and negotiated nature.

José Esteban Muñoz's discussion of *chusmería* as a strategy of disidentification in his seminal study of performances by queers of color offers an important theoretical grounding to my discussion of intra-Latina/o queer class differentiation.[21] *Chusma,* a pejorative colloquialism, marks lower-class status within the Cuban community. As Muñoz explains, *chusmería* "is a form of behavior that refuses standards of bourgeois comportment. *Chusmería* is, to a large degree, linked to stigmatized class identity. Within Cuban culture, for instance, being called *chusma* might be a technique for the middle class to distance itself from the working class; it may be a barely veiled slur suggesting that one is too black; it sometimes connotes gender nonconformity."[22] The term circulates with equal weight in Mexican culture, where it was successfully cemented into the popular imaginary through the infamous expression performed by Doña Florinda in skit after skit of Chespirito's *El Chavo del Ocho* television series: "¡Vámonos, tesoro! ¡No te juntes con esta chusma!"[23] In this instance, calling her son Kiko away from the rest of the children, a resident of a Mexican *vecindad* (residential complex) used the term to mark class differentiation within their specifically low-income geography. The emphasis on class difference nuances the generalized majority/minority dyad that tends to position latinidad only in relation to a dominant other outside of the latinidad proper. This move recognizes that friction might figure as prominently as does collective cohesion in latinidad.[24]

The cultural economies of class in circulation at the Latina/o queer dance club rely on performance—from music and dance to conversation and fashion—as the constitutive elements of a public sphere that becomes recognizable through the behavioral repertoires of its participants. The presentational aesthetics of the club are thus significant indices of the varying collective categories constituting queer latinidad and its manifestations at particular sites. That is, the music and dance practices that make the soundscape and choreoscape of the club evidence borders and boundaries that delimit local specificity, including those of class. However, musical cultures—attached to specificities of nationality, ethnicity, race, and class as they are—present us with marked differences, cultural borderings if you will, but never with impermeable divisions. The local practices of class inclusion and exclusion that govern the Latina/o queer club traverse local, national, and transnational scales.

I situate the queer club as central to contemporary debates over Latina/o class, especially in relation to the more recent narratives of Latina/o mainstreaming. I take my cue from the recent work of anthropologist Arlene Dávila, who has noted the adjustments and expectations that structure Latina/o narratives of "respectability" and "class ascendancy." She explains that mainstreaming "projects and policies that claim to advance a 'Latina/o' agenda are not always inclusive, [that] referencing 'Latina/o' culture provides little guarantee of a lack of complicity with neoliberal interests and policies, and that distinctions and inequalities among Latinas/os are not being reproduced and fostered."[25] I highlight similar dynamics within the local realm of the Latina/o queer dance club. Here, ethno-racial collective identifications negotiate, amid their queering, what I would describe as the class hierarchies of a contemporary LGBTQ public sphere. I am referring to the centralization of the marriage equality agenda, the gays-in-the-military debate, and consumer-based versions of LGBTQ politics. These have tended to leave behind the still-marginalized versions of queerness that oftentimes include queers of color, the poor, and other less palatable subjects.[26] That is, only specific versions of queerness ascend to "metrosexual hipness" and mainstream agendas. The queer club displays similar mainstreaming tendencies.

Inter-Latina/o affiliations do produce quotidian frictions. This has been the subject of much research in the field, including the pioneering work of anthropologists Elena Padilla in the 1970s and Nicholoas de Genova and Ana Y. Ramos-Zayas in the 1990s on Mexican and Puerto Rican relations in Chicago[27] and dance scholar Cindy García's ethnographic research into the queer negotiations of pan-latinidad in the heteronormative context of the salsa dance scene in Los Angeles.[28] The scholarly work of Frances Aparicio is instrumental here. Her definition of "interlatino sites" as "sites where two or more Latinas/os from various national origins encounter, construct, and transculturate each other" describes the kinds of intersections that rule the experience of the club.[29] Like her, I want to highlight the convergences as well as the divergences of inter-Latina/o relations and imaginaries relative to queer latinidad.[30] I do so by choreographing a critical dance between two Latina/o queer dance clubs in Phoenix.

Club Zarape and Club Karamba anchor the Latina/o queer nightlife in the central district of the city. In fact, they are adjacent to each other and share a parking lot. Both establishments cater to a primarily working-class Mexican and Mexican-American gay community. Club Zarape and Club Karamba showcase the diversity of orientations in queer latinidad as they embrace distinct performance practices corresponding to varying musical subcultures. Club Zarape caters to a northern Mexico ranchero scene that favors *moda vaquera* (cowboy wear) and musical genres such as *banda, norteña,* and *cumbia.* Club Karamba favors contemporary Mexican pop that relies heavily on a techno beat. Most recently at Karamba, reggaetón and hip-hop fiercely intrude in counterpoint to Mexican music.

Club Zarape invests in a traditional *norteño* masculinity. Femininity is most publicly performed by *transexuales*/transsexuals and *transvestistas*/transvestites, often dressed in sequined gowns with shoulder pads, big *moño*/bun hairdos, and bold fantasy (often plastic) jewelry that recall the fabulous *señoras ricas* / rich ladies of the 1980s *telenovela* / soap opera tradition. Club Karamba, on the other hand, often traffics in a metrosexual image of international queer modernity that incorporates gender variance as long as it conforms to appropriate trends in contemporary urban-wear and stylistics.

Fig. 15. Karamba (left) and Club Zarape, Phoenix. Photo by Lucas Messer.

Club Zarape centers on a working-class regional aesthetic, while Club Karamba, although serving a primarily working-class community as well, aspires to a middle-class aesthetic that references the tourist environs of coastal queer life in Mexico. Not surprisingly, Club Karamba borrows its name from a popular gay club in Cancún frequented by national and international tourists alike.[31] While both Karamba and Zarape cater to a primarily working-class Mexican immigrant and Mexican-American community, their design, musical repertoires, and quotidian performances mark differences that are grounded on the nuances of cultural taste and assumed distinctions based precisely on class, regional identity, time of migration, and so on. These differences are often articulated relative to musical taste and its concomitant cultural subsidiaries— from fashion to speech. Despite the stark differences between these two musical scenes, and their corresponding social practices, we cannot understand one space without the other. Their reputations throughout the city owe much to the competition created by their sheer proximity to each other and their shared iconic status as the center of a Latina/o queer public sphere in Phoenix. To borrow Aparicio's conceptualization, they constitute an "interlatino space."

Cultural Ascendancy: Queer Nightlife and the Mexican Modern

Although Club Zarape is the oldest of the establishments in this Latina/o queer complex, it never appeared in the club listings in LGBTQ publications in Phoenix such as *Echo*, *'N Touch News*, and *IONAZ* magazines.[32] Club Zarape was never covered in the colorful documentary pictorials or included in the entertainment maps that both authorize and orient the city's queer cultural scene in these magazines. During the three years I spent conducting fieldwork, Zarape was virtually invisible in queer media—with the exception of a 2007 mention as the Best Va-Queer-O Bar in *Phoenix New Times'* "Best of Phoenix" issue, a category it occupied all on its own, excerpted in one of the epigraphs to this chapter.[33]

The first review of the club appeared in a column for *Latino Perspectives* magazine: Arizona's leading publication for professional, middle-class, and upwardly mobile Latinas/os. Published monthly and distributed to some 25,000 households in Phoenix and Tucson, the magazine emerged at a time when the economic wealth of the state, funded by the speculative investment in new construction real estate, fueled the optimism of many Latinas/os who saw in the changing landscape of Arizona's economic boom an opportunity for class ascendancy. In advocating for a new Latina/o Phoenix, with an imagined affluent Latina/o middle class at its core, *Latino Perspectives* positioned Zarape as a sign of the past; things to leave behind in a move toward economic and cultural integration into the Valley's elite. Performance artist and journalist Marcos Nájera opened his review as follows:

> I totally thought I was in Nogales the first time I walked into Club
> Zarape on West Macdowell near downtown Phoenix. From the
> looks of the place, I had either flitted into a John Waters makeover
> of a norteño bar or a wacked out produce section of my neighbor-

Fig. 16. Entrance to Club Zarape, Phoenix. Photo by Lucas Messer.

hood Food City. Who knew that the supermarket's gaudy décor would years later inspire the interior of a hot night club.

Club Zarape's tragic décor aside, I was thirsty. So without a thought, I clip-clopped past the oh-so-queer vaqueros, con belt buckles the size of Frisbees, as they grabbed-assed each other on the dance floor. Another clue that I actually wasn't at Food City.[34]

The author positions himself as a border crosser in this scene. Confusing the club with the border city of Nogales or the interior of a Food City does not only mark the space as quintessentially Mexican but also as particularly classed. The Food City chain of supermarkets was acquired in 1993 as a subsidiary brand of Chandler-based Bashas' Incorporated. Food City fit the parent company's lowest consumer profile. It catered to a primarily Mexican and working-class to poor demographic. This distinction was made explicit by the company's other two retail portfolios: the middle-class Bashas' and the high-end gourmet profile of AJ's. Nájera's performed disorientation serves to both support the caricature of otherness and place him as a distanced, but in the know, arbiter of good taste.

Nájera's description of Club Zarape performs a comic condescension that transforms the space into a temporary stage to showcase his own hipness. Nájera, not Club Zarape, becomes the protagonist of this column in a descriptive exuberance that is geared toward a showcasing of his good taste and clever wit. He continues:

> I ordered a drink. Breezing by a gaggle of Latina lesbians with oversized haircuts swapping *chisme* under a canopy of piñatas, I marched up to the bartender and proudly ordered "un appletini, por favor" (that's Spanish "for one apple martini please"). Silence. Peering over my shoulder, I imagine the Thalia music come to a screeching halt, replaced by the strains of "the good, the bad and the ugly." "Como?" [*sic*] said the bartender. That means, "What?" My homeboys, Guillerma and Trina, they are comfortable enough with their feminine side that I don't have to refer to them by their given names, looked stunned. Still, they managed a polite laugh to smooth over the situation. Trina suggested, "Marcos, why don't you just get a beer? You already had an apple martini at Amsterdam tonight?" But I was all, "OOOOH, nah Trina if I feel like a beer, I would have ordered one." "He'll have a beer." Trina blurted to the bartender. Moments later, I found myself being served a Bud Light in a can, with a lime wedge, and a cute little *paquete de sal*. I would have been pissed if it wasn't for the clever garnishes that come with every beer. Just another strange moment in my club hopping adult life.[35]

This narrative adventure into an exotic working-class queer latinidad served as the inaugural column for "Nájera Nites," a series of commentaries about Latina/o life in Phoenix published in *Latino Perspectives* magazine.[36] Nájera's description of Zarape for a mainstream Latina/o publication could be seen as a daring intervention into the scripts of respectability operative in what was then a young and aspirationally middle-class print venue, unprecedented in recent Phoenix history. Intentions aside, the piece does indeed queer *Latino Perspectives* by documenting and circulating knowledge about heretofore ignored aspects of the Latina/o community in Phoenix. His queering of *Latino Perspectives* remained curiously guarded in nature. He enacts a narrative distance from his subject matter by assuming the judgmental ironic stand of a middle-class outsider before the *chusma* excess, to return to Muñoz, of the Mexican working-class bar.

Fig. 17. Inside of Zarape, Phoenix. Photo by Lucas Messer.

Nájera closes his article not just by highlighting the anomalous and temporary nature of his presence in this space: "just another strange moment in my club hopping life," but by offering an apology, a historical caveat, and future itinerary. This complicated sign-off absolves him of the transgression incurred by not only visiting but profiling Zarape as a Latina/o social space. He qualifies his night out as simply a moment: "A moment I hope, that you don't mind me sharing." This small moment indexes monumental changes in his classed world. He continues: "Arizona's changed in ways big and small since my dad's Food City days and so have I. And nothing, in my humble opinion, has changed more than our nightlife." Zarape is described here as a beacon of change, an underdeveloped but hopeful harbinger of better queer things to come.[37] "For the record," he continues, "my central question is and always will be: Where do the Brown get down?" And thus begins "Nájera Nites," an adventure into the waterholes, restaurants, social, and cultural spaces that make the Latina/o nightlife in the metropolitan Phoenix area a thriving scene. Not letting this thrifty queer inaugural adventure taint the image of a respectable latinidad, Nájera has his eye on better and more intriguing places. As he closes his essay he reminds us that he already has his "lens fixed on the new James Hotel in Scottsdale (recently profiled in *Travel & Leisure Magazine*)."[38] It is clear that Nájera's piece synchs with the upwardly mobile middle-class orientation of *Latino Perspectives* and its assumed audience or market niche. Zarape figures as both a marker of authenticity, "where the Brown get down," and a signpost in a progressive narrative of Latina/o ascendancy from low-end *chusma* environs of Food City to the affluent hipsterdom of the Scottsdale hotel. The move here is not single-handedly malicious but nonetheless participates in a strategic categorization of Mexican *chusma* in ways that formalize and circulate specifically classed understanding of public culture in Arizona.

If Club Zarape, with its excessive *chusma* Mexicanness, elicits an apologetic stance before the middle-class Latina/o readership and is simply nonexistent before the LGBTQ mainstream, its next-door neighbor, Karamba, was embraced enthusiastically by mainstream gay communities in Phoenix and well beyond the Valley when it opened its doors in 2004. In fact, Karamba became a hot spot destination that housed a clientele embodying a latinidad that Zarape could only spectacularly fail to possess. In an article about Karamba in L.A.'s *Adelante Magazine* (a Latina/o queer publication that has never featured Zarape), Carlos Manuel, another performer turned queer journalist, reported Karamba as "the best Phoenix had to offer."[39] He clarifies that this is not just his personal opinion. All the people he interviewed for his article (a total of six different voices are cited in the short one-page review) indeed mention Karamba as less "trashy when comparing [it] to other clubs." What Carlos Manuel seems to value the most in his assessment of this social space is its ability to offer a dignified—meaning properly middle class—version of queer latinidad that might integrate Latina/o queers into the broader LGBTQ scene in the city and beyond. The club splashed into the broader queer scene in Phoenix when in 2006, 2008, and 2009 it won the Best Gay Latin Dance Club award from *Phoenix New Times*. Such recognition positions the club as a central stop in the barhopping itineraries of Valley queer socialites. The ascendancy of the club into the gay mainstream includes being listed as one of the best gay bars in the world, according to the October 2007 issue of *Out* magazine. Ongoing inclusion in the photomontages of the fabulous that appear in the glossy back pages of mainstream LGBTQ press in Arizona ensures that buffed boys in search of the spotlight continue to flock to its realm.

Fig. 18. Karamba flyer

What is most poignant about Karamba's successful appeal to a broader queer community is precisely its showcasing of a commercial pan-Latina/o, aspirationally middle-class aesthetic. As Carlos Manuel points out:

> The owner of the club opened Karamba because he saw the need to offer a place of entertainment to that community who didn't have a more modern and diverse locale to go. "Being Latino is not only Mexico, it's also Latin America," he explained. And in my personal opinion this is what separates Karamba form the rest of the Latino Clubs. Karamba's entertainment repertoires goes from cumbia, norteño, banda, and Spanish pop on Vaquero Thursdays with Susana's show, to rock & roll, disco punk, indie, electronica, dance rock, brit pop y new wave every Friday with its Hot Pink and Teenage Kicks After Hours program, to salsa, merengue, rock and pop en español, cumbia y reggaeton every Saturday and Sunday. With such variety, the club administrator tries to offer

a unique entertainment service to the Latino gay community of Phoenix and surrounding area.[40]

The club's "global repertoires" mark its difference from the "rest." The international diversity of musical material evidences Karamba is "more than" Mexico and its competition. This necessary "service," as the owner explains, offers a "modern" option for entertainment not previously available. Karamba, according to this narrative, appropriately "modernizes" *mexicanidad*. The pan-Latina/o appeal advances a rhetoric of commerce intent in the competitive expansion of the geography and the clientele of the dance club. This is not surprising, considering the connections Karamba establishes to the aesthetics of tourism. Karamba's image as appropriate mainstream entertainment cites the dramaturgies of touristic performance associated with its "sister" club in Cancún. Latina/o entertainment is rendered the component product or service that more appropriately packages and supplements *mexicanidad* as modern. This model of commercial latinidad assumes that an investment in the trends of globally current musical cultures favors innovation over tradition.

Frictions between tradition and innovation are especially salient in the original iteration of Karamba as a destination of queer travel to Cancún. In the context of the tourist experience of the greater Yucatán Peninsula, Karamba represents a concerted effort to move beyond a market geared toward encounters with history into one that focuses on ahistorical leisure. The aesthetics of tourism in the region initially banked on the monumental ancient Maya architecture of the area to stage indigenous culture as consumable object. The simultaneous dismissal and dependence on living Mayan communities was and continues to be a key component of this dynamic. Starting in the 1980s, Cancún began to develop a new profile oriented toward global trends of luxury. The image for this profitable niche market favored modern architecture and interior design, international influences in cuisine, and high-end services. This segment of the tourist district retreated from indigeneity to render the hotel experience as the familiar nowhere of the contemporary global resort. Indigeneity does not fully disappear from this experience. Day tours to the pyramids or purchasing of crafts remain key experiences for the visitor. The aesthetics of tourism in the region have rendered indigeneity a motif instead of the central defining feature. You can still touch history in these new resorts. You do so within the comforts of an Italian-designed couch, martini in hand, or the air-conditioned tour bus with

CNN World playing on your individual screen. The tourist is in Cancún, and she is also in her luxurious global home.

The investment by Cancún's Karamba Bar in a correspondingly modern notion of entertainment, itself predicated on assumptions about its clientele, counting on expendable income and high-end tastes, cemented its iconic standing as Cancún's top queer destination. Established in 1986, Karamba Bar opened at a time of significant growth in the tourist economy of the region. Karamba has also been a key participant in Cancún's transition from a destination built exclusively on the showcasing of historically specific features to more recent trends in leisure standards. Its presence in downtown Cancún has been key for the area's courtship of the pink dollar. Airfare and lodging services, hotels, tourist guides, and transportation services benefit from the development of the region advertised as an LGBTQ tourist destination. This puts the club in a critical position within an industry that stands as the area's primary source of income. Its pivotal role in the local economy has helped authorize Karamba's presence in Cancún.

The presence of U.S. and European citizens supported the development of the club and influenced its aesthetics and business practices in a variety of ways. Visitors impacted the club most directly through consumption. The out queer club community in Cancún is not sufficiently large to fill its space, with a capacity close to five hundred. Without the constant influx of traffic from the nearby hotel district, the cavernous facility would sit empty. The club courts its clientele by catering design, musical programming, bar offerings—from featured brands to drink menus—to an imagined USAmerican or European patron. Karamba's techno-influenced musical tracks, remixes of the latest American pop music, and up-to-date laser lighting technologies rival clubs at any other urban location in Mexico. However, the club also cultivates an image or motif of "exotic" Mexico meant to satisfy the tourist trade's thirst for brown bodies.

The citational practices of Phoenix's Karamba extend the tourist rhetoric of the club space to a city where the primary clientele is in fact Mexican.[41] The modernizing aesthetic of touristic performance signifies differently in this cross-border location. In Phoenix, the image of the iconic club in Mexico makes what is generally a leisure space oriented toward the foreign visitor available and affordable to Mexican working-class patrons, generally regarded as outside the realm of the tourist map or middle-class sections of the Mexican city. Queer tourism is made accessible here as domestic experience for both local and transmigrated *mexicanas/os* who venture in to experience queer *mexicanidad.* The club also animates conceptions and experiences of class attached to the aesthetics of the modern. These opportunities to be—or, rather, perform being—modern is central to the culture of this club. To be current or in the know enables public enactments of class differentiation. These practices of localized distinction and friction are enhanced by the presence of Zarape across the parking lot as a counterexample.

The different characterizations of the two clubs in Arizona queer and Latina/o media point to a significant investment in the traditional and modern dyad. Zarape's focus on Mexican regional genres is derided for being "tacky," traditional, and passé. If in Nájera's account it is a reminder of what Arizona Latina/o life used to look like, for Carlos Manuel it is the void Karamba's modernity comes to fill. For Nájera, Zarape allows the middle-class Latina/o "native" the opportunity to recognize how far he has climbed the ladder of upwardly mobile Latina/o Arizona. Contrastingly, for Carlos Manuel, Karamba welcomes patrons into a performed modernity that imagines class mobility as a relocation from the myopically *mexicano* into the transnationally Latina/o.

The disparities in décor and clientele between Zarape and Karamba need to be understood as deeply invested in class hierarchies at a time when increased anti-immigrant activism against recent arrivals threatened Latina/o middle-class ascendancy in Phoenix. While some middle-class Latinas/os rose in public visibility across the Valley, lower-class migrants became increasingly maligned. In the heated debates about Arizona's emergence as the central corridor for Mexican undocumented migration into the United States, to be lower class and *mexicano* was to spoil the party of affluence. To be Mexican and chic, on the other hand, became an easy sign of Phoenix's newly achieved cosmopolitanism. Arizonans became familiar and enamored of the new "modern" Mexico during this period. Mexican beach leisure developments boomed in places such as Rocky Point along the coastal regions of the bordering state of Sonora. For the Valley's wealthy, they provided second-home opportunities across the border. High-end Mexican restaurants with minimalist décor also proliferated, often replacing the more folkloric renderings of an earlier, less "global" Arizona.

A story of Latina/o ascendancy does not correspond fully with the performances of class in the Latina/o queer nightlife of Phoenix. Despite the distinctions outlined in the publicly circulated descriptions above,

actual interactions on the ground pointed in a markedly different direction. Regardless of the best efforts by club owners, media observers,
and some scenesters to dichotomize the relationship between the social
scenes in Zarape and Karamba, between a humble Mexican past and
a middle- and upper-class Latina/o future, and between the aesthetics
of *chusmería* and the queer modern, the cultural practices unraveling
at these two clubs were interconnected. The social and cultural scenes
crossed from one club to another, from one musical and choreographic
format to another. Instead of a clearly delineated border, what governed
individual and collective experience at Phoenix's Latina/o queer club
complex was the tense porousness of Chicana feminist scholar Gloria
Anzaldúa's borderlands.[42]

Between *Chusma* and *Fresas*: Practices of Belonging

The frictions between Zarape and Karamba are exemplary of larger
politico-economic negotiations in Latina/o Arizona. As I explained
above, traditional *mexicana/o* social spaces and cultural practices became
increasingly upgraded by globally homogenous standards of tourism
and affluent modernism. They retained watered-down versions of their
Mexican flavor.[43] Pan-latina/o music and techno-based pop mixes were
the musical modernizing forces in Karamba's club scene. The slick metal
surfaces, contemporary lamps, and large flat video screens throughout
the club also contributed to the enhanced identity of the space as *mexicano* but with a very "modern" difference. The divergences outlined in
the portrayals of Karamba and Zarape found significant parallels in the
on-the-ground distinctions expressed among participants of this cultural complex. Within the club itself, the standards for valuing cultural
markers included fashion, choreography, musical taste, and speech and
relied heavily on the established competition between the spaces. For instance, when I asked a group of Zarape patrons (four Mexican-born men
in their middle to late twenties, who arrived in the United States between
eight and twelve years of age) whether they ever went to Karamba, I got
an immediate response from one and a raucous endorsement from the
affirmative laughter of his companions: "¡No! ¡Allí son fresitas!" (No!
They are *fresitas* there!)

Fresitas, or little strawberries, is a colloquial term originating in the
1960s by Mexican countercultural groups, *nueva ola* rock-and-rollers

and later, punks, to describe conservatives, especially women, who were characterized as prudes and unable to participate in the freedoms from decorum espoused by the rising youth cultural movements. In marking this difference, the term often referred to the identified group's wealth or attitudinal orientation toward upward mobility in terms of class. By the late 1970s and early 1980s, the term was used to describe generally middle- to upper-class youth, men, and women in Mexico City and other urban centers. In its current usage, *fresa* can identify both an attitude and an aesthetic. Its public display generally relies on consumptive practices and performative displays of a modern Mexico, often characterized by an articulate internationalization of taste (e.g., fashion labels, national and international pop music, incorporation of trendy phrases into everyday speech—from pop culture anglicisms to haute couture frenchisms). To the extent that *fresa* seeks to mark class difference, it could be assumed to represent the putative opposite to *chusma*.

The use of this term by my Zarape interlocutors does not necessarily indicate a reference to Mexico City or an actual belonging to the upper class, but points to the perceived class aspirations of Karamba's social scene. As the young man explained:

> Esos son de Sinaloa, Chihuahua, norteños de por ahí, pero se quieren pasar de fresas. Ahí van vestiditos a todo dar. No más cuando abren la boca ya sabes que son de estas partes. ¡Pero como se chulean a lo bonito!

> (They are from Sinaloa, Chihuahua, northerners from around there, but they want to pass as *fresas*. There they go dressed up to the max. As soon as they open their mouths you realize that they are from over here. Oh, but how they flirt with all that is beautiful!)[44]

In his punning of the Karamba crowd, this young man does not necessarily mark a difference based on the actual class status or regional precedence of his imagined others. Instead, he describes their performances of *fresa* as aspirational dramaturgies whereby men very much like themselves (working class and from the northern region of Mexico) attempt to pass into a more affluent social scene. As he comments, the efforts to perform in this scene are often frustrated by the interjection of an unavoidable working-class habitus.[45] By dressing in the latest fashions the *fresitas* perform a desire to belong to Karamba's scene, but these efforts are at times betrayed by speech habits that identify them as working-class *norteños*.

Distinctions between the two social and musical spaces are also performed at sites of exchange that precede and exceed the inside of the club. These ancillary spaces, what communication studies scholar Lucas Messer has termed "peri-club" spaces, are just as framed by assumptions around class.[46] In peri-club spaces, such as the entrance to the club and the adjacent alleyway and parking lot, the differences in experience about belonging to a particular scene are just as evident as inside the club. Crucial to the understanding of peri-club space is the notion that club cultures extend well beyond the contained publicity of the dance floor. For Messer, this move allows him to extend the pleasures of the club to other places. He documents how the soundtrack of the club may enable performance repertoires to reactivate the emotional charge inside it. He joins club patrons as they get ready in their homes or rides with them in their automobiles, sharing in the exhilaration and expectation of getting to the club but also performing the club before actually arriving at its environs. But attending to the peri-club also entails noticing the less pleasurable aspects of the club's encounter with the rest of the world. As I explained in the previous chapter, getting ready for the club or getting to the club often entails an immense amount of risk. Assuming the dress codes or even the celebratory attitudes of the club may expose queerness in places where there might be hurtful consequences. Messer observed in his qualitative study of Latina/o queers in the Karamba-Zarape club complex that approaching the club's entrance became an increasingly difficult transaction. The brutal anti-immigration debate came knocking at the club's door.

During this period, Maricopa County Sheriff Joseph "Joe" Arpaio increased the harassment of all Mexicans, documented or not, as suspect citizens. In a clear deviation from the law, which relegates all immigration enforcement procedures to the federal government, Arpaio used the resources of the Sheriff's Office to conduct raids of undocumented immigrants at work sites throughout the Valley. At the same time the Arizona State Legislature (aided by the reinvigorated anti-immigrant policies of a post-9/11 federal government) debated additional restrictions on services and identification requirements directed at the growing population of recently arrived Mexican migrants to the region.[47] The political debate brought a cloud of bad feelings upon the Valley, with anti-immigration

Fig. 19. Karamba entrance, Phoenix. Photo by Lucas Messer.

activists and politicians adopting an increasingly violent rhetoric and proposing equally aggressive measures that matched Arpaio's hateful irrationality. Activist groups, like the Minutemen, joined Arpaio in the media spotlight. They stood at the border ready, before the cameras, to "hunt down" Mexicans who crossed the border. While the sounds and flavors of Mexico, transformed by chic minimalist design, emerged as the signature motif of southwestern sophistication in the tourist industry, Mexicans became the scapegoats of an economy about to crash.

The rodeo around immigration escalated significantly during this period. These changes in attitude and policy toward Mexicans had specific repercussions for the region's nightlife. Under such conditions, clubs like Zarape, which served and depended on a recently migrated crowd for its viability, suffered. Patrons concerned about their well-being and safety became increasingly wary of such public rituals as the entry point ID check. Mexican passports or driver's licenses, a common form of identity prior to the advent of the anti-immigration campaign, were no longer acceptable forms of ID. At Karamba, where the aspirationally middle-class aesthetics of "Cancún tourism" had begun to attract a larger population of second- and third-generation Mexican-Americans, other Latinas/os, and non-Latina/o U.S. citizens, the performative rituals of admission into the club gained a particularly classed significance. As Phoenix's economy worsened and anti-immigrant sentiment grew, Karamba's bordered geography became progressively more apparent. As a way to comply with government agents and conservative citizens invested in the persecution of undocumented immigrants, the club stepped up security measures at its door. Door staff began to require U.S.-issued identification.[48]

The appeal of a touristic dramaturgy of space and the accompanying media attention it garnered Karamba as a friendly "Mexican modern" destination, worked to keep out working-class-identified *mexicanas/os*. These practices worked in tandem with capitulations to increased pressure from police and the political climate of the city, to seal the identity of the club as aspirationally middle class. Belonging to a space like Karamba required a repertoire of behaviors—from dress code to gestural approaches—that sought to evidence insider status in *mexicana/o moderno* style. A Mexican-American security staff member in her midfifties once described it to me: "In Karamba you have to look like you belong here; anyone can get into Zarape." The *mexicanidad* performed at the club's entrance, invested as it was in the touristic performance aesthetics of the Mexican queer club scene and the anxieties over migratory status, delimited differences that collapsed migrant experience with class status. Legality was posited as an observable condition that relied on the performance of class (*fresa sí pero chusma no*).

To a certain extent the public rhetoric circulating about these clubs in Latina/o and queer media prescribed the participation of particular groups in each of the clubs. The statements by the young man at Zarape and the security guard at Karamba certainly suggest some acceptance of this portrayal. However, patrons crossed from one establishment to the other with much more frequency than official accounts let on. Just a second look at the young man's statement shows his comedic emasculation of fellow *mexicanas/os* as *fresitas* to be narratively supplemented by a recognition of their commonality. Although he describes the men in Karamba as invested in performing class difference, he acknowledges that they are "de estas partes" (from here). This shared geography, the north of Mexico, is established at the instance of a failed performance, "cuando abren la boca" (when they open their mouths). The differences and commonalities articulated in this Latina/o queer scene rely on performance. Live acts in public spaces determine the legibility of queer latinidad. These performances are contingent on cultural border crossings that exceed simple narrative categorization. I want to turn now turn to an example that further complicates the role class plays in *mexicano* queer Phoenix and its serendipitous or accidental crossings into latinidad.

Ricanstructing the Border, or How Reggaetón Brought the *Chusma* into the Cancún Club

The positioning of Karamba atop the hierarchy of Latina/o queer clubs in Phoenix depended on a class identification that relied on an international, tourist-oriented dramaturgy of space as a sign of queer modernity. It was precisely this very investment in the "queer modern," a disciplinary performance that required an emphasis on the latest trends, that opened the doors for the arrival of reggaetón, Puerto Rico's most recent music and dance cultural export, into the club. Radio was a protagonist in this transition. In 2005, Phoenix's 91.5 FM radio station changed briefly from Mexican-regional to an exclusively reggaetón / Latin hip-hop format. It was the sudden and increased presence of reggaetón across the desert's airwaves that signaled the possibility of a trend. And it was reggaetón's potential fashioning of a commercial culture that borrowed from the present sounds of commercial hip-hop that allowed for its smooth adoption. From 2005 to 2007 reggaetón was everywhere across the Valley. It was continuously announced by the station's DJs and in the promotional signature "91.5, Reggaetón." Karamba's soundscape changed in keeping with this new trend.

It was the pressure to keep current, *a la moda,* that brought this new musical genre into Karamba. With it came a new population of patrons, Puerto Ricans, Dominicans, and African-Americans from across the Valley who ventured into Karamba and quite dramatically expanded not only its demographic profile but its choreographic and linguistic registers as well. *Mexicanas/os,* very much like the couple described at the opening of this chapter, began to experiment with articulating the hip in circular and back-and-forth isolations and mimicking sexual acts in polyrhythmic moves more common to Jamaican dance hall and African-American hip-hop than the basic two-step *cumbia* or the even-beat structure of the techno-inflected pop ballad. These experiments with articulating the body in "tropicalized" aesthetics of Caribbean hip-hop challenged both the assumed choreographic protocols of Karamba as a club and opened up the space for valuing the performance repertoires of Caribbean Latinas/os and African-Americans in the Valley, who gained local notoriety for their ability to execute movements correctly.[49] The temporary choreographic shift from a *norteño* aesthetic, or even a pop aesthetic, to the movements of reggaetón represents a significant transformation of the scripts of queer *mexicanidad* in Phoenix. Karamba's patrons also playfully incorporated the explicit and coded language about sexuality circulated in reggaetón's music. Many participants in Karamba's scene appropriated a Puerto Rican or more broadly Spanish Caribbean accent, specific words for the body, or expressions describing the sexual act and deployed them in flirtatious local exchanges where the newness of Puerto Rican Spanish added sexual charge and queer potentiality to the scene.

As the transformation of Karamba's scene suggests, reggaetón's currency in the club was certainly not only about keeping up with commercial popular culture trends. The genre gained some of its appeal as Karamba's soundscape because of the queer potentialities it could mobilize. Calle 13's "Atrévete-te-te," which I discuss at the opening scene of this chapter, was an often-cited example by my interlocutors. A twenty-one-year-old Mexican-born gay man, Luis had been living in Phoenix for less than a year when Juan introduced us. "Atrévete-te-te" came on as he popped out of his bar stool, grabbed my hand and pulled me and his boyfriend, Michael, onto the dance floor, "Este es nuestro himno! A mover el culo! Fuera del closet! Epa!" Luis delivered his enthusiastic appraisal of the song while imitating a Puerto Rican accent in exaggerated fashion. He substituted all the "r's" for "l's." He also accentuated his use of the word *culo,* a word frequently used in colloquial Puerto Rican speech to refer to the buttocks. He finished his statement with the typical "*epa,*" a Puerto Rican exclamation that expresses celebration and invites the listener to join in the jubilation. In his excited prelude to an equally ecstatic dance routine, Luis establishes the critical interconnections between ethno-racial and queer embodiments that make reggaetón such an appealing format for the Mexican club-goer.

To come out of the closet for him means to "mover el culo." He embodies his queerness as he bumps and grinds with his friends on the dance floor. Reggaetón facilitates this playfully assertive performance by offering an intimate difference. To *mover el culo* is to simultaneously step into a queer and a Puerto Rican mode of performance that mixes the pleasurable freedoms of sexualized abandon with the racialized and classed stereotype of Puerto Ricans as lower-class, black Latinas/os. These frictive encounters across identitarian and aesthetic platforms center queer latinidad as a social intersection or *convivencia diaria* riddled with layers of historical and contemporary affectivities. Reggaetón as genre is proximately Latina/o in its Puerto Ricanness while introducing a sufficiently "new" or "queer" way of moving, speaking, perhaps even being.

To *mover el culo* also points to a political economy of latinidad configured from the circulation of global popular music. Luis's expression of the phrase in the club recalls the Argentinean hip-hop group Illya Kuryaki and the Valderramas, who, during the late 1990s, rode the Latin-infused soundwaves of the club scenes I describe in the previous chapter. Their hit song "Coolo," featured in their 1999 album *Leche,*[50] popularized the phrase *a mover el culo* as the musical hook in a fast-paced dance track that mixes electronica with rap metal vocals and a funk backbeat. The song continues to make frequent appearances in the Latina/o club scenes of today. Luis recognized the reference and understood his own expression as a citation of this popularized expression. Not surprisingly, he attributes Puerto Rican authorship to the song, further demonstrating how the aesthetics of musical blackness and explicit bodily articulation tended to land upon a Puerto Rican identity despite its origins.

Adrián, a twenty-two-year-old Mexican-American college student and frequent patron of the club, further demonstrates how Puerto Ricanness fueled the queerness of the Mexican club. He explains, "*Atrévete* is totally it these days. How could it not! I mean, hello. *Tanta jotería en una canción, que nó?* [So much queerness in a single song, right?]." When I asked him to identify the queerness of the song, expecting the obvious reference to the coming out of the closet narrative or the thematization of sexual freedom in the lyrics, he responded: "It's the accent silly! I mean, that Puerto Rican talk speaking [*sic*] is like all sex for me. Can't you hear it? *Es mas rápido, mas fuerza* [It's faster, more forceful]. They talk the way they dance and they dance the way they fuck." Speech becomes embodiment in this example. Puerto Rican Spanish, especially the colloquial stylizations that characterize the MC's (René Joglar) delivery (strength, force), allude to a Puerto Rican masculinity read and appropriated as queer otherness in the realm of the Mexican club. What is more, the aesthetics of Puerto Rican music in song and dance lead to a clear articulation of queer sexual fantasy. Puerto Rican queerness, what we might term *patería,* is nowhere asserted in this dynamic. Instead,

Adrián translates Puerto Ricanness as a cultural script into his specifically Mexican queerness, or *jotería*. The move from talk to dance to fuck banks on established sexualized racial stereotypes that imagine the repertoires of Puerto Rican masculinity within a tradition of tropicalizing representations.[51]

Luis's and Adrián's tropicalized engagements with Puerto Ricanness reveal the avowals and disavowals the identitarian figurations of *jotería* entail within the Mexican modern. Friction, as a theory in practice of queer latinidad, lies therein. Frances Aparicio and Susanna Chávez-Silverman's adaptation of Edward Said's theorization of Orientalism is useful here. They describe a similar tradition of representational otherings whereby Latin American and Latinas/os are imagined as tropical dark hypersexual beings. They term these "tropicalizations." "To tropicalize," they explain, is "to trope, to imbue a particular space, geography, group, or nation with a set of traits, images and values."[52] The troping of tropicalization includes aggressively discriminatory and erotically desirous characterizations of latinidad's otherness. In their account, Latin American and Latina/o ethno-racial difference is aligned with histories of colonial and neocolonial relations to Europe and the United States. These representations they term "hegemonic tropicalizations."[53] However, they also discuss the ways in which Latinas/os engage these representations, and their ideological vestiges, in consumptive, complicitous, and oftentimes radical ways. I argue that latinidad as a practiced identity or affect maintains and exploits the friction between the hegemonic and the radical.

Tropicalization takes a particularly queer turn in Luis's and Adrián's accounts. In stereotyping Puerto Ricanness as not them—the ethno-racial difference of hegemonic tropicalization—they appropriate the historically subordinate status of Puerto Ricans in order to possess or assume their sexual currency in a consumptive gesture. They trope Puerto Ricans through the discriminatory caricaturing and the desirous characterization of their difference and sexual appeal. At the same time, their embodiment of the repertories of Puerto Ricanness endow a queer agency otherwise suppressed in the heteronormativity of Mexican and U.S. Anglo cultural contexts. Furthermore, in their engagements with tropicalized performance codes, Mexican queer men find ways to flaunt their latinidad in the context of Phoenix's rampant xenophobia. The queer intersections in latinidad presented in their accounts refuse the easy categorizations proposed in definitive identitarian thinking.

They propose instead queer latinidad as a doing or becoming where the contingencies involved are global in their incorporation of cultural material. Most importantly, they evidence the significance of the local in the particularities of their individual and collective dynamics. Friction dominates the dance floor.

Juan, a Mexican-born gay man in his midthirties with more than a decade residing in the United States, illustrates these frictions in his own entanglements with Calle 13's tropicalized anthem in the Mexican queer club. When asked about the song, he responds,

> Esa canción se escucha en todas partes. Ya han de ser por lo menos dos años desde que yo la escucho por primera vez. Aquí la andan sonando a cada rato.

> (You can hear this song everywhere. It's been at least two years since I first heard it. Here [in Karamba] they play it all the time.)

Two years after the release of Calle 13's song, Juan remarks on its enduring influence. He demonstrates how the soundscapes of the club move into peri-club geographies beyond it. In acknowledging that the song plays everywhere and that it plays all the time, he marks the extended time-space endurance of these traveled cultural objects. His use of *andan*, which means to walk or to be, in "andan sonando," playfully puts sound in motion. I read this simple phrase with my own Latina/o queer intentions. I recognize in this double meaning of walking and being, the very economies of becoming with which I endow Latina/o queer performance. To walk or to set the body in motion is to become what the body does. Queer latinidad relies on the technologies of performance to make the worlds we imagine inhabiting real in their enactment. Pleasure is key to queer latinidad's motivation and doings. It is the desire to be in the pleasure of queer latinidad that motivates the (e)motion of becoming.

When I ask Juan if he enjoyed the song he responded,

> Sí y no. Me gusta la música. Es alegre. También es sexy ver a los chavitos bailando. Pero yo no acostumbro a bailar esa música. Es mas para los chavos que se pueden mover. . . . A veces pues me hace sentir mayor. Pero la mayoría de las veces si me gusta el ánimo de la música. Es un poco ya de otras regiones, de la playa o del D.F., pero se disfruta igual aquí.

(Yes and no. I like the music. It is happy. It is also very sexy to see the young men dancing. But I do not usually dance to that music. It is more for the young ones who can move. . . . Sometimes it makes me feel older. But most of the time I enjoy the energy of the music. It belongs more to other regions—the beach or the D.F. [Mexico City], but you can enjoy it the same here.)

What compels me the most about Juan's account is his simultaneous embrace and distancing from reggaetón, and "Atrévete-te-te" in particular. To the extent that he identifies the genre and the song as belonging to the club (it has been playing for over two years) and derives pleasure from its energetic or emotional stimulation (*ánimo*) or the choreographies it incites in the younger dancers, he establishes a clear connection to it. But he is also quick to mark the song as corresponding to a younger way of moving he rarely attempts. Reggaetón positions him within a generational hierarchy in the club where youth reigns supreme. His regard of the young dancers is both a site of spectatorial pleasure and generational distance.

Juan's mapping of his relationship to reggaetón offers a critical outline of the place of class in queer latinidad. Class follows a complicated pattern here through established assumptions about musical styles and tropicalized characterizations of place. In his narrative, Juan identified reggaetón as belonging elsewhere, the beach or Mexico City. When I pursued his geographic outline of the song's difference further, he responded,

> Pos, esta música es mas de gran ciudad pero también caliente. Los puertorriqueños son así de ciudad y calientes. No sé porqué pienso del mar cuando pienso en esta música. Han de ser los movimientos asi muy puertorriqueños. Nosotros los mexicanos somos mas tranquilos. A menos que seas del D.F. Por eso creo que pienso D.F. y Puerto Rico juntos. Aquí en Arizona ya es muy distinto.

(Well, this music is from big cities and also very hot. Puerto Ricans are like that, from the city and hot. I don't know why I think of the ocean when I think of this music. I suppose it is because of the very Puerto Rican movements. We Mexicans are much mellower. Unless you are talking about Mexico City. That's why I think of Mexico City and Puerto Rico together. Here in Arizona it is very different.)

Juan attributes the appeal and the distance of Puerto Ricanness to an urbanity shared with Mexico City and not with the northern Mexico where he comes from, or the southwest United States where he has lived for over a decade now. His recurrence to images of the beach or the ocean to define the choreographic displays of Puerto Rican dancers and other Latinas/os performing within a Puerto Rican aesthetic suggests regional distinctions (city, tropics) across a transnational geography (Puerto Rico, Mexico, the United States). In the first instance, this characterization registers a racialized engagement with an assumed Puerto Rican blackness. The beach connotes choreographic repertoires most often ascribed to Caribbean Latinas/os, including Puerto Ricans. Correspondingly, the undulations of the back, the isolation of the hip and buttocks, and the emphasis on rhythm that characterize the dancing of reggaetón map the dance aesthetics of reggaetón outside of *mexicana/o* queer Phoenix. In the tropicalized vision of his narrative, Juan offers a cartography of tourism whereby inhabitants of warm locales are themselves hot. Hotness stands here for both an excessive corporeality and sexuality and the simultaneous desirability for those bodies. That said, the difference introduced by the aesthetics of blackness facilitates ventures into sexual freedom enacted through racial impersonation (dancing) or racialized spectatorship (looking). In simulating the sexual act in the performance of *perreo*, or doggy-style dancing, for example, Mexican dancers in the club are at once performing a stereotype of Latina/o blackness while engaging deeply in queer sexual play.

Nevertheless, the narrative of racial impersonation offers only a partial view of the dynamics at play in Juan's narrative. The connections Juan establishes between Puerto Rico and Mexico City invite a significant adjustment to an exclusively racialized reading. Recall that in his narrative Mexico City and Puerto Rico share urban, or modern, qualities. The shared "big-city hotness" marks them as centers of cultural production and circulation. Consequently, both locations may suggest an economy and an aesthetic of normativity, if not homonormativity, based on the assumed superiority of the exclusive know-how or cultural legitimacy of the urban center. The narrative of reggaetón in Juan's explanation not only documents regional and transnational frictions inherent in the flow of cultural material across Latina/o soundscapes but points to the peripheral status of the Arizona-Sonora region in the musical imaginaries of queer latinidad. This reading proposes Puerto Ricanness as a supplementary aesthetic of the Mexican modern and thus the aspirationally middle-class queerness centered in Karamba's ascendancy as an entertainment destination in Phoenix.

I want to dwell on the repercussions of Juan's (from here on AZ-Juan)[54] account of reggaetón for a moment as a clear example of the productive frictions characteristic of "interlatino" exchanges. In doing so, I introduce two more Juanes into this dialogue: Puerto Rican cultural critic Juan Flores and Juan (from here on NY-Juan), a Nuyorican informant in Suzanne Oboler's ethnographic study of Latina/o identities in the United States. In an extended quote, NY-Juan ruminates on the origin of hegemonic ethnic and racial labels in the United States. He says, "So you got Hispanics over here which includes whatever race you want to put in it south of the border. Then you got your blacks, anything from the Congo down. Then you got your whites which is Americans."[55] In the analysis that follows the quote, Oboler understands NY-Juan's notion of identity in terms of racial classification in the United States. It demonstrates NY-Juan's understanding of U.S. conceptualizations of racial others through groupings (Hispanics, blacks) that justify their exclusion from the ideal of the white nation (American). From a more experiential vantage point, Juan Flores considers this informant's declaration to be an exception to the understanding of Latina/o as a label. He brilliantly observes, "Oboler notes that [NY] Juan is voicing his recognition that the ethnic labeling process in the U.S. context involves the conflation of race and nationality, but she does not acknowledge that he is the only one of her informants to pose the issue into those terms, nor does she make anything of this 'exceptional' perspective."[56] In surveying the scholarly literature of pan-latinidad, Flores revisits the quote to particularize the Puerto Rican experience in the United States without falling into an easy assumption of pan-latina/o cohesiveness. The colonial history of Puerto Ricans and the structural inequities that position them as second-class citizens of the United States, despite their holding of a U.S. passport, beg for sociological nuancing of the argument around latinidad. Flores offers "translation" as a more appropriate term for understanding the historical pressures of the transnational in the local figurations of Latina/o experience. By the same token, the exception of Puerto Rico's national limbo and its history of circular migration, productively troubles narratives that would otherwise rely on the certainty of national border crossings.

Puerto Rican reggaetón performs a similar kind of trouble to the binational or border understandings of latinidad, as AZ-Juan exemplifies, in the *mexicana/o* clubs of Phoenix. This argument does not work strictly along identitarian logics nor does it assume full knowledge by participants of the historical and material nuances of the various communities and cultural materials engaged in the queer club. That is, I do not suggest that queer Mexicans and Mexican-Americans in Karamba always identified with Puerto Ricanness in explicit ways. I suggest, instead, that the Puerto Ricanness circulated in Karamba, and many other Latina/o public spaces in Arizona that incorporated reggaetón into their soundscape, was more of an affect and an aesthetic that was "mexicanized" in translation. It offered an opportunity to be queer within the sphere of latinidad in a primarily Mexican region.

The incorporation of reggaetón into Karamba enacts the practices of class exclusivity that the Mexican modern aesthetics of the Cancún club seek to perform, while contradicting its exclusionary gesture. In bringing reggaetón into the club, Karamba opened its doors to the very same communities it wanted to keep out: the visibly poor and working class. Puerto Ricanness introduced into the club an aesthetics born of the *caseríos* and urban ghettoes where reggaetón speaks a language that is outspokenly, and often vulgarly, from below. Dancers and patrons in the Mexican queer club who appropriated these aesthetics into their vision of cultural capital became, in their doings, the excessively *chusma* bodies they sought to distance themselves from. This friction is generally unresolvable. Quite simply, it is the condition of a queer latinidad that spans a vast terrain with an equally diverse catalog of histories, identities, and affects. But there is something deliciously rich, and of course problematic, about the ways stepping into tropicalized conceptions of latinidad at the Latina/o queer club derive pleasures, queer and otherwise, out of historical and contemporary power differentials. I don't want to suggest that these contingencies be forgotten for the sheer moment of pleasure achieved on the dance floor. I do, however, want to argue that queer latinidad, as a practiced orientation to the world and an optic from which to understand it, offers important frictions that productively trouble how we have come to either celebrate or dismiss pan-ethnic queer affiliations.

Queer latinidad as an analytic allows us to attend to these intersections and explore the cultural frictions at hand. Puerto Ricans began to frequent Karamba at a time when reggaetón intruded into the club scene. That is, the cultures of exclusion that brought reggaetón into the club ended up inviting actual Puerto Rican queers from the Valley into it. This awkward or accidental placement is neither definitively enabling nor limiting. Rather it illustrates the complicated points of friction and interaction that characterize the homogenizing trends of Latina/o commercial culture and its localizations in subcultural practice.

In approaching queer latinidad on the move, we must pursue what bodies do as much as what identity seeks to tell of their doing. Class, as a particular positionality, is central to the dynamics of cultural friction because it signals an aspirational futurity (that may or may not congeal as an identity) and an aesthetic that enables both purposeful and accidental crossings. The title of this chapter, "Dancing Reggaetón with Cowboy Boots," documents actual transitions, negotiations, and acts of (mis)translation taking place in Latina/o Phoenix but also present across the nation as Latinas/os with varying histories of arrival and settlement, experiences of class, race, and ethnicity, and orientations to gender and sexuality meet in a quickly changing demographic map. Inter-Latina/o cultural crossings have become more frequent and consequential. Dancing under these circumstances offers a theoretical paradigm to approach these and other sites and sights of encounter where both inter-Latina/o commonality and friction play equal part. Pursuing of these "contradictory movements," as Ian Barnard has described Anzaldúa's conceptualization of the borderlands, I too seek to break away from fixed identitarian scripts that render Latina/o queer bodies as static. Anzaldúa has explained in the preface to *Borderlands / La Frontera,* "the Borderlands are physically present wherever two or more cultures edge each other, where people of different races occupy the same territory, where under, lower, middles and upper classes touch, where the space between two individuals shrinks with intimacy."[57] Dancing reggaetón with cowboy boots seeks to document these intimacies, no matter how contradictory they are, because that is the space where queer Latina/o theories in practice emerge. This chapter looks for intimacies in ever-shifting geographies where learning to be pleasurably in the world results from movements across categories of comfort and discomfort. Friction is central to our understanding of these dynamics as it reminds us that cultural exchanges demand adjustments, involve appropriations, and incite conflicts that are formative and simply routine to cohabitation. Focusing on friction allows us to understand latinidad and queer latinidad in particular as always dynamic, negotiated. It asks us to produce a scholarship that is more ethnographically grounded. Learning to articulate reggaetón's hip while proudly displaying a Jalisco belt buckle, daring to move publicly in intimate proximity to another queer body, negotiating the pressures of anti-immigrant sentiment in the United States, and navigating the complicated class hierarchies within Latina/o communities are all part and parcel of living Latina/o and queer in a place like Phoenix. But daring to move seems to be the key maneuver across these various levels of engagement. To dare a step, a touch, a laugh . . . *atrévete-te-te*.

EPILOGUE

Moving Forward—Between Fragility and Resilience

I want to close this book at the very scene where I began it. I return to the Orgullo en Acción Annual Picnic in Chicago's Humboldt Park. It is July 30, 2011, more than two years after my first visit, and the rain really did pour this time. On the morning of the picnic my Facebook newsfeed displays a message from the event organizers, "Due to flooding picnic will b on humboldt drive and cortez by basketball courts. Furthur down from original location. [syc]" In 2009 I was skeptical about attending due to the threat of inclement weather and my unfamiliarity with Chicago. This time I know the weather has passed but I am deep in the process of revising the very manuscript before you and dread the idea of pausing to participate in what might be considered a distraction. I look at my computer screen once again and notice that right below the relocation notice for the picnic there is yet another message from the organizers. This one, written before knowledge of the flooding that forced the relocation of the event a few yards from its intended location, reminds us of the time and place of the picnic and signs off with, "Let's Get Together and Feel Alright!"

The expression is a citation of Bob Marley's "One Love / People Get Ready" song for which a YouTube link is provided in the message. The 1977 reggae number recorded for the Tuff Gong label in Jamaica is here circulated as an anthem of fellowship in a specifically Latina/o queer context. I click on the video link and am taken by the simplicity of this communication and moved by its affective depth. The easygoing rhythm of the song eases in powerful lyrics that invite collective unity, "one love, one heart," and forward-looking politics "is there place for the hopeless children?" The message performed on my Facebook page is clear: Orgullo en Acción organizers argue that the event of the picnic is as pleasurable as it is political. There are significant resonances between the use of the Marley song to promote the Orgullo en Acción event and the theories in practice I have pursued throughout this book. The message calls for an arrival at the home of queer latinidad, in the hopeful, utopian, and frictive practices of performance. "One Love" was steeped in the traditions of Rastafarianism but was also a commercial success. The album on which it was originally included, *Exodus,* propelled Marley into international fame. "One Love" could be arguably positioned at the center of the Jamaican music explosion that influenced popular music cultures globally during the 1980s. The song has also been frequently appropriated in commercial media as a global sound of comfort.[1] For example, during the 1990s the Jamaica Tourist Board notoriously used it to welcome tourists, imaged as white in the television ads circulated in the United States, to an idyllic tropical landscape serviced by the happy Jamaicans featured in the background. It has circulated as a countercultural text that imagines an alternative, more just, world, at demonstrations and rallies very much like the Orgullo en Acción picnic. I also heard it chanted in Phoenix during the marches for immigrant rights in 2006 and printed in large bold type below a triptych of red, green, and yellow portraits of Barack Obama on T-shirts in support of his campaign of hope in 2008. "One Love" is a commodity and much more.

The song's effect on me as I stare at my computer screen, like any other communicative practice, draws on its history of circulation and its related meanings and affects across varied contexts. In this instance, it gains its significance in the local, particular contexts of Latina/o queer identities and desires. That is, the Orgullo en Acción announcement translates the song as optimistic collectivism, a wish for what the social event of performance could be. In the proposition "let's get together" we are called into participation through performance (music) and into performance (the collection of staged and quotidian displays that constitute the picnic event I described at the opening of this book). To "feel alright," as an objective, connotes a commitment to the pleasurable instances of performance but also to its potential outcomes. But for me the invitation to attend this Latina/o queer performance intervention into public space is also an act of history. This is a history carried and felt on the body. As Diana Taylor has convincingly argued, "Performed, embodied practices make the past available as a political resource in the present by simultaneously enabling several complicated multilayered processes."[2] The appeal of the Orgullo en Acción event lies precisely in this reaching back to embodied experiences, tactics, and emotional memories of a past, perhaps as recent as last year's picnic but potentially as distant as the beginnings of the Puerto Rican antigentrification movement in Chicago or the gay and lesbian rights movement nationally. It may also prompt embodied memory for those who like me have been there before, at the site of Latina/o queer publicity, and reveled in the joyful and festive sharing of time in public space here in Chicago or elsewhere. As I did two years ago, I ready to walk out, moved by the hope of making home with others.

As I have stressed throughout, to "feel alright" or to coalesce at the site of Latina/o queer performance is not to be elevated uncritically from the societal restraints that in large part compel us to seek out moments of respite. While joyful, these gatherings also introduce an important level of discomfort. As Laura G. Gutiérrez explains in her study of Mexican and Chicana cabaret performance, Latina/o queer counterpublic events "by their very own constitution, however performative and ephemeral these worlds may be, are simultaneously spaces of desire and fear."[3] And thus, our journey through the various Latina/o queer performance worlds across the United States has showcased how home, hope, and utopia are in fact built upon and in friction. If the Facebook invitation to the Orgullo en Acción event compels me to the home of performance to "get together" with others in hopes that I might experience community as a utopian embodiment, it does not do so by glossing over the obstacles and fears to be encountered en route or in the midst of pursuing such goals. To temporarily rise above the flooded terrain of the park in order to be "alright" with others means to recognize, engage, and oftentimes confront the source of the downpours that have so altered the landscapes of our being. The "floods" negotiated by queer Latinas/os between the 1990s and early 2000s—a time in which both Latina/o and queer visibility were on the rise in the USAmerican public sphere as commoditized identities—were plentiful and not always easily avoided by a simple adjustment in location. From the renewed push out from urban space to the conservative pushback by homophobic and xenophobic conservative activism and legislation, performing queer latinidad assertively in public space was not a safe stance or movement pattern to assume. However, countless queer Latinas/os, some whose lives and efforts have been recorded in this book, took to the streets, opened arts organizations, confronted governmental authorities, and danced the night away in pleasure and defiance.

I do not want to give the impression that the stories or histories this book documents have reached resolution, that by the closing of each chapter we are simply up to date or have arrived at the finality of the now. That is perhaps the most tempting of impulses in rendering the ethnographic present into the recent past. I also want to make sure that we recognize the fragility of the historical and enduring politico-economic contexts that make performance interventions necessary as continued, repeated, hopeful efforts for Latina/o queer communities. Each of the chapters presented in this book offered a snapshot in a temporal continuum that has involved successes and pleasures as much as failures, contradictions, and discomforts in the years that followed the time frame of fieldwork.

For example, since opening its doors in 1999, Arthur Aviles and his collaborators at the Bronx Academy of Arts and Dance have continued to expand the organization's offerings throughout the Hunts Point community. For more than a decade Aviles and his collaborators have hosted Latina/o queer cultural and artistic events in the neighborhood— including the Out Like That, BAAD ASSS WOMEN, and Blacktino Festival showcasing the works by queers, women, and black Latina/o artists. Aviles also continued to develop choreography for his dance company, the Arthur Aviles Typical Theatre, and produce the work of other queer, Latina/o, and African-American local dancers and theater artists. He received an incredible amount of attention for his efforts and so did the neighborhood. The work of Aviles at BAAD! and other cultural workers and organizations in Hunts Point, including the Point, became one of the centerpieces in the neighborhood's marketing to potential investors. The growth in arts activity and the neighborhood pride it fostered enabled alternative narratives that supplemented the "industry only" focus of much economic growth advocacy, including the always ongoing pressures to incentivize the food distribution industries in Hunts Point out of fear of losing them to competing locations. Aviles also inserted a queer perspective into the conversation about the future of the neighborhood.

However, Paul Lipson's warning in the epigraph to chapter 2 that "art spurs investment, and then investment spurs displacement" became part of the reality encountered by cultural developers in Hunts Point.[4] With the improved image the arts have helped secure for Hunts Point has come an onslaught of investors drawn to the possibility of profit. In 2007, real estate developers purchased the Bank Note Building where BAAD! is housed and set out to draft remodeling plans focused on turning the building into a mixed-use facility of corporate rentals, arts and educational organizations, and retail. All seemed like a positive influx of much-needed investment into a neighborhood that continues to suffer economically until the plans called for the displacement of the Living Room, a drop-in facility for the homeless.[5] Aviles's journey as a New York Rican queer man returning to the Bronx to make home, connected as it was to the history of housing activism by Latinas/os equally intent in claiming the neighborhood as their own, now lived uncomfortably between the roles of the homemaker and of the potential evictor.

Many more changes have come to BAAD! with the passing of time. At the time of writing, Aviles and Charles Rice-González are no longer the "real life" romantic couple I so enthusiastically narrated as collapsing the materiality of being in the performance space with the representational world of the stage. They do, however, continue to collaborate as codirectors of the BAAD! operation and as active artists and activists in Hunts Point. But despite their real-life risks in becoming Hunts Point's most visible queer couple during the mid-1990s and into the early 2000s and their untiring labor to create a queer home within the Latina/o neighborhood, homophobia persists in Hunts Point. The last time I found BAAD! mentioned in a major New York City publication was in a 2010 article in the *New York Times* reporting on incidents of violence against gay men in the neighborhood.[6] Latina/o queer homemaking in Hunts Point continues to be a difficult, at times dangerous task.

In San Antonio, the Esperanza Center has experienced similar ups and downs over the years. During and shortly after their viewpoint discrimination lawsuit against the City of San Antonio, Esperanza received an incredible amount of national attention from individuals and groups. Academic, political, and arts organizations invited Esperanza representatives, especially Graciela Sánchez, to speak about the case and to opine on general matters of culture and activism. Foundations allocated their financial support, including sizable contributions from the Ford Foundation and the Rockefeller Foundation. Esperanza artists and activists remained true to their mission and continued to organize across a variety of causes during the early 2000s—from water rights issues to the protection of historical buildings associated with the Mexican community in the city. Their public interventions remained grounded in the traditions of Mexican and Latina/o expressive cultures and built around participatory models of communication. Much as they made the case about their discriminatory funding to the broader community, they translated the complicated issues of water permits and historic preservations laws through engaging performances embedded in tradition but intent on safeguarding the future of Latina/o, queer or straight, San Antonio. Nonetheless, the organization has also experienced significant challenges along the way.

As is expected of large multigenerational organizations, some of the art activists present during my initial fieldwork, especially some of the youngest, moved on to other projects or life pursuits. Others simply burned out or found themselves in conflict with the direction of the strengthened organization post–Todos Somos Esperanza. Nonetheless, the organization retained a substantial number of its core constituency and continued to welcome new members. They continued to take to the streets, cutting across the carefully drawn-out maps of the tourist center, to engage San Antonio citizens in practices of hope.[7] Not surprisingly, in 2007 the San Antonio City Council passed an ordinance mandating permits and charging fees for any public processions, marches, parades, as well as runs, walks, and cycling events taking place in the city streets.[8] The city justified the measures as part of a revenues argument, but many in the Esperanza perceived it as a direct attack on their art and activism since the late 1980s. The ordinance required organizers to pay a permit-processing fee and assume responsibility for any municipal government expenses incurred in managing or policing the public site involved. Events organized by cash-strapped grassroots organizations such as the International Women's Day would incur between $1,700 and $7,500 total costs to secure and cover permits and service fees associated with walking in the streets during their annual event.

Esperanza activists saw this as an affront to free speech, an attempt to both limit and profit from the movements of groups along the city streets. They launched a San Antonio Free Speech Coalition, a yearlong campaign, and a lawsuit against the City of San Antonio over the issue. Over the course of two years (2008–10) Esperanza Center activists mobilized to the streets under the Free Speech Coalition, standing in front of court buildings, marching southward from their headquarters on San Pedro Street into the festive Mexican realm of downtown tourism, mouths muzzled with packing tape, holding banners and signs reading "Las Calles No Se Callan! Our Streets Will Not Be Silenced!"or "Pay Up or Shut Up." Despite their efforts, the decisions from the municipal courts up to the Fifth Court of Appeals were disappointingly not in their favor. Moving hope into the streets from then on would cost more than tired feet or wounded egos. There is increasingly a reason for Esperanza's hope to be an angry one.

Much like the performances that happen within them, the spaces of Latina/o queer nightlife are also ephemeral, fragile. The nightlife scenes that I described in chapters 4 and 5 changed over the course of my return visits and my writing of this project. Many of my informants ceased to attend the dance clubs where I first encountered them. Some said they had aged out of the scene or had grown tired of the routine. Others found newer clubs or scenes. But in the volatile business of nightlife entertainment, owners, DJs, bartenders, and promoters also came and went. With each minor shift the cultural ecology of the entire club changed and so did its constituencies. Moreover, while some of the clubs I visited during my fifteen years of fieldwork have lasted a long time (for example Escuelita in New York City is still going strong at the time of writing), the vast majority of them have been short lived. In Rochester, the club where Nestor worked his imaginary catwalk relocated twice over the course of my research before finally shutting down. The crowds who patronized the club dispersed across the city; some went back to older, more stable watering holes, while others ventured into newer clubs. Krash, in Queens, New York, closed its space and became an itinerant party event hosted at various locations across the city. During my last visit to Phoenix, in 2010, the effects of the anti-immigration crisis had become increasingly palpable on the Latina/o queer club scene. Club Zarape's dance floor was empty all three nights I attempted to check in with my informants during a weekend trip. No more than ten patrons sat on their chairs looking at the empty dance floor lit through the enthusiastic reflections of a disco ball. "People are scared to come out," said the young man who brought me my drink, "You come out for a beer and a little dancing *con los que te gustan y terminas en México* [with the ones you like and you end up in Mexico]." Many times during that weekend I heard similar stories about the increased threat of deportation and about the cloud of suspicion that had descended over every single Latina/o in Phoenix, documented or not. It was not so much the ID check or even deportation they feared, it was their lives they felt were threatened by the hate circulated over the immigration debate. And yet, the ten or so queer Latinas/os who braved the streets of Phoenix on that Saturday night eventually stood up under the disco ball and danced into the night.

Performing Queer Latinidad has argued for the resiliency of Latina/o queer communities who navigated the complications of cultural mainstreaming and material disenfranchisement at the close of the twentieth century and the beginning of the twenty-first. During this period perfor-

mance became both a site and a strategy for the articulation of queer latinidad as a counterpublic. But as I have demonstrated throughout, these
practices have histories. Latina/o queer performance engages past aesthetic and political legacies, as well as historical traumas and conflicts,
to practice new ways of being and being together, Latina/o and queer.
The artists, activists, and social dancers discussed in this book have carried forth, in performance, critical embodied knowledge and affective
resources that are likely to remain significant understandings and figurations of queer latinidad into a future, seemingly turbulent but possible.

NOTES

Chapter 1

1. Orgullo en Acción, Facebook post, June 13, 2009.

2. In its usage by organizations like Orgullo en Acción, LGBTQQ stands for lesbian, gay, bisexual, transgender, queer and questioning.

3. See Gina M. Pérez, *The Near Northwest Side Story: Migration, Displacement, and Puerto Rican Families* (Berkeley: University of California Press, 2004).

4. The steel flags are located at the corners of Division Street and Western Avenue and Division Street and California Street respectively. For a discussion of the use of national performances such as the use of the flag in Puerto Rican struggles against gentrification in Humboldt Park, see Ana Y. Ramos Zayas, *National Performances: The Politics of Class, Race, and Space in Puerto Rican Chicago* (Chicago: University of Chicago Press, 2003).

5. Orgullo en Acción (Pride in Action) and the Association for Latino Men in Action (ALMA) are Chicago-based organizations dedicated to both social and political Latina/o LGBTQQ community development. For more information on these groups, see http://www.orgulloenaccion.org and http://www.almachicago.org. Amigas Latinas focuses similarly on organizing the Latina lesbian community in the region. For more information see http://www.amigaslatinas.org.

6. On tacit modalities of Latina/o queer sexuality see Carlos Ulises Decena, *Tacit Subjects: Belonging and Same-Sex Desire among Dominican Immigrant Men* (Durham, NC: Duke University Press, 2011).

7. In my usage throughout this book "inter-Latina/o" refers to actual encounters and exchanges among diverse Latina/o constituencies. "Pan-Latina/o" refers to their resulting collective imaginaries.

8. Micaela di Leonardo, "Introduction: New Global and American Landscapes of Inequality," in Jane L. Collins, Micaela di Leonardo, and Brett Williams, eds., *New Landscapes of Inequality: Neoliberalism and the Erosion of Democracy in America* (Santa Fe, NM: School for Advanced Research Press, 2008), 5.

9. David Román, *Performance in America: Contemporary U.S. Culture and the Performing Arts* (Durham, NC: Duke University Press, 2005), 12.

10. For a theoretical discussion of the engagements with history performance reenactment entails see Rebecca Schneider, *Performance Remains: Art and War in Times of Theatrical Reenactment* (London: Routledge, 2011).

11. On the Stonewall riots and the ensuing repertoires of commemoration see David Carter, *Stonewall: The Riots That Sparked The Gay Revolution* (New York: St. Martin's Press, 2004) and Martin Duberman, *Stonewall* (New York: Dutton, 1993).

12. The films *Zoot Suit* (1981), *Crossover Dreams* (1985), *La Bamba* (1987), *Born in East LA* (1987), *Stand and Deliver* (1988), *Salsa* (1988), and *Lambada* (1989) further supported the notion of "Decade of the Hispanic" and helped to launch the Hollywood careers of many Latina/o actors, including Edward James Olmos, Elizabeth Peña, Ruben Blades, Lupe Ontiveros, Andy García, and Raúl Juliá. In art, the 1980s saw major exhibitions of Mexican and Latin American art and the inclusion of U.S. Latina/o artists in mainstream museum exhibitions. Musical acts that gained national attention in the 1980s U.S. popular markets include the Gloria Estefan and Miami Sound Machine, starting with their CBS International debut album *Miami Sound Machine* in 1980 and Linda Ronstadt's 1987 album *Caciones de mi Padre*. Key exhibitions include "Diego Rivera: A Retrospective" (1985) at the Detroit Institute of Arts, "Hispanic Art in the United States: Thirty Contemporary Painters and Sculptors" (1987) at the Houston Museum of Fine Art and the Corcoran Gallery, "Art and Artists in the United States, 1920–1970" (1988) at the Bronx Museum, and "Mexico: Splendors of 30 Centuries," which opened in 1990 at the Metropolitan Museum of Art in New York.

13. Deborah Paredez has similarly offered a historical perspective on the Latin boom by tracing a genealogy of dead Latina icons—from Frida Kahlo to Eva Perón to Selena Quintanilla—upon which the image of Latina/o stardom was developed in the United States. See Deborah Paredez, *Selenidad: Selena, Latinos, and the Performance of Memory* (Durham, NC: Duke University Press, 2009), 5–13.

14. Toraño commented: "We haven't had the Vernon Jordans and the Jesse Jacksons. We haven't had the civil-rights battles. But we are being sensitized. The blacks had the decade of the '60s; women had the '70s. The '80s will be the decade for Hispanics." "Hispanics Push for Bigger Role In Washington," *U.S. News & World Report*, May 22, 1978, 58.

15. See Katherine Roberts and Richard Levine. "Coors Extends a $300 Million Peace Offering," *New York Times*, November 4, 1984, 4.8.

16. For a detailed discussion of Latinas/os and the census see Marta Tienda and Vilma Ortiz, "Hispanicity and the 1980 Census," *Social Science Quarterly* 67.1 (1986): 3–20; and Clara E. Rodríguez, *Changing Race: Latinos, the Census, and the History of Ethnicity in the United States* (New York: New York University Press, 2000).

17. What is more, the embrace of the "Decade of the Hispanic" story resulted in collaborative relationships among unexpected bedfellows. The demands for inclusion and representation in the *US News and World Report* statement in 1978 and the suspicious media campaign by the embattled beer company in 1983 have been assumed as distinct origin stories to the popularization of the term "Hispanic" in the U.S. However, by 1987 these seemingly independent roots of the "Decade of the Hispanic" led to increasingly interconnected routes into the nation. "Hispanic" as a collective designation propelled partnerships between mainstream Latina/o politics and corporate interests such as Toraño's founding of the National Hispana Leadership Institute (NHLI), an organization initially charted with increasing the presence of Latinas in the nation's corporate boards, with funding from no other than Coors Brewing Company. The agenda for representation and inclusion in government was quickly turned into an agenda for

representation and inclusion in corporate governance. Latina/o political power became subsumed into a story of Latina/o purchasing power.

18. See Arlene Dávila, *Latinos Inc.: The Marketing and Making of a People* (New York: New York University Press, 2001).

19. Licia Fiol-Matta, "Pop Latinidad: Puerto Ricans in the Latin Explosion, 1999," *Centro Journal* 14.1 (2002): 45.

20. The Immigration Reform and Control Act of 1986 provided amnesty measures for immigrants already residing in the United States and the Immigration Act of 1990 reinforced family reunification measures. However, both pieces of legislation included measures that further criminalized the lives of undocumented migrants and those who assisted or employed them.

21. On Proposition 187 see Robin Dale Jacobson, *The New Nativism: Proposition 187 and the Debate over Immigration* (Minneapolis: University of Minnesota Press, 2008) and Kent A. Ono and John M. Sloop, *Shifting Borders: Rhetoric, Immigration and California's Proposition 187* (Philadelphia: Temple University Press, 2002). On SB 1070 see Lisa Magaña, ed., *Latino Politics and International Relations: The Case of Arizona's Immigration Law SB 1070* (New York: Springer, 2012).

22. For a cultural history and analysis of AIDS see the work of Cindy Patton, especially *Sex and Germs: Politics of AIDS* (Montreal: Black Rose Books, 1988) and *Globalizing AIDS* (Minneapolis: University of Minnesota Press, 2002). For pioneering work on AIDS activism see Douglas Crimp's edited collection *AIDS: Cultural Analysis, Cultural Activism* (Cambridge: MIT Press, 1988) and his *Melancholia and Moralism: Essays on AIDS and Queer Politics* (Cambridge: MIT Press, 2004). For a discussion about AIDS, activism, and performance see David Román, *Acts of Intervention: Performance, Gay Culture, and AIDS* (Bloomington: Indiana University Press, 1998).

23. See Lisa Peñaloza, "We're Here, We're Queer, and We're Going Shopping! A Critical Perspective on the Accommodation of Gays and Lesbians in the U.S. Marketplace," in Daniel Wardlow, ed., *Gays, Lesbians, and Consumer Behavior: Theory, Practice, and Research Issues in Marketing* (Binghampton, NY: Haworth Press, 1998), 9–41.

24. Lisa Duggan, "The New Homonormativity: The Sexual Politics of Neoliberalism," in Dana Nelson, ed., *Materializing Democracy: Towards a Revitalized Cultural Politics* (Durham, NC: Duke University Press, 2002), 179.

25. "Don't Ask Don't Tell" has since been repealed and expired as official policy on September 20, 2011.

26. See Lisa Duggan and Nan D. Hunter, *Sex Wars: Sexual Dissent and Political Culture*, 10th anniversary ed. (New York: Routledge, 2006).

27. The 1989 revision of the National Endowment of the Arts to include a decency clause and the revocation of funds awarded to feminist and/or queer performance artists Karen Finley, Holly Hughes, Time Miller, and John Fleck because of their engagement with explicit representations of the body and sexuality and the litigation that ensued became an iconic example that received national attention. See Richard Bolton, ed., *Culture Wars: Documents from the Recent Controversies in the Arts* (New York: New Press, 1992).

28. These organizations include the American Family Association, the Christian Broadcasting Network, Focus on the Family, Concerned Women For America, and the Christian Coalition.

29. On the influence of Juanito Extravaganza on Keith Haring see Arnaldo Cruz-Malavé, *Queer Latino Testimonio, Keith Haring, and Juanito Extravaganza* (New York: Palgrave Macmillan, 2008). On Warhol superstar Holly Woodlawn, Jean Michelle Basquiat, and Madonna see Frances Negrón-Muntaner, *Boricua Pop: Puerto Ricans and the Latinization of American Culture* (New York: New York University Press, 2004).

30. See for example Michael Hames-García and Ernesto Javier Martínez, eds., *Gay Latino Studies: A Critical Reader* (Durham, NC: Duke University Press, 2011); Lawrence La Fountain-Stokes, *Queer Ricans: Cultures and Sexualities in the Diaspora* (Minneapolis: University of Minnesota Press, 2009); and Lawrence La Fountain-Stokes, Lourdes Torres, and Ramón H. Rivera-Servera, "Toward an Archive of Latina/o Queer Chicago: Arts, Politics, and Social Performance," in Jill Austin and Jennifer Brier, eds., *Out in Chicago: LGBT History at the Crossroads* (Chicago: Chicago Historical Society, 2011), 127–53.

31. See José Quiroga, *Tropics of Desire: Interventions from Latino America* (Durham, NC: Duke University Press, 2000).

32. On gentrification of Latina/o neighborhoods see Arlene Dávila, *Barrio Dreams: Puerto Ricans, Latinos, and the Neoliberal City* (Berkeley: University of California Press, 2004). For an example of the advocacy for queer communities as gentrifiers see Richard Florida, *The Rise of the Creative Class: And How It's Transforming Work, Leisure, Community and Everyday Life* (New York: Perseus, 2002).

33. See Dávila, *Latinos Inc.*

34. See Louis DeSipio, *Counting the Vote: Latinos as a New Electorate* (Charlottesville: University of Virginia Press, 1996).

35. See Miriam Jiménez Román, "Looking at that Middle Ground: Racial Mixing as Panacea?" in Juan Flores and Renato Rosaldo, eds., *A Companion to Latino Studies* (Malden, MA: Blackwell, 2007), 325–36.

36. For a notable and recent exception see Alicia Arrizón, *Queering Mestizaje: Transculturation and Performance* (Ann Arbor: University of Michigan Press, 2006).

37. See José Quiroga, "From Republic to Empire: The Loss of Gay Studies," *GLQ* 10.1 (2003): 133–35.

38. See Moraga's "Chicana Feminism as Theory in the Flesh," in Gloria Anzaldúa and Cherríe Moraga, eds., *This Bridge Called My Back: Writings by Radical Women of Color* (San Francisco: Aunt Lute Press, 1981).

39. Dwight Conquergood, "Rethinking Ethnography: Towards a Critical Cultural Politics," in D. Soyini Madison and Judith Hamera, eds., *The Sage Handbook of Performance Studies* (Thousand Oaks, CA: Sage, 2006), 351–65.

40. See Paredez, *Selenidad*. See also Raúl Coronado, "Selena's Good Buy: Texas Mexicans, History, and Selena Meet Transnational Capitalism," *Aztlán* 26.1 (2001): 59–100.

41. José Esteban Muñoz, "Feeling Brown: Ethnicity and Affect in Ricardo Bracho's *The Sweetest Hangover (and Other STDs)*," *Theatre Journal* 52 (2000): 68.

42. I use the term "USAmerica" as a gesture against imperial geographical constructions of U.S. nationalism. I borrow the term from Gretchen Murphy's usage in her book-length study *Hemispheric Imaginings: The Monroe Doctrine and Narratives of U.S. Empire* (Durham, NC: Duke University Press, 2005).

43. Diana Taylor, "Opening Remarks," in *Negotiating Performance: Gender, Sexuality & Theatricality in Latin/o America* (Durham, NC: Duke University Press), 4.

44. Juan Flores, *The Diaspora Strikes Back: Caribeño Tales of Learning and Turning* (New York: Routledge, 2009).

45. Paul Allatson, *Key Terms in Latina/o Cultural and Literary Studies* (Malden, MA: Blackwell, 2007), 102.

46. See David Harvey, *A Brief History of Neoliberalism* (Oxford: Oxford University Press, 2005).

47. Tomás Ybarra-Frausto, introduction to Don Adams and Arlene Goldbard, eds., *Community, Culture and Globalization* (New York: Rockefeller Foundation, 2002), 5.

48. For a discussion of U.S. interventionism in Latin America, see Harold Molineu, *U.S. Policy toward Latin America: From Regionalism to Globalism* (Boulder, CO: Westview Press, 1986). For a discussion of U.S. international policy and immigration to the United States, see Ruben G. Rumbaut, "Origins and Destinies: Immigration to the United States since World War II," *Sociological Forum* 9.4 (1994): 583–621. See also Alberto Sandoval-Sánchez's discussion of U.S. interventionism relative to the politics of representation in U.S. theater and film in his chapter "Carmen Miranda and Desi Arnaz: Foundational Images of 'Latinidad' on Broadway and in Hollywood," in *José Can You See? Latinos On and Off Broadway* (Madison: University of Wisconsin Press, 1999), 21–61.

49. For an account of these pressures in the case of Mexico, see Devon G. Peña, *The Terror of the Machine: Technology, Work, Gender and Ecology on the U.S.-Mexico Border* (Austin, TX: CMAS Books, 1997).

50. David Harvey, *Spaces of Hope* (Berkeley: University of California Press, 2000), 63.

51. Betsy Guzman, *The Hispanic Population: Census 2000 Brief* (Washington, DC: U.S. Census Bureau, 2001).

52. Abby Goodnough, "Hispanic Vote in Florida: Neither a Bloc Nor a Lock," *New York Times,* October 17, 2004, 1.31. For a discussion of the growth of the Puerto Rican population in Florida, see Jorge Duany and Félix V. Matos-Rodríguez, *Puerto Ricans in Orlando and Central Florida,* Report for the Hispanic Chamber of Commerce of Metro Orlando, http://hispanicchamber.net/images/pdf/puerto_ricans-orl.pdf (accessed on July 20, 2009).

53. See, for example, Felix Padilla's groundbreaking study, *Latino Ethnic Consciousness: The Case of Mexican Americans and Puerto Ricans in Chicago* (South Bend, IN: Notre Dame University Press, 1985) and Nicholas De Genova and Ana Y. Ramos-Zayas, *Latino Crossings: Mexicans, Puerto Ricans and the Politics of Race and Citizenship* (New York: Routledge, 2003). For a discussion of how the particular case of Chicago might relate more broadly to the formation of Latina/o studies, see Frances Aparicio, "Reading the 'Latino' in Latino Studies: Toward Re-imagining Our Academic Location," *Discourse* 21.3 (1999): 3–18. See also Mérida Rúa, *A Grounded Identidad: Places of Memory and Personhood in Chicago's Puerto Rican Neighborhoods* (forthcoming, Oxford University Press).

54. Taylor, "Opening Remarks," 9.

55. French scholars Gilles Deleuze and Félix Guattari introduced the concept of

rhizome, based on the botanical definition for the rootstalk of plants, to offer a model for philosophical thinking that accounts for simultaneous multiplicities of origins and directions. This model is supposed to contrast traditional approaches in Western thought that favor linearity and narrative coherence. See Gilles Deleuze and Félix Guattari, *A Thousand Plateaus*, trans. Brian Massumi (New York: Continuum, 2004).

56. Juana María Rodríguez, *Queer Latinidad: Identity Practices, Discursive Spaces* (New York: New York University Press, 2003), 22.

57. Alicia Arrizón, *Latina Performance: Traversing the Stage* (Bloomington: Indiana University Press, 1999), 2.

58. Sandoval-Sánchez, *José Can You See?* 15.

59. Aparicio's borrowing of term "decolonial" references Emma Pérez's *The Decolonial Imaginary: Writing Chicanas into History* (Bloomington: Indiana University Press, 1999). In this book Pérez offers alternative Chicana feminist methodologies for historiography that seek to undo the knowledge produced within colonial academic production and its usage by Chicano historians to the exclusion of gender as a critical vector.

60. Frances Aparicio, "Jennifer as Selena: Rethinking Latinidad in Media and Popular Culture," *Latino Studies* 1.1 (2003): 93.

61. See Juan Flores, "The Latino Imaginary: Dimensions of Community and Identity," in Frances Aparicio and Susana Chávez-Silverman, eds., *Tropicalizations: Transcultural Representations of Latinidad* (Hanover, NH: Dartmouth College Press, 1997), 183–93.

62. Angharad N. Valdivia, "Is My Butt Your Island? The Myth of Discovery and Contemporary Latina/o Communication Studies," in Angharad N. Valdivia, ed., *Latina/o Communication Studies* (New York: Peter Lang, 2008), 9.

63. Rodríguez, *Queer Latinidad,* 27

64. Michael Warner, introduction to *Fear of a Queer Planet* (Minneapolis: University of Minnesota Press, 1993), xiii.

65. For an example of what reading queerly entails for academic analysis, see Alexander Doty, *Making Things Perfectly Queer: Interpreting Mass Culture* (Minneapolis: University of Minnesota Press, 1993) and Stacy Wolf, *A Problem Like Maria: Gender and Sexuality in the American Musical* (Ann Arbor: University of Michigan Press, 2002).

66. E. Patrick Johnson, "'Quare' Studies, or (Almost) Everything I Know about Queer Studies I Learned from My Grandmother," *Text and Performance Quarterly* 21.1 (2001): 1–25.

67. For another important critique of queer theory, also cited in Johnson's article, see Cathy Cohen, "Punks, Bulldaggers, and Welfare Queens: The Radical Potential of Queer Politics?" *GLQ* 3 (1997): 437–65.

68. Johson, "Quare," 10.

69. See E. Patrick Johnson, *Appropriating Blackness: Performance and the Politics of Authenticity* (Durham, NC: Duke University Press, 2003) and José E. Muñoz, *Disidentifications: Queers of Color and the Performance of Politics* (Minneapolis: University of Minnesota Press, 1999).

70. On the intersections of queer theory and migration studies, see Martin Mana-

lansan IV, "Queer Intersections: Sexuality and Gender in Migration Studies," *International Migration Review* 40.1 (2006): 224–49.

71. I use the term "traveling subjects" as an adaptation of James Clifford's important discussion of traveling cultures. See James Clifford, *Routes: Travel and Translation in the Late Twentieth Century* (Cambridge: Harvard University Press, 1997).

72. Queer theorist Judith Halberstam offers an apt critique of the tendency to situate queer cultures exclusively within urban spaces. See Judith Halberstam, *In Queer Time and Space: Transgender Bodies, Subcultural Lives* (New York: New York University Press, 2005), 35–36. For exemplary scholarship on rural queer studies, see Scott Herring, *Another Country: Queer Anti-urbanism* (New York: New York University Press, 2010). For work on queer suburbia, see Karen Tongson, *Relocations: Emergent Queer Suburban Imaginaries* (New York: New York University Press, 2011).

73. Anthropologist Martin Manalansan has observed that "sexual marginals experience their displacements as part of this global ecumene in particular ways." See Martin Manalansan IV, "Diasporic Deviants/Divas: How Filipino Gay Transmigrants 'Play with the World," in Cindy Patton and Benigno Sánchez-Eppler, eds., *Queer Diasporas* (Durham, NC: Duke University Press, 2000), 185. See also Brad Epps, *Passing Lines: Sexuality and Immigration* (Cambridge, MA: David Rockefeller Center for Latin American Studies, 2005).

74. Lionel Cantú Jr., *The Sexuality of Migration: Border Crossings and Mexican Immigrant Men,* ed. Nancy A. Naples and Salvador Vidal-Ortiz (New York: New York University Press, 2009), 142.

75. Gloria Anzaldúa discusses the slippage between homophobia and home in *Borderlands / La Frontera* (San Francisco: Aunt Lute Press, 1999). See especially: "Fear of Going Home: Homophobia," 41.

76. For a media studies assessment of these representations, see Mary Beth Oliver, "Race and Crime in the Media: Research from a Media Effects Perspective," in Angharad N. Valdivia, ed., *A Companion to Media Studies* (Malden, MA: Blackwell, 2003), 421–26.

77. Michel de Certeau,. *The Practice of Everyday Life,* trans. Steven Rendall (Berkeley: University of California Press, 1984), 117.

78. Priscilla Peña-Ovalle's book *Dance and the Hollywood Latina: Race, Sex, and Stardom* (New Brunswwick, NJ: Rutgers University Press, 2011) is an important addition to the field focused primarily on the representation of Latina dancers on the Hollywood screen.

79. Andrew Hewitt, *Social Choreography: Ideology as Performance in Dance and Everyday Movement* (Durham, NC: Duke University Press, 2005), 12.

80. Randy Martin, *Critical Moves: Dance Studies in Theory and Politics* (Durham, NC: Duke University Press, 1998).

81. Susan Leigh Foster, "Choreographies of Protest," *Theatre Journal* 55.3 (2003): 412.

82. For a panoramic introduction to performance and to the field of performance studies with a sampler of representative scholarship in the field, see D. Soyini Madison and Judith Hamera, eds., *Sage Handbook of Performance Studies* (Thousand Oaks, CA: Sage, 2006).

83. Anthropologist Victor Turner defines these structured events of performance exchange as cultural performances. Cultural performances are announced as public events within a defined framework understood by all participating. Turner divides performance into three different categories: cultural performance, social performance, and social drama. See Victor Turner, *From Ritual to Theater: The Human Sciences of Play* (New York: Performing Arts, 1982).

84. Erving Goffman, *The Presentation of Self in Everyday Life* (New York: Anchor, 1959).

85. Pierre Bourdieu, *Distinction: A Social Critique of the Judgement of Taste,* trans. Richard Nice (Cambridge: Harvard University Press, 1987).

86. Richard Schechner, *Performance Theory,* 2nd ed. (New York: Routledge, 1994).

87. This formulation is echoed in David Savran's exhortation to develop a sociological methodology for the study of theater. See his "Choices Made and Unmade," *Theater* 3.2 (2001): 89–95.

88. Schechner, *Performance Theory,* 169.

89. See Elin Diamond, introduction to *Performance and Cultual Politics* (New York: Routledge, 1996), 1–14.

90. I draw here from Michael Warner's thinking on counterpublics. I develop this argument in the next chapter. See his *Publics and Counterpublics* (New York: Zone, 2005).

91. Jill Dolan, *Utopia in Performance: Finding Hope at the Theater* (Ann Arbor: University of Michigan Press, 2005).

92. Dolan, *Utopia in Performance,* 5.

93. For a beautiful and thoughtful account of the importance of these public sex spaces, see Samuel R. Delaney, *Times Square Red, Times Square Blue* (New York: New York University Press, 1999). For a discussion of the transformation of Times Square by family-friendly retail and theater, see Maurya Wickstrom, "Commodities, Mimesis, and *The Lion King*: Retail Theater for the 1990s," *Theatre Journal* 51.3 (1999): 285–98.

94. Tsing centers friction in her ethnographic work in global connections in Indonesia. See Ana Lowenhaupt Tsing, *Friction: An Ethnography of Global Connection* (Princeton, NJ: Princeton University Press, 2005).

95. Milagros Ricourt and Ruby Danta, *Hispanas de Queens: Latino Panethnicity in a New York City Neighborhood* (Ithaca, NY: Cornell University Press, 2003), xi.

96. Arjun Appadurai, "Grassroots Globalization and the Research Imagination," *Public Culture* 12.1 (2000): 3.

97. Jill Dolan, "Performance, Utopia and the 'Utopian Performative,'" *Theatre Journal* 53.3 (2001): 478.

Chapter 2

1. Brent Owens, Director, *Hookers at the Point: Five Years Later,* 2002.

2. Cited in Douglas Gillison, "Close-up on Hunts Point," *Village Voice,* February 4, 2003, http://www.villagevoice.com/2003-2-4/nyc-life/close-up-on-hunts-point/ (accessed on August 28, 2009).

3. Arthur Aviles Typical Theatre, *Arturella*, 1996.

4. Cass Gilbert (1859–1934) was a prominent American architect best known as an early proponent of the skyscraper. He designed landmark projects such as the Woolworth Building in New York City, the state capitol buildings for Minnesota and West Virginia, and the U.S. Supreme Court building. His stylistic approach ranged from neoclassical to neogothic and drew optimistically from the history of European architectural traditions as a way of connecting American notions of progress with an imagined legacy of "great civilization." For more on Gilbert, see Marta Heilburn, ed., *Inventing the Skyline: The Architecture of Cass Gilbert* (New York: Columbia University Press, 2000).

5. For a history of the Bronx that includes an account of Hunts Point's affluent past and struggles with economic decline since the 1940s, see Evelyn Diaz Gonzalez, *The Bronx* (New York: Columbia University Press, 2004) and Jill Jonnes, *South Bronx Rising: The Rise, Fall, and Resurrection of an American City* (New York: Fordham University Press, 2002).

6. Hunts Point was primarily an area of wealthy estates and farmlands until the early 1930s. Working-class Jewish, Irish, and Italian settlers, most of whom worked in Manhattan, developed modest housing in the area as an alternative to the higher cost of living in the city once the subway lines made the area accessible. Businesses soon followed, but with the departure of much of this population to newer housing stock made available further north in the borough and in suburban locations such as Long Island, the economy stalled soon after the end of World War II. See Gary Hermalyn and Lloyd Ultan, "One Hundred Years of the Bronx," *Bronx County Historical Society Journal* 35.2 (1998): 63–68.

7. 2000 U.S. census. Summary data accessed through the New York City's Department of City Planning Census Fact Finder: http://www.nyc.gov/html/dcp/ (accessed on August 28, 2009).

8. Hunts Point Community Profile presented by the Hunts Point Development Corporation, http://www.hpedc.org (accessed on August 28, 2009).

9. The global South refers to the countries in the Southern Hemisphere, including the regions of Africa, Central and South America, and most of Asia. The broad geographical designation seeks to identify the large group of nations generally positioned on the receiving end of global political and economic decision-making. Comparative economic "underdevelopment" is generally cited as the primary shared characteristic of this geographical expanse. This distinction generally extends the maps of historic European colonization and its concomitant extension in USAmerican neoimperialism. For scholarship dedicated to the comparative understanding of this broad region, see Indiana University Press's journal *The Global South*.

10. For a discussion of the economic transformation of Manhattan, see Saskia Sassen, *The Global City: New York, London, Tokyo* (Princeton, NJ: Princeton University Press, 1991).

11. Owens's films include *Hookers at the Point* (1996); *Hookers at the Point: Goin' Out Again* (1997), and *Hookers at the Point: Five Years Later* (2002).

12. As early as 1972, urban geographers Michael R. Greenberg and Thomas D. Boswell suggested that the negative perception of neighborhoods like Hunts Point may have been primary factors in outward intracity migration from the area. See Green-

berg and Boswell, "Neighborhood Deterioration as a Factor in Intraurban Migration: A Case Study in New York City," *Professional Geographer* 24.1 (1972): 11–16.

13. French sociologist Pierre Bourdieu introduced the term to refer to the advantages gained by subjects by sheer participation in social networks. See Pierre Bourdieu, "The Forms of Capital," in J. G. Richardson, ed., *Handbook of Theory and Research in the Sociology of Education* (New York: Greenwood Press, 1985), 241–58.

14. 2000 U.S. census.

15. 2000 U.S. census figures show that 30.7 percent individuals and 28 percent of families in the Bronx live under poverty level. These figures are higher for the residential core of Hunts Point, where close to 56 percent of the population qualifies for some form of financial assistance through city, state, or federal programs.

16. 2000 U.S. census. Summary data accessed through the New York City's Department of City Planning Census Fact Finder: http://www.nyc.gov/html/dcp/ (accessed on August 28, 2009).

17. For a discussion of the economic transformation of Manhattan and its particular pressures on historically low-income housing see Sassen, *The Global City*.

18. Dean Brackley, "South Bronx: Past Destruction and the Rebuilding Process, The Symposium on Poverty and the Law," *Harvard Civil Rights–Civil Liberties Law Review* 22.1 (1987): n. 16.

19. Brackley, "South Bronx," 4.

20. See Jill Jonnes's *South Bronx Rising*. In his account of community organizing in the South Bronx, Jim Rooney offers a compelling analysis of the conditions that led to the region's economic downfall, including rapid deindustrialization and federal government housing regulations that provided incentives for single-family housing development for returning veterans and froze rents, leaving property owners without resources to maintain increasingly deteriorating properties. See Jim Rooney, *Organizing the South Bronx* (Albany: State University of New York Press, 1995).

21. See Marilyn Adler Papayanis, "Sex and the Revanchist City: Zoning Out Pornography in New York," *Environment and Planning D: Society and Space* 18 (2000): 341–53.

22. See Brian Sahd, "Community Development Corporations and Social Capital," in Robert Mark Silverman, ed., *Community-based Organizations: The Intersection of Social Capital and Local Context in Contemporary Urban Society* (Detroit: Wayne State University Press, 2004), 90. The Community Action Program was a federally funded component of the 1964 Economic Opportunity Act signed into law by President Lyndon B. Johnson. Designed to fight poverty by promoting self-sufficiency, the program distributed block grants in areas such as health, education, housing, labor, and justice. Most of the programs sponsored under this act have been heavily modified or eliminated since, especially through the Omnibus Reconciliation Act of 1981, which resulted from President Ronald Reagan's request to reduce eighty-five different antipoverty grant programs into nine broad categories with significantly smaller budgets than initially allocated. In the case of housing, funding continues to be provided through the Community Services Block Grants program administered through the Office of Community Services in the Administration for Children and Families of the Department of Health and Human Services. The Model Cities program was also a component program of Lyndon Johnson's "Great Society" legislation targeting urban development

and social services. Authorized through the 1966 Demonstration Cities and Metropolitan Development Act, this program was designed to offer economic assistance to blighted urban areas. The Housing and Urban Development (HUD) program was a component of this act. For a historical account of the block grants programs, see Kenneth Feingold, Laura Wherry, and Stephanie Schardin, "Block Grants: Historical Overview and Lessons Learned," Urban Institute whitepaper in *New Federalisms: Issues and Options of the States Series* A, no. A-63 (April 21, 2004).

23. See Sahd, "Community Development."

24. Barretto Street Park, 1975.

25. Baretto Street Garden, n.d.

26. For information on the Barretto Street Garden (636 Barretto St.), see Peter Stein, "Criteria for Urban Land Trusts," in Russell L. Brenneman and Sarah M. Bates, eds., *Land-Saving Action: A Written Symposium by 29 Experts on Private Land Conservation in the 1980s* (Covelo, CA: Conservation Law Foundation of New England / Island Press, 1984), 48–52; and Mark Francis, Lisa Cachan, and Lynn Paxson, *Community Open Spaces: Greening Neighborhoods through Community Action and Land Conservation* (Covelo, CA: Island Press, 1984). For a profile of the Barretto Street Garden (645 Barretto St.) see http://www.placematters.net/node/1020.

27. Sahd, "Community Development," 88–89.

28. See Jill Dolan's *Utopia in Performance,* especially chapter 4, "Def Poetry Jam: Performance as Public Practice."

29. Deborah Paredez has been working on a book-length study on this subject tentatively titled *Burn, Break, Boogie: Arts and Activism in the Bronx.*

30. Lawrence M. La Fountain-Stokes, "Dancing *La Vida Loca*: The Queer Nuyorican Performances of Arthur Avilés and Elizabeth Marrero," Arnaldo Cruz-Malavé and Martin F. Manalansan, eds., *Queer Globalizations: Citizenship and the Afterlife of Colonialism* (New York: New York University Press, 2002), 166.

31. Juan Flores, *Divided Borders: Essays on Puerto Rican Identity* (Houston: Arte Público Press, 1993), 176.

32. Tato Laviera, *La Carreta Made a U-turn* (Houston: Arte Público Press, 1992), 16.

33. Homi Bhabha, *The Location of Culture* (London: Routledge, 1994).

34. For a discussion of Bill T. Jones's critical engagement with the politics of community, see Ann Daly, "Dancing the Unsayable: Bill T. Jones's *Still/Here* Becomes a Meditation on the Possibilities of Postmodernist Art," *Texas Observer,* March 22, 1996, 18–19. Reprinted in Ann Daly, *Critical Gestures: Writing on Dance and Culture* (Hanover, NH: Wesleyan University Press, 2002), 60–63.

35. Arlene Croce, "Discussing the Undiscussable," *New Yorker.* December 26, 1994, 54–60.

36. Warner, *Publics and Counterpublics,* 11.

37. Jürgen Habermas, *The Structural Transformation of the Public Sphere: An Inquiry into a Category of Bourgeois Society,* trans. Thomas Burger (Cambridge: MIT Press, 1989).

38. Nancy Fraser, "Rethinking the Public Sphere: A Contribution to the Critique of Actually Existing Democracy," in Craig Calhoun, *Habermas and the Public Sphere* (Cambridge: MIT Press, 1992), 109–42.

39. Warner, *Publics and Counterpublics,* 57.

40. Chelsea, a neighborhood in midwest Manhattan, is considered an LGBT community. El Barrio, a neighborhood in northeast Manhattan, is a historic Puerto Rican community. Interestingly, what is now Chelsea contained from the mid-twentieth century onward a significant Puerto Rican population. El Barrio has also seen significant demographic transformation and is currently undergoing rapid gentrification from the south and diversification of its residential Latina/o community as Mexicans, Dominicans, and other groups continue to make the neighborhood home.

41. Luis Aponte-Parés identifies a trend in the development of specifically Latina/o LGBT activist organizations and social spaces within Latina/o neighborhoods in New York City beginning in mid-1980s through the early 1990s. In this study I focus on efforts from the mid-1990s onward. See his essay "Outside/In: Crossing Queer and Latino Boundaries," in Agustín Laó-Montes and Arlene Dávila, eds., *Mambo Montage: The Latinization of New York* (New York: Columbia University Press, 2001), 363–85.

42. Arthur Aviles, in discussion with the author, July 2003.

43. Judith Hamera, *Dancing Communities: Performance, Difference and Connection in the Global City* (Basingstoke: Palgrave Macmillan, 2007).

44. Arthur Aviles, in discussion with the author, July 2003.

45. http://www.thepoint.org.

46. Don Adams and Arlene Goldbard, *Creative Community,* 61.

47. Dan Friedman, "What's the Point?" *Bronx Times Reporter,* October 15, 1998.

48. The New York Dance and Performance Awards (Bessies) have been awarded annually since 1983 in recognition of excellence in the downtown dance scene. The Off-Broadway Theatre Award (Obies) have been awarded annually since 1956 in recognition of excellence in off-Broadway theatre in New York City. Since 1964 the Obies have recognized off-off-Broadway productions for the award.

49. Arthur Aviles, in discussion with the author, July 2003.

50. Warner, *Publics and Counterpublics,* 75.

51. Ricourt and Danta, *Hispanas de Queens,* 56.

52. Cherríe Moraga, *Giving Up the Ghost: Teatro in Two Acts* (Los Angeles: West End Press, 1986), 58.

53. See Richard T. Rodríguez, *Next of Kin: The Family in Chicano/a Cultural Politics* (Durham, NC: Duke University Press, 2009); Marivel T. Danielson, *Homecoming Queers: Desire and Difference in Chicana Latina Cultural Production* (New Brunswick, NJ: Rutgers University Press, 2009); and Sandra K. Soto, *Reading Chican@ Like a Queer: The De-mastery of Desire* (Austin: University of Texas Press, 2010).

54. Rodríguez, *Next of Kin,* 176.

55. The vast majority of the migrants during the 1940s and 1950s were dark-skin Puerto Ricans who were, because of racist hierarchies, the most impoverished sector of the island's population. For an important historic and contemporary assessment of racial identification in Puerto Rican and Latina/o communities in the United States, see Clara E. Rodríguez, *Changing Race: Latinos, the Census, and the History of Ethnicity in the United States* (New York: New York University Press, 2000).

56. Performance studies scholar Jan Cohen Cruz has discussed Aviles's *El Yunque is in the Laundromat* (2005), a site-specific dance piece performed at a neighborhood coin-operated laundry, as part of a broader assessment of socially engaged art prac-

tices in the South Bronx. See Jan Cohen Cruz, ""Twixt Cup and Lip': Intentions and Execution of Community-Based Art as Civic Expression," in Mary Schmidt and Randy Martin, eds., *Artistic Citizenship: A Public Voice for the Arts* (New York: Routledge, 2006), 163–80. See also David Román, "Comment—Theatre Journals," *Theatre Journal* 54.3 (2002): xii–xix; and Ramón H. Rivera-Servera, "Latina/o Queer Futurities: Arthur Aviles Takes on the Bronx," *Ollantay Theatre Magazine* 25.29–30 (2007): 127–46.

57. La Fountain-Stokes, *Queer Ricans*; "A Naked Puerto Rican Faggot from America: An Interview with Arthur Avilés," *Centro Journal* 19.1 (2007): 314–29; "Dancing *La Vida Loca*."

58. La Fountain-Stokes, *Queer Ricans*, 132.

59. Adams and Goldbard, *Creative Community*, 13.

60. Ann Daly, "When Dancers Move onto Making Dances," *New York Times*, April 6, 1997, C12.

61. *El Pato Feo* cowritten by Marlyn Matias and produced by Arthur Aviles Typical Theater (AATT) and the Point Community Development Corporation. It premiered at the Bronx Academy of Arts and Dance in 2000 and was presented at Dixon Place, an alternative performance venue in downtown Manhattan, later that year. *Maeva de Oz*, written and choreographed by Arthur Aviles, premiered at the Point in 1997. It was restaged with revisions as *Super Maeva de Oz* at BAAD in 2000.

62. Arthur Aviles, in discussion with the author, July 2003.

63. Ramona Fernandez, "Pachuco Mickey," in Elizabeth Bell, Lynda Haas, and Laura Sells, eds., *From Mouse to Mermaid: The Politics of Film, Gender, and Culture* (Bloomington: Indiana University Press, 1995), 248.

64. *Arturella* was developed at the Point and premiered at Hostos Community College in 1996. The piece was performed by Arthur Aviles as Arturella; Elizabeth Marrero as the Evil Stepmother, Maeva the narrator, and the King; and Jorge Merced as the Prince. The ensemble included Ben Quiñones, Mildred Ruiz, Steven Sap, Richard Baretto, Maria Torres, Paul Lipson, Malina Mckale, Pepper and Angel Rodriguez. Costumes designed by Liz Prince. The piece was restaged in February 2003 at the Dance Theater Workshop in Manhattan. All citations are from video documentation of the Hostos Community College performance. For reviews of the piece, see Jennifer Dunning, "New Spin on 'Cinderella': Prince Finds a Dream Guy," *New York Times*, November 5, 1996, C16; and Anna Kisselgoff, "'Cinderella' Set in a Puerto Rican Ghetto," *New York Times*, February 3, 2003, C6.

65. Teatro Pregones is a Bronx-based Latina/o experimental theater troupe. Merced has become well known for his performance of *Loca de La Locura*, an adaptation of Puerto Rican queer writer Manuel Ramos Otero's short story about a transsexual convict imprisoned for murdering her lover. For more information on Teatro Pregones, see Eva Vasquez's *Pregones Theatre: A Theatre for Social Change in the South Bronx* (New York: Routledge, 2003).

66. A Sweet Sixteen celebration would be the U.S. equivalent. The *quinceañero* has been used in previous queer performance including Paul Bonin-Rodriguez, Beto Araiza, and Michael Marinez's *Quinceañera*, which premiered at Jump Start Performance Space in San Antonio, Texas, and toured nationally during 1998–99. The script can be found in Roberta Uno and Lucy Mae San Burns, eds., *The Color of Theater: Race, Cul-*

ture, and Contemporary Performance (New York: Continuum Press, 2002), 261–301. See also Alberto Sandoval-Sánchez's essay "Quinceañera: A Latino Queer and Transcultural Party for AIDS," in the same volume (303–12).

67. See Molineu, *U.S. Policy toward Latin America*.

68. See Charles Ramírez Berg, *Latino Images in Film: Stereotypes, Subversion, and Resistance* (Austin: University of Texas Press, 2002).

69. See Alberto Sandoval-Sánchez's *José Can You See?* for a discussion of Broadway and early Hollywood's relationship to the Good Neighbor Policy. See also Julianne Burton's important essay "Don (Juanito) Duck and the Imperial-Patriarchal Unconscious: Disney Studios, the Good Neighbor Policy, and the Packaging of Latin America," in Andrew Parker, Vito Russo, Doris Sommer, Patricia Yaeger, eds., *Nationalisms and Sexualities* (New York: Routledge, 1992).

70. Henry A. Giroux, *The Mouse That Roared: Disney and the End of Innocence* (Lanham, MD: Rowman & Littlefield, 1999), 126.

71. I attended the 1996 performance at Hostos Community College. At the time I was not researching Latina/o performance; my analysis of this piece is based on my recollections of that event and video documentation provided by the artist.

72. Elizabeth Marrero began her performance career as a drag king in New York City's Latina lesbian bar scene. After an initial collaboration with Arthur Aviles in *Maeva: A Puerto Rican Ensalada* in which the character of Maeva was developed, she has continued to collaborate in AATT productions. She has also gone on to develop solo performances of her own that have premiered at BAAD.

73. The critical side of this equation reads more poignantly in the Dance Theater Workshop performances where audience members looked at the representation of the Bronx from a downtown New York perspective.

74. "It's OK baby, 'cause I'm gonna hook you up!"

75. "What do you think, that this is a big Broadway production?"

76. La Fountain-Stokes, "Nyorico," 168.

77. Ricardo Trancoso, "Dancer Sheds Inhibitions (& Clothes) at Hostos," *Bronx Times Reporter*, 1996.

78. *This Pleasant and Grateful Asylum* was premiered at the Bronx Academy of Arts and Dance in 1999.

79. Arthur Aviles Typical Theater, promotional packet.

80. The reaction of the audience was evident even in the video recording. In conversation with Aviles I learned that this reaction was not exclusive to my experience of the piece but is a common one whenever it is performed in the Bronx and elsewhere.

81. The stereotype of the Latino gang member is a recurrent representation in gay and straight pornography. See for example the productions of the Latino Fan Club.

82. It is important to note here that although from the perspective of experimental queer theater history these acts may not represent much of a groundbreaking or revolutionary model of performance practice, within its local context in Latino South Bronx it constitutes a serious, even radical, political intervention.

83. Ann Cooper Albright, *Choreographing Difference: The Body and Identity in Contemporary Dance* (Hanover, NH: Wesleyan University Press, 1997), 149.

84. Arthur Aviles, in discussion with the author, July 2003.

85. Shannon Jackson, *Social Works: Performing Art, Supporting Publics* (London: Routledge, 2011).

86. Arthur Aviles, in discussion with the author, July 2003.

87. In conversation he explained, "One thing I have to say about BAAD is that it comes out of the struggles of the 1960s when our parents struggled to make sure they had a place in the community that they come to and that they felt they owned. It's theirs, too." Arthur Aviles in discussion with the author, July 2003.

88. Arthur Aviles in discussion with the author, July 2003.

89. Arthur Aviles in discussion with the author, July 2003.

90. Román, "Comment—Theatre Journals," xv.

91. Arthur Aviles in discussion with the author, July 2003.

Chapter 3

1. Graciela I. Sánchez, "La Cultura, la Comunidad, la Familia, y la Libertad," in Antonia Castañeda, Susan H. Armitage, Patricia Hart, and Karen Weathermon, eds., *Gender on the Borderlands: The Frontiers Reader* (Lincoln: University of Nebraska Press, 2007), 79.

2. Ann Cvetkovich, *An Archive of Feelings: Trauma, Sexuality, and Lesbian Public Cultures* (Durham, NC: Duke University Press, 2003).

3. San Antonio counts with the largest concentration of Spanish missions within the U.S. territory. These include Mission San José, Mission Concepción, Mission San Juan, and Mission Espada. The Alamo is also mission in the original Spanish colonial plan but stands as an iconic site on its own in the tourist maps of the city. Tourists traveling through the missions often experience the Catholic mass with mariachi and other folkloric entertainments.

4. See Lisa Duggan, "The New Homonormativity: The Sexual Politics of Neoliberalism," in Russ Castronova and Dana D. Nelson, eds., *Materializing Democracy: Toward a Revitalized Cultural Politics* (Durham, NC: Duke University Press, 2002), 175–94; David Greene, "Why Protect Political Art as 'Political Speech?'" *Hastings Communications and Entertainment Law Journal* 27.2 (2004–5): 359–82; and Sarah F. Warren, "Art: To Fund or Not to Fund? That Is *Still* the Question," *Cardozo Arts and Entertainment Law Journal* 19.1 (2001): 149–81.

5. Susana M. Guerra, "Semillas de Milagro," *La Voz de Esperanza* 19.10 (2006–7): 5.

6. Hannah Arendt, *The Human Condition* (Chicago: University of Chicago Press, 1958).

7. The term "political affect" is critically developed in John Protevi's *Political Affect: Connecting the Social and the Somatic* (Minneapolis: University of Minnesota Press, 2009).

8. Barack Obama, *The Audacity of Hope: Thoughts on Reclaiming the American Dream* (New York: Crown/Three Rivers Press, 2006).

9. Jeremiah Wright, "The Audacity to Hope," audio file and transcript, 1990, http://www.preachingtoday.com/sermons/outlines/2010/july/theaudacitytohope.html (accessed February 28, 2011).

10. Performance theorist Jill Dolan explains practiced hope in her theorization of the "utopian performative," which I discuss extensively in chapter 4. Attending to philosopher Ernst Bloch's discussion of hope in his understanding of humanism, she

states: "The performatives I'm engaging here aren't iterations of what *is*, but trans-formative doings of what *if*. This kind of hope represents an opening up, rather than a closing down, of consciousness of the past and the future in the present; this kind of hope relies on the active doing of faith, which too often, too daily, I feel slip when I listen to the radio or read the newspaper. Hope, like faith, demands continual reaf-firmation; theater gives me faith and persistently shores up my ability to hope." See Dolan, *Utopia in Performance*, 141.

11. Anzaldúa and Moraga, *This Bridge*, 23

12. Antonia I. Castañeda, "Respect and Defend Our Democratic Rights: Commu-nity Support for Esperanza Litigation," *La Voz de Esperanza* 11.7 (1998): 4.

13. *Esperanza v. City of San Antonio*, Civil Action Case SA98CA0696-OG, U.S. Dis-trict Court, Western District of Texas, San Antonio Division. For journalistic accounts of the defunding see Barbara Renáud-González, "Remembering the Alamo, Part II," *The Nation*, http://www.thenation.com/article/remember-alamo-part-ii?page=0,1 (ac-cessed March 15, 1999); Dianne Monroe, "The Art of DeFunding: An Examination of the Forces That Caused City Council to Deny Taxpayer Money to the Esperanza Peace and Justice Center," *San Antonio Current*, November 6–12, 1997.

14. Until October 2010 Adam McManus hosted his conservative talk show, *Take a Stand*, on weekdays 3:00–6:00 p.m. on KSLR, 630 AM in San Antonio.

15. Esperanza Center had been previously targeted and had some of its funds cut (as early as 1994) by conservative activists and politicians. Then city councilman How-ard Peak was one of the most vocal legislators opposing the political nature of Esper-anza's work and challenging its status as an arts organization.

16. Linda Kintz, *Between Jesus and the Market: The Emotions That Matter in Right-Wing America* (Durham, NC: Duke University Press, 1997), 17.

17. The flyer was presented during the legal case as evidence of the hostile environ-ment under which the defunding decision took place. See records of the *Esperanza v. City of San Antonio* case for more information. Martha Breeden, executive director of the Christian Pro-Life Foundation, testified in court that she had indeed designed and distributed the flyer to approximately 1,200 of her supporting members (Breeden Deposition, at 38–39, 47–48)

18. For an important discussion of right-wing activism and performance, see Peggy Phelan, "White Men and Pregnancy: Discovering the Body to be Rescued," in *Un-marked: The Politics of Performance* (New York: Routledge, 1993). Her analysis sheds light on the circulation of alarmist discourses by the Right and the authoritative claims to representation that antiabortion activists recur to in relation to women's bodies. For an extensive study of antiabortion activism, see Faye Ginsburg, "Saving America's Souls: Operation Rescue's Crusade against Abortion," in Martin Marty and R. Scott Applebee, *Fundamentalists and the State: Remaking Politics, Economies, and Militants* (Chicago: University of Chicago Press, 1992).

19. Esperanza Center was expected to receive close to $76,000 in arts grants for op-erational as well as programming costs for the 1998 fiscal year. The Esperanza Center served as the fiscal sponsor for two of the affiliated organizations: Out at the Movies and VAN. The San Antonio Lesbian and Gay Media Project sponsored the Out At the Movies Film Festival, which was the primary target of anti-Esperanza activists. The

San Antonio Lesbian and Gay Media Project was recommended to receive a $7,000 allocation for the 1998 film festival. VAN functioned as a networking organization busing artists and other cultural practitioners visiting Texas to the San Antonio region for public programs. Artists that benefited from this arrangement included nationally known queer performance artists Peggy Shaw, Lois Weaver, Alina Troyano aka Carmelita Tropicana, and others.

20. Exh. 5, DACA Strategic Plan; Diaz Deposition, at 3–5, 9, 11–12, 16–18, 28–29, 25; see also Exh. 3, Blue Ribbon Commission for the Arts Report to City Council, August, 1998, at 1; Exh. 8, Peer Panel Handbook; Exh. 4, Resolution No. 98-8-5 February 26, 1998.

21. Judith H. Dobrzynski, "San Antonio Reduces Aid to the Arts by 15 Percent," *New York Times,* September 13, 1997, A17.

22. Tomás Ybarra-Frausto, a senior Chicano scholar, testified on the historical role of politics in the arts and especially within the Chicano/Latino tradition. His argument was fundamental in challenging the easy disqualification of Esperanza's work as not belonging to the realm of artistic practice. See Ybarra-Frausto's Deposition (TR 482–87, 489), *Esperanza v. City of San Antonio.*

23. Dobrzynski , "San Antonio Reduces Aid."

24. Cvetkovich, *An Archive of Feelings, 7.*

25. *Esperanza vs. City of San Antonio,* plaintiff exhibit P-54.

26. *Esperanza vs. City of San Antonio,* plaintiff exhibit P-54.

27. *Esperanza vs City of San Antonio,* plaintiff exhibit P-54.

28. The law against same-sex sodomy was not struck down until the *Lawrence v. Texas* U.S. Supreme Court decision in 2003.

29. *Esperanza v City of San Antonio,* plaintiff exhibit P-54.

30. Gilbert Herdt, "Introduction: Moral Panics, Sexual Rights, and Cultural Anger," in Gilbert Herdt, ed., *Moral Panics, Sex Panics: Fear and the Fight Over Sexual Rights* (New York University Press, 2009), 4.

31. Herdt, *Moral Panics,* 5.

32. See John O'Neill, "AIDS as a Globalizing Panic," in *Global Culture: Nationalism, Globalization and Modernity* (London: Sage, 1990), 329–42.

33. See Adam McManu's website for this and other comments: http://www.takeast and.net/adamsstands.asp (accessed August 10, 2007).

34. See Barbara Browning, *Infectious Rhythm: Metaphors of Contagion and the Spread of African Culture* (New York: Routledge, 1998) for a discussion of race and AIDS contagion in the African diaspora.

35. David Montejano, *Anglos and Mexicans in the Making of Texas, 1836–1896* (Austin: University of Texas Press, 1987), 1.

36. Montejano, *Anglos and Mexicans,* 1.

37. Richard Flores, *Remembering the Alamo: Memory, Modernity and the Master Symbol* (Austin: University of Texas Press, 2002), 34.

38. Flores, *Remembering the Alamo,* 34.

39. Sianne Ngai, *Ugly Feelings* (Cambridge: Harvard University Press, 2005).

40. See Daniel D. Arreola, *Tejano South Texas: A Mexican American Cultural Province* (Austin: University of Texas Press, 2002) and *Arnoldo De León, Tejano Community, 1836–1900* (Albuquerque: University of New Mexico Press, 1982).

41. Raquel R. Marquéz, Louis Mendoza, and Steve Blanchard, "Neighborhood Formation on the West Side of San Antonio, Texas," *Latino Studies* 5 (2007): 296.

42. They also argue that barriological factors, or the positive elements resulting from cohabitation at the margins, also shape the development of communities.

43. See Robert B. Fairbanks, "The Texas Exception: San Antonio and Urban Renewal, 1949–1965," *Journal of Planning History* 1.2 (2002): 181–96.

44. Miguel de Oliver, "Marketing Latinos as Development Policy: San Antonio and the Reproduction of Underprivilege," *Latino Studies* 2 (2004): 402.

45. See http://thesanantonioriverwalk.com for additional historical information as well as current programming in San Antonio's tourist district.

46. Richard Flores, *Los Pastores: History and Performance in the Mexican Shepherd's Play of South Texas* (Washington, DC: Smithsonian Institution Press, 1995), 160.

47. I do not mean to suggest that these performances are completely devoid of agency. For a discussion of agency within tourist performance see Christopher B. Balme "Staging the Pacific: Framing Authenticity in Performances for Tourists at the Polynesian Cultural Center," *Theater Journal* 50.1 (1998): 70.

48. See Barbara Kirshenblatt-Gimblett, *Destination Cultures: Tourism, Museums, and Heritage* (Berkeley: University of California Press, 1998).

49. De Oliver, 402.

50. Lisa Duggan and José Esteban Muñoz. "Hope and Hopelesness: A Dialogue," *In Women & Performance* 19.2 (2009): 275–83.

51. Graciela Sánchez, in discussion with the author, San Antonio, March 19, 2001.

52. Renáud-González, "Remembering the Alamo, Part II."

53. The Peace Market is an annual sale of arts and crafts, many of them created in many of Esperanza's programs hosted at the Center.

54. See José Limón, *Dancing with the Devil: Society and Cultural Poetics in Mexican-American South Texas* (Madison: University of Wisconsin Press, 1994).

55. Bárbara Renáud-González, "The Trial of Our Lives," *La Voz de Esperanza* 13.7 (2000): 3.

56. Graciela Sánchez, in discussion with the author, San Antonio, March 2001.

57. In *Geographies of Learning*, Jill Dolan stresses the need for activist communities in politics, theater, and the academy to translate the specialized knowledge produced within disciplinary boundaries in order to make the process of politics more accessible and efficient. *Geographies of Learning: Theory and Practice, Activism and Performance* (Middletown, CT: Wesleyan University Press, 2001).

58. Virginia Grise, in discussion with the author, San Antonio, March 21, 2001.

59. D. Soyini Madison, *Acts of Activism: Human Rights as Radical Performance* (Cambridge: Cambridge University Press, 2010), 5.

60. See Jorge Huerta, *Chicano Theater: Themes and Forms* (Ypsilanti, MI: Bilingual Press, 1982);Yolanda Broyles-González, *El Teatro Campesino: Theater in the Chicano Movement* (Austin: University of Texas Press, 1994); and Harry Elam Jr., *Taking It to the Streets: The Social Protest Theater of Luis Valdez and Amiri Baraka* (Ann Arbor: University of Michigan Press, 2001). Another notable troupe was Teatro de la Esperanza in Santa Barbara, CA.

61. Teatro Mascarrones performed political theater in Mexico during the height of the student movement in the early 1970s.

62. Pete Haney, in discussion with the author, March 19, 2001.

63. In the 1970s San Antonio became an important center for the Chicana/o movement arts programs. The Guadalupe Arts Center on the west side of the city hosted important national theater festivals.

64. Jorge Huerta, *Chicano Drama: Performance, Society and Myth* (Cambridge: Cambridge University Press, 2000), 3.

65. Teatro Callejero's appeal was its perception as tradition. As Haney explained, "I felt at times that we were doing *teatro* because we thought it was important to do *teatro* and not necessarily because we thought *teatro* was going to be what got us on television. There was a strong sense that we just did it because of what it meant for the community." Pete Haney, in discussion with the author, March 19, 2001.

66. Originally a *corrido* of Spanish origin, "La Cucaracha" became a popular song during the Mexican Revolution. Since then it has served a dual function as popular Mexican tradition and U.S. iconic stereotype.

67. Imported from the United Kingdom, *Who Wants to Be a Millionaire* first aired in the United States in 1999. Regis Philbin was the original host for the program. Margaret Viera assumed the position in 2002.

68. Jan Cohen Cruz, *Local Acts: Community-Based Performance in the United States* (New Brunswick, NJ: Rutgers University Press, 2005), 84.

69. Virginia Grise, "Teatro Callejero," *La Voz de Esperanza* 13.7 (2000): 14.

70. See Tim Miller and David Román, "Preaching to the Converted, "*Theatre Journal* 47.2 (1995): 169–88.

71. Jane C. Desmond, *Staging Tourism: Bodies on Display from Waikiki to Sea World* (Chicago: University of Chicago Press, 1999), 251.

72. Foster, "Choreographies of Protest,"408.

Chapter 4

1. This chapter developed out of ethnographic research conducted in eight different dance clubs in Austin, San Antonio, New York City, and Rochester from 1998 to 2003. Three clubs were identified as Latina/o gay clubs; the other five clubs were identified as mainstream gay clubs (often this meant a primarily Anglo clientele). The interviewees here cited were selected through a combination of snowball sampling and on-site solicitation. Formal interviews were conducted by appointment outside of the club premises. A total of twenty-eight initial interviews were conducted, with an additional eleven follow-up interviews. Initial interviews ran from fifteen to forty-five minutes. Additional information was gathered from interviewed informants and others not formally interviewed through participant observation at the clubs. The data relayed in this book have been selected as representative sample after coding for frequency of themes. Informants have been assigned substitute names in order to protect their privacy.

2. Florida, *Rise of the Creative Class.*

3. See Ernest Sternberg, "The Sectoral Cluster in Economic Development Policy: Lessons from Rochester and Buffalo, New York," *Economic Development Quarterly* 5.4 (1991): 342–56.

4. See Lara Becker Liu, "Puerto Ricans Build on Rich History in Rochester," *Rochester Democrat and Chronicle*, February 26, 2006 (accessed online May 10, 2010).

5. Dolan, "Utopia, Performance," 455.

6. In Puerto Rico and other Spanish-speaking regions of the Americas the *piropo* has become a repertoire of courtship phrases that range from elegant poetry to crass, but creative, harassment. These advances are not always read as offensive.

7. A similar aesthetic of Latino masculinity may be observed in the tradition of the zoot suit in the southwest United States.

8. See Ricourt and Danta, *Hispanas de Queens*.

9. In her discussion of Danny Guerrero's solo performance *¡Gaytino!* literary critic Rita Urquijo uses the concept of the "queer comfort zone" as a space "created and inhabited by a Chicana/o and Latina/o queer subject after negotiating his/her conflicts" (148). While I do not agree with the notion of a resolved identity position suggested in her analysis, I find the concept useful to imply a temporary moment of comfort or rest where the subject may satisfy one or more aspects of his/her self. See Rita E. Urquijo-Ruiz, "Comfortably Queer: The Chicano Gay Subject in Dan Guerrero's *¡Gaytino!*" *Ollantay Theater Magazine* 25.29–30 (2007): 147–67.

10. See Winifred Curran, "Gentrification and the Nature of Work: Exploring the Links in Williamsburg, Brooklyn," *Environment and Planning A* 36. 7 (2004): 1243–58.

11. I frequented these bars between 1991 and 1999.

12. See David Diebold, *Tribal Rites: San Francisco's Dance Music Phenomenon* (Northridge, CA: Time Warp, 1986); and Richard Dyer, *Only Entertainment* (New York: Routledge, 1992).

13. See Walter Hughes, "In the Empire of the Beat: Discipline and Disco," in Andrew Ross and Tricia Rose, eds., *Microphone Friends: Youth Music and Youth Culture* (New York: Routledge, 1994), 147–57.

14. Jonathan Bollen, "Queer Kinesthesia: Performativity on the Dance Floor," in Jane C. Desmond, ed., *Dancing Desires: Choreographing Sexualities On and Off the Stage* (Madison: University of Wisconsin Press, 2001), 287.

15. While carnival has been traditionally accepted as a temporary break from tradition in ways that allow for public displays of sexuality (although not always queer sexuality), gay and lesbian dance clubs have historically developed in relation to aggressive regulatory restrictions against the public display of homosexuality. See Fiona Buckland, *Impossible Dance: Club Culture and Queer World-Making* (Middletown, CT: Wesleyan University Press, 2002), on the crackdown on New York City clubs during the 1990s.

16. Hughes, "Empire of the Beat," 147–48.

17. Bollen, "Queer Kinesthesia," 297.

18. For a discussion of some of these relationships from the perspective of a recent Puerto Rican migrant in one of the clubs discussed in this essay, see Manuel Gúzman, "Pa' la Escuelita con Mucho Cuida'o y por la Orillita: A Journey through the Contested Terrains of Nation and Sexual Orientation," in Frances Negrón-Muntaner and Ramón Grosfogel, eds., *Puerto Rican Jam: Rethinking Colonialism and Nationalism* (Minneapolis: University of Minnesota Press, 1997), 209–28.

19. Gay clubs circulate models of appropriate bodies, ornamentation, and comportment that offer equally hierarchical notions of gay identity that further layer notions of normativity within these locales. See, for example, Fiona Buckland's comparative

study of queer clubs in New York City, *Impossible Dance*. She notes significant differences in expectations of body type, dress code, and class performance among the various gay communities she engaged during her four-year ethnography.

20. In referring to the "world-making" power of club dancing I am indebted to Buckland's coining of the term as the critical point of analysis in *Impossible Dance*. In my own work I seek to address some of the same issues from the perspective of queer Latinas/os.

21. Dolan, "Performance, Utopia," 457.

22. David Román, "Theatre Journals: Dance Liberation," *Theatre Journal* 55.3 (2003): xi.

23. Buckland, *Impossible Dance*, 7.

24. In his discussion of dance and gay liberation, Román observes that in a local bar in Wisconsin "gay men and lesbians were forced to forge alliances for political gain, and . . . met across class, gender, and racial lines to do so." "Theatre Journals," iii.

25. For a recent discussion of queer *latinidad*, see Rodríguez, *Queer Latinidad*.

26. See José E. Muñoz's engagement with queer Latina/o affect in "Feeling Brown."

27. For a foundational theorization of *communitas* in performance, see Turner, *From Ritual to Theatre*. For an application of his theory to African-American and Chicana/o theatre, see Elam, *Taking It to the Streets*.

28. Dolan, "Performance, Utopia," 479.

29. "Sometimes I get scared because my family doesn't know. I sneak out. You know, with my perfume and all . . . but I just say that I'm going to go out and that's it. Then I just rush a couple of blocks and get into Krash!" (All translations are my own.)

30. Nestor is not a go-go boy and does not stand on the platform during his performance.

31. Bollen, "Queer Kinesthesia," 299.

32. In his essay on dance liberation, "Theatre Journals," David Román also mentions that the emergence of community may also be based on the political radicalization of participants who identified as a group based on their marginalization from society and the urgent need for intervention in relation to this position.

33. "Latin" refers here to the music industry label for music produced by Latin American and Latina/o musicians. It also defines the aesthetic codes and conventions of these musical styles and their appropriation and incorporation into other musical practices. John Storm Roberts discusses this phenomena in the Latin music industry up to the 1970s in his study *The Latin Tinge: The Impact of Latin American Music on the United* (New York: Oxford University Press, 1979). He comments that Cuban musical traditions of the nineteenth century influenced greatly the social dance and musical publishing industry throughout Latin America. Through the influence of early Hollywood conceptions of Latin America, this focus on Afro-Caribbean musical tradition developed into a stereotypical characterization of all Latin American–derived cultures through the concept of rhythm and to the expense of the more melody-driven genres of Mexican and South American traditions, with the exception of tango and bolero.

34. Celeste Fraser Delgado and José E. Muñoz, eds., *Everynight Life: Culture and Dance in Latin/o America* (Durham, NC: Duke University Press, 2004), 16.

35. See Fernando Ortiz, *Cuban Counterpoint: Tobacco and Sugar,* trans. Harriet de Onis (Durham, NC: Duke University Press, 1995).

36. Ana M. López, "Of Rhythms and Borders," in Fraser Delgado and Muñoz, *Everynight Life,* 340.

37. George, Lipsitz, *Dangerous Crossroads: Popular Music Postmodernism and the Poetics of Place* (London: Verso, 1994), 3.

38. For a discussion of salsa in a pan-Latina/o context, see Frances Aparicio, *Listening to Salsa: Gender, Latin Popular Music, and Puerto Rican Cultures* (Middletown, CT: Wesleyan University Press, 1998). See also Juan Flores's discussion of bebop and hip-hop in *From Bomba to Hip-Hop: Puerto Rican Culture and Latino Identity* (New York: Columbia University Press, 2000) and Ramón H. Rivera-Servera's "Exhibiting Voice / Narrating Migration: Performance-Based Curatorial Practice in *Azúcar! The Life and Music of Celia Cruz," Text and Performance Quarterly* 29.2 (2009): 131–48.

39. *Banda,* which means band in translation, is a Mexican musical genre derived from the traditions of the marching band and polka. *Norteñas* are yet another Mexican regional genre that denotes music from the northern portions of Mexico. Both these genres are notorious for their use of the accordion.

40. *Quebraditas* is a fast-paced musical genre derived from *banda.* It is rarely performed in Rochester, New York, with the exception of *jaripeos*—northern Mexico cowboy festivities that include music, dance, food, and rodeo competitions—organized by local Mexican merchants during the summer season when Mexican migrant workers labor in the fields of western New York.

41. References to *banda* and *norteñas* in the Northeast were less frequent, but some informants, especially those of Mexican and Central American descent, did express an interest in listening and dancing to those styles in their New York state clubs.

42. For example, Cuban producer Emilio Estefan, with his Florida-based associates, has been one of the central figures in launching the Spanish-language leg of the Latin Explosion. His production house has also been involved in the production of some of Ricky Martin's crossover work. Sont Latino and Latin BMG operate as niche market subsidiaries of multinational recording corporations. Their market strategy is often outlined from corporate headquarters, leaving limited space for the local decision-making characteristic of earlier developments in the Latin music industries.

43. San Antonio, for example, featured an impressively healthy recording industry from the 1930s until the 1950s.

44. For a discussion of Selena's role as a Mexican-American and pan-Latina icon, see Paredez, *Selenidad.*

45. It is important to note, however, that Mexico had served up to the 1980s as the musical capital of Latin American music. Most crossover acts have been developed and produced out of Mexico into the United States. Furthermore, musical crazes such as the mambo, rumba, and cha-cha entered the United States filtered through the popular entertainment circuits of Mexico.

46. My reference to Afro-Caribbean music here is not musicologically discrete in the sense that I include under this category musical genres influenced by the Caribbean but oftentimes developed in the diaspora such as salsa in New York City. Furthermore, this musical category stretches its regional reach to the musical productions of Colombia, Panama, Venezuela, and other Latin American countries with coastal communities in proximity to the Caribbean.

47. In New York City, DJ Junior Vasquez became legendary at the Palladium for his spiced-up mixes of popular hits. He went on to mix and produce dance versions and later pop release versions of songs by some of the top American popular music, most notoriously Madonna.

48. Brian Currid, "We Are Family: House Music and Queer Performativity," in Sue-Ellen Case, Phillip Brett, and Susan Leigh Foster, eds., *Crusing the Performative: Interventions into the Representations of Ethnicity, Nationality, and Sexuality* (Bloomington: Indiana University Press, 1995), 174.

49. Sarah Thornton, *Club Cultures: Music, Media, and Subcultural Capital* (Middletown, CT: Wesleyan University Press, 1996), 3.

50. Other examples of mediatized transmission of dance practices include television programs such as *Soul Train*; Univision's *Sábado Gigante*, which often presents social dance competitions as part of its four-hour variety show (interestingly this is the world's most-watched television show, based on audience numbers in Latin America and the United States); and MTV's many live dance shows, such as *MTV Beach House*, which showcases MTV groupies dancing to the top-selling tracks of American pop music.

51. The dance steps I describe here were observed in 1998. I did not interview Wilbert until the summer of 2002, after running into him at Escuelita in Manhattan.

52. It is important to note here that the exoticism assigned to forms like salsa is often present in local manifestations. That is, the location of the practice within a Latina/o context does not eliminate the possibility of racist representation, especially in regard to blackness.

53. See Aparicio, *Listening to Salsa*.

54. The face-to-face position in close proximity characterizes much Latin American social dance. The term has, however, been standardized in formal social dance training in both Anglo and Latin American dance studios.

55. Lisa Sánchez González, *Boricua Literature: A Literary History of the Puerto Rican Diaspora* (New York: New York University Press, 2001), 168.

Chapter 5

1. "Best of 2007," *Phoenix New Times*, http://www.phoenix newtimes.com/bestof/2007/ award/best-va-queer-o-bar-553472 (accessed January 7, 2008).

2. "Karamba," *Phoenix New Times*, http://www.phoenixnew times.com/locations/karamba-9663 (accessed March 22, 2011).

3. Matt Woosley, "America's Fastest-Growing Cities," *Forbes Magazine*, October 31, 2007, http://www.forbes.com/2007/10/31/property-cities-growth-forbeslife-cx_mw_1031realestate.html (accessed May 11, 2010).

4. See Mireya Navarro, "Mad Hot Reggaeton," *New York Times*, July 17, 2005, 9.1; and Kaleefa Sanneh, "Reggaeton's Rise on Radio Shows Change Isn't Bad," *New York Times*, June 30, 2005, E1.

5. Jon Pareles "Reggaeton Rides the Next Latin Wave," *New York Times,* September 11, 2005, 2.77.

6. Niki D'Andrea "¡Viva La Danza! Phoenix sizzles with the latest dance music from Puerto Rico," *Phoenix New Times,* Thursday, December 15, 2005.

7. See Douglas Massey, *New Faces in New Places: The Changing Geography of American Immigration* (New York: Russell Sage Foundation, 2010).

8. Dan Nowicki, "Arizona Immigration Law Ripples through History, U.S. Politics," *Arizona Republic,* July 25, 2010.

9. Tamara L. Underiner discussed Joe Arpaio as a performance artist in her commentary "After SB 1070: Art and Activism in Arizona," presented during the panel "Global Trends, Local Narratives: Performative Responses to Anti-immigrant Sentiment," Association for Theatre in Higher Education Annual Conference, August 14, 2011.

10. Sylvia R. Lazos Vargas, "The Immigrant Rights Marches (Las Marchas): Did the 'Gigante' (Giant) Wake Up or Does It Still Sleep Tonight?" *Nevada Law Journal* 7 (2006–7): 780–825.

11. Wayne Marshall's groundbreaking essay "From Música Negra to Reggaeton Latino: The Cultural Politics of Nation, Migration and Commercialization" is an important contribution from this debate. While his focus remains primarily on the production and marketing of reggaetón, his apt reading of the inter-Latina/o dynamics at play in these negotiations are foundational to any consideration of the genre's traversing into *pan-latinidad.* In Raquel Z. Rivera, Wayne Marshall, and Deborah Pacini Hernandez, eds., *Reggaeton* (Durham, NC: Duke University Press, 2009).

12. See Cvetkovich, *An Archive of Feelings* and my discussion of the concept in chapter 2.

13. This chapter developed out of ethnographic research conducted at Club Karamba and Club Zarape in Phoeniz from 2004 to 2007 with subsequent check-in visits in 2008 and 2009. The interviewees here cited were selected through a combination of snowball sampling and on-site solicitation. Most interviews were conducted at or near the club premises. A total of twelve initial formal interviews were conducted, with an additional five follow-up interviews. Initial interviews ran from thirty to ninety minutes. Additional information was gathered from interviewed informants and others not formally interviewed through participant observation at the clubs. The data relayed in this essay has been selected as representative sample after coding for frequency of themes. Informants have been assigned substitute names in order to protect their privacy.

14. Calle 13, "Atrévete-te-te," *Calle 13,* Sony US Latin, 2005, CD.

15. As Wayne Marshall, Raquel Z. Rivera, and Deborah Pacini Hernandez observed in the introduction to their edited volume on reggaetón: "Reggaeton [sic] differs from earlier Latin pop or dance 'explosions' in its widespread grassroots popularity, especially among Spanish speakers, as the genre's basis in digital tools of production and distribution has facilitated a flowering of aspiring producers and performers across the United States and Latin America." *Reggaeton,* 3. Nonetheless, the practices I document in this essay developed in close relationship to reggaetón's commercial promotion and distribution as a new Latin boon with potential market reach in Arizona. Thus, the practices I represent here offer examples of grassroots rearticulations of mass-

mediated cultural commodities of the Latin Explosion phenomenon. For a discussion of the Latin Explosion, see María Elena Cepeda, *Musical ImagiNation: U.S.-Colombian Identity and the Latin Music Boom* (New York: New York University Press, 2010).

16. Dare yourself, come out of the closet.
  Escape, take your nail polish off.
  Stop covering yourself cause nobody's gonna photograph you
  Rise up, get hyper
  Turn on, bring out sparkles out of your engine's starter.
  Turn on fire like a lighter
  Shake your sweat off as if you were a wiper
  Cause you are of the streets, a street fighter.

17. For a discussion of the gender dynamics of reggaetón dancing, see Jan Fairley, "Dancing Back to Front: *Regeton,* Sexuality, Gender and Transnationalism in Cuba," *Popular Music* 25.3 (2006): 471–88.

18. Alfredo Nieves Moreno offers an important alternative to the narrative positioning of women in this song. In his analysis of this song he proposes that the freedom women are invited to experience remains conditional on the presence of the hypermasculine male partner who must still be present in the *perreo* dance scenario to authorize her supposed freedom. See "A Man Lives Here: Reggaeton's Hypermasculine Resident," in Rivera, Marshall, and Hernandez, *Reggaeton,* 252–79.

19. See Zaire Zenit Dinzey-Flores, "*De la Disco al Caserío*: Urban Spatial Aesthetics and Policy to the Beat of Reggaetón," *Centro Journal* 20.2 (2008): 35–69.

20. In addition to Wayne Marshall's important intervention, Bernadette Marie Calafell's discussion of reggaetón is a notable exception. See Bernadette Marie Calafell, *Latina/o Communication Studies* (New York: Peter Lang, 2007).

21. Muñoz's exploration of *chusmería* is grounded in his analysis of Alina Troyano's dystopian futuristic fantasy play *Chicas 2000*. This piece premiered in 1997 at Dixon Place, one of New York City's leading spaces for experimental performance. For a published version of the script, see Alina Troyano, "Chicas 2000," in *I Carmelita Tropicana: Performing Between Cultures* (Boston: Beacon Press, 2000), 72–122.

22. Muñoz, *Disidentifications,* 182.

23. "El Chavo del 8" is a Mexican sit-com originated in 1971 as a short skit in Chespirito's weekly show and then became a weekly half-hour serial for Televisa. The show ran successfully in Mexico and Latin America throughout the 1970s. It was later incorporated in a skit version back into Chespirito's own show through the 1980s and early 1990s. With reruns continually circulated on TV and other media venues, and its most recent reappearance as an animated series, "El Chavo del 8" continues to circulate its type characters and their phrases, including its reference to *chusma* across the Spanish- and Portuguese-speaking world. The show has circulated in the United States through Spanish television networks since the early 1980s.

24. The idea that Latino identity involves investments in an identitarian collectivity while engaging notions of difference has been a central tenet and debate within Latino studies as a field. In terms of Latino performance, Diana Taylor's early introduction to these differences continues to serve as an important starting point. See Diana Taylor, "Opening Remarks." David Román's 1995 survey essay on Latina/o performance discusses how Latina/o performers in the 1990s insisted "on the visibility and coherence

of Latina/o identity even as they refuse to stabilize that identity as any one image, role, stereotype, or convention" (163). See David Román, "Latino Performance and Identity," *Aztlán* 22.2 (1997): 151–67.

25. Arlene Dávila, *Latino Spin: Public Image and the Whitewashing of Race* (New York: New York University Press, 2008), 171.

26. For an important critique of these tendencies, see Lisa Duggan's brilliant analysis in "The New Homonormativity," and "Equality, Inc." in *The Twilight of Equality? Neoliberalism, Cultural Politics, and the Attack on Democracy* (Boston: Beacon Press, 2008).

27. See Elena Padilla, "Puerto Rican Immigrants in New York and Chicago: A Study in Comparative Assimilation," master's thesis, University of Chicago, 1947; and Nicholas De Genova and Ana Y. Ramos-Zayas, *Latino Crossings: Mexicans, Puerto Ricans, and the Politics of Race and Citizenship* (New York: Routledge, 2003).

28. Cindy García, "Don't Leave Me, Celia! Salsera Homosociality and Pan-Latina Corporealities," *Women and Performance* 18.3 (2008): 199–213.

29. Aparicio, "Jennifer as Selena," 94.

30. See Aparicio, "Jennifer as Selena."

31. Located in downtown Cancún, Karamba was founded in 1986 and it advertises itself as the only survivor of the 1980s club scene in the city. Its website, exclusively in English, also evidences its outward courtship of foreign tourism over local clientele as its publicized intended audience. See http://www.karambabar.com.

32. To date the maps of *'N Touch* and *Echo* do not include Club Zarape. Both maps are available on the publications' respective websites: http://www.ntouchaz.com/-content/map.php and http://www.echomag.com/bar_map.cfm (both accessed April 20, 2010).

33. See http://www.phoenixnewtimes.com/bestof/2007/award/best-va-queer-o-bar-553472 (accessed April 20, 2010). The copy for this short article was authored by Marcos Nájera, whom I discuss later.

34. Marcos Nájera, "Nájera Nites," *Latino Perspectives,* September 2004, 10.

35. Nájera, "Nájera Nites," 10–11.

36. Nájera's column was later picked up by the more mainstream yet alternative *Phoenix New Times* (the Valley's version of the *OC Weekly* or the *Village Voice*) under the title "Browntown."

37. This framing of a past referent from which to evidence the modern is aptly identified by Carlos Monsiváis in his portrait of Mexico City and its representations in photography by Francis Alÿs. See Francis Alÿs and Carlos Monsiváis, *The Historic Center of Mexico City* (Madrid: Turner, 2006).

38. Nájera, "Nájera Nites," 11.

39. Carlos Manuel, "Review of Club Zarape," *Adelante Magazine,* October 2005, http://www.karambanightclub.com/days_of_week_html/Tuesday.html (accessed April 20, 2010).

40. Manuel, "Review of Club Zarape."

41. In Phoenix, the introduction of the modern within the Latina/o queer club relies on similar distinctions between tradition and innovation. They also respond to significant shifts in the image of the city as a rising metropolitan area. Much like Cancún, the Phoenix metro area counts on a significant tourist economy. It was best known for its location in the warm desert lands of the Southwest, the folklores of the Wild West attitude, and its proximity to Native American ruins, arts, and crafts. In the

1980s, but most precipitously from the late 1990s, it also began to upgrade its lucrative resort industry to the standards of luxurious minimalism. In this move to capture the new trend in the industry it also distanced itself from traditional aesthetics.

42. See Anzaldúa, *Borderlands / La Frontera.*

43. Spaces within the traditionally white and affluent Valley tourist corridors of Camelback Street and Scottsdale Road also shifted their engagement with Mexicanness from one that banked on a rustic image of México to one that increasingly invested in similar upgrades into an image a Mexican modern that retained a sense of distanced otherness while aesthetically merging with new codes and conventions of international luxury.

44. Translation by the author.

45. In invoking *habitus* I am referring to Pierre Bourdieu's important theorization of the sedimentation of cultural patterns and attitudes as naturalized behaviors and orientations. See Pierre Bourdieu, *Outline of a Theory of Practice* (London: Cambridge University Press, 1977).

46. Lucas Messer, "Queer Migrant Culture: Undocumented Queer Latinos and Queer Clubs in Phoenix," PhD diss., Arizona State University, 2010.

47. SB 1070 (with amendments from House Bill 2162) was signed into law by Governor Janet Brewer on April 23, 2010. The law proposes requirements that immigrants in the state carry proof of citizenship or residency status at all times and makes the inability to produce such document a misdemeanor. It also authorizes state law enforcement officials to enforce federal immigration law and criminalizes anyone providing any form of support to undocumented immigrants in the state. Scheduled to activate on July 29, 2010, its most controversial proposals were halted in a federal court injunction pending full consideration of legal challenges against it.

48. As Lucas Messer observes, these policies were implemented inconsistently and oftentimes subverted in myriad strategies of distraction and persuasion performed by queer migrants themselves in gaining access to this scene.

49. See Aparacio and Chávez-Silverman, *Tropicalizations.*

50. Illya Kuryaki and The Valderramas, *Leche,* Universal International, 1999, CD.

51. Sydney Hutchison and Cathy Ragland have argued for radio's centrality to the popularization of Mexican popular music in the United States in their respective studies of *quebradita* and *norteña* music. See Sydney Hutchinson, *From Quebradita to Duranguense: Dance in Mexican American Youth Culture* (Tucson: University of Arizona Press, 2007) and Cathy Ragland, *Música Norteña: Mexican Migrants Creating a Nation Between Nations* (Philadelphia: Temple University Press, 2009).

52. Aparicio and Chávez-Silverman, *Tropicalizations,* 8.

53. For examples of studies that addressed these hegemonic representations see Isabel Molina-Guzmán, *Dangerous Curves: Latina Bodies in the Media* (New York: New York University Press, 2010) and Myrna Mendible, ed., *From Bananas to Buttocks: The Latina Body in Popular Film and Culture* (Austin: University of Texas Press, 2007).

54. It is important to note here that my interlocutor's name is his chosen alibi for the purposes of this study. I did not influence his decision to assume Juan as a name.

55. Suzanne Oboler, *Ethnic Labels, Latino Lives: Identity and Politics of (Re)presentation in the United States* (Minneapolis: University of Minnesota Press, 1997), 155.

56. Flores, *From Bomba to Hip-Hop,* 154.

57. Anzaldúa, *Borderlands / La Frontera,* 19.

Epilogue

1. The song has been featured in countless mainstream popular culture projects from the 2008 film *Marley and Me* to a 2010 episode of the Fox network television show *Glee*.

2. Diana Taylor, "Performance and/as History," *Drama Review* 50.1 (2006): 67.

3. Laura G. Gutiérrez, *Performing Mexicanidad: Vendidas y Cabareteras on the Transnational Stage* (Austin: University of Texas Press, 2010), 19.

4. Gillison, "Close-up on Hunts Point."

5. Susan Dominus, "Big Visions for Building Don't Include People Inside," *New York Times,* March 10, 2008, B1.

6. Sam Dolnick, "Openly Gay in the Bronx, but Constantly on Guard," *New York Times,* October 16, 2010, A13.

7. I reference here Michel de Certeau's statement that "what the map cuts up, the story cuts across" (see *Practice of Everyday Life*, 129) as cited by Dwight Conquergood in his essay "Performance Studies: Interventions and Radical Research," *Drama Review* 46.2 (2002): 145–56.

8. San Antonio City Council Ordinance 2007-11-29-1193, approved on November 29, 2007. The ordinance repealed precious articles of the City Code and created Article XVII to amalgamate all public events taking place on the city streets. The application fee was set at $75 with the expectation that the applicant would assume financial responsibility for any city services used in the process, including traffic control staff, police, and barricade equipment.

BIBLIOGRAPHY

Albright, Ann Cooper. *Choreographing Difference: The Body and Identity in Contemporary Dance.* Hanover, NH: Wesleyan University Press, 1997.

Allatson, Paul. *Key Terms in Latina/o Cultural and Literary Studies.* Malden, MA: Blackwell, 2007.

Alÿs, Francis, and Carlos Monsiváis. *The Historic Center of Mexico City.* Madrid: Turner, 2006.

Anzaldúa, Gloria. *Borderlands / La Frontera: The New Mestiza.* San Francisco: Aunt Lute Press, 1999.

Aparicio, Frances. *Listening to Salsa: Gender, Latin Popular Music, and Puerto Rican Cultures.* Middletown, CT: Wesleyan University Press, 1998.

Aparicio, Frances. "Reading the 'Latino' in Latino Studies: Toward Re-imagining Our Academic Location." *Discourse* 21.3 (1999): 3–18.

Aparicio, Frances. "Jennifer as Selena: Rethinking Latinidad in Media and Popular Culture." *Latino Studies* 1.1 (2003): 90–105.

Aparicio, Frances, and Susana Chávez-Silverman, eds. *Tropicalizations: Transcultural Representations of Latinidad.* Hanover, NH: Dartmouth College Press, 1997.

Aponte-Parés, Luis. "Outside/In: Crossing Queer and Latino Boundaries." In *Mambo Montage: The Latinization of New York,* edited by Agustín Laó-Montes and Arlene Dávila, 363–85. New York: Columbia University Press, 2001.

Appadurai, Arjun. "Grassroots Globalization and the Research Imagination." *Public Culture* 12.1 (2000): 1–19.

Arendt, Hannah. *The Human Condition.* Chicago: University of Chicago Press, 1958.

Arreola, Daniel D. *Tejano South Texas: A Mexican American Cultural Province.* Austin: University of Texas Press, 2002.

Arrizón, Alicia. *Latina Performance: Traversing the Stage.* Bloomington: Indiana University Press, 1999.

Balme, Christopher B. "Staging the Pacific: Framing Authenticity in Performances for Tourists at the Polynesian Cultural Center." *Theatre Journal* 50.1 (1998): 53–70.

Becker Liu, Lara. "Puerto Ricans Build on Rich History in Rochester." *Rochester Democrat and Chronicle,* February 26, 2006. Accessed May 10, 2010.

Bhabha, Homi. *The Location of Culture.* London: Routledge, 1994.

Bollen, Jonathan. "Queer Kinesthesia: Performativity on the Dance Floor." In *Dancing Desires: Choreographing Sexualities On and Off the Stage,* edited by Jane C. Desmond, 285–314. Madison: University of Wisconsin Press, 2001.

Bolton, Richard, ed. *Culture Wars: Documents from the Recent Controversies in the Arts.* New York: New Press, 1992.

Bourdieu, Pierre. *Distinction: A Social Critique of the Judgement of Taste.* Trans. Richard Nice. Cambridge: Harvard University Press, 1987.

Bourdieu, Pierre. "The Forms of Capital." In *Handbook of Theory and Research in the Sociology of Education,* edited by J. G. Richardson, 241–58. New York: Greenwood Press, 1985.

Bourdieu, Pierre. *Outline of a Theory of Practice.* London: Cambridge University Press, 1977.

Browning, Barbara. *Infectious Rhythm: Metaphors of Contagion and the Spread of African Culture.* New York: Routledge, 1998.

Broyles-González, Yolanda. *El Teatro Campesino: Theater in the Chicano Movement.* Austin: University of Texas Press, 1994.

Buckland, Fiona. *Impossible Dance: Club Culture and Queer World-Making.* Middletown, CT: Wesleyan University Press, 2002.

Burton, Julianne. "Don (Juanito) Duck and the Imperial-Patriarchal Unconscious: Disney Studios, the Good Neighbor Policy, and the Packaging of Latin America." In *Nationalisms and Sexualities,* edited by Andrew Parker, Vito Russo, Doris Sommer, and Patricia Yaeger, 21–41. New York: Routledge, 1992.

Calafell, Bernadette Marie. *Latina/o Communication Studies.* New York: Peter Lang, 2007.

Calle 13. "Atrévete-te-te." *Calle 13.* Compact disc. Sony US Latin. 2005.

Cantú Jr., Lionel. *The Sexuality of Migration: Border Crossings and Mexican Immigrant Men,* edited by Nancy A. Naples and Salvador Vidal-Ortiz. New York: New York University Press, 2009.

Carter, David. *Stonewall: The Riots That Sparked the Gay Revolution.* New York: St. Martin's Press, 2004.

Castañeda, Antonia I. "Respect and Defend Our Democratic Rights: Community Support for Esperanza Litigation." *La Voz de Esperanza* 11, no. 7 (1998): 4.

Cepeda, María Elena. *Musical ImagiNation: U.S.-Colombian Identity and the Latin Music Boom.* New York: New York University Press, 2010.

Clifford, James. *Routes: Travel and Translation in the Late Twentieth Century.* Cambridge: Harvard University Press, 1997.

Clifford, James. "Traveling Cultures." In *Cultural Studies,* edited by Laurence Grossberg, Cary Nelson, and Paula Treichler, 96–117. London: Routledge, 1992.

Cohen, Cathy. "Punks, Bulldaggers, and Welfare Queens: The Radical Potential of Queer Politics?" *GLQ* 3 (1997): 437–65.

Cohen-Cruz, Jan. *Local Acts: Community-Based Performance in the United States.* New Brunswick, NJ: Rutgers University Press, 2005.

Conquergood, Dwight. "Performance Studies: Interventions and Radical Research." *Drama Review* 46.2 (2002): 145–56.

Conquergood, Dwight. "Rethinking Ethnography: Towards a Critical Cultural Politics." In *The Sage Handbook of Performance Studies,* edited by Soyini Madison and Judith Hamera, 351–65. Thousand Oaks, CA: Sage, 2006.

Coronado, Raúl. "Selena's Good Buy: Texas Mexicans, History, and Selena Meet Transnational Capitalism." *Aztlán* 26.1 (2001): 59–100.

Crimp, Douglas, ed. *AIDS: Cultural Analysis, Cultural Activism.* Cambridge: MIT Press, 1988.

Crimp, Douglas. *AIDS Demographics.* Seattle: Bay Press, 1990.

Crimp, Douglas. *Melancholia and Moralism: Essays on AIDS and Queer Politics.* Cambridge: MIT Press, 2004.

Croce, Arlene. "Discussing the Undiscussable." *New Yorker,* December 26, 1994, 54–60.

Cruz Malavé, Arnaldo. *Queer Latino "Testimonio," Keith Haring, and Juanito Extravaganza.* New York: Palgrave Macmillan, 2008.

Cruz Malavé, Arnaldo. "Toward an Art of Transvestism: Colonialism and Homosexuality in Puerto Rican Literature." In *¿Entiendes? Queer Readings, Hispanic Writings,* edited by Emilie Bergmann and Paul Julian Smith, 137–67. Durham, NC: Duke University Press, 1995.

Curran, Winifred. "Gentrification and the Nature of Work: Exploring the Links in Williamsburg, Brooklyn." *Environment and Planning A* 36.7 (2004): 1243–58.

Currid, Brian. "We Are Family: House Music and Queer Performativity." In *Cruising the Performative: Interventions into the Representations of Ethnicity, Nationality, and Sexuality,* edited by Sue-Ellen Case, Phillip Brett, and Susan Leigh Foster. Bloomington: Indiana University Press, 1995: 165–96.

Cvetkovich, Ann. *An Archive of Feelings: Trauma, Sexuality, and Lesbian Public Cultures.* Durham, NC: Duke University Press, 2003.

Daly, Ann. "Dancing the Unsayable: Bill T. Jones's *Still/Here* Becomes a Meditation on the Possibilities of Postmodernist Art." *Texas Observer,* March 22, 1996, 18–19. Originally published in Ann Daly, *Critical Gestures: Writing on Dance and Culture.* Hanover, NH: Wesleyan University Press, 2002.

D'Andrea, Niki. "¡Viva La Danza! Phoenix Sizzles with the Latest Dance Music from Puerto Rico." *Phoenix New Times,* December 15, 2005.

Danielson, Marivel T. *Homecoming Queers: Desire and Difference in Chicana Latina Cultural Production.* New Brunswick, NJ: Rutgers University Press, 2009.

Dávila, Arlene. *Barrio Dreams: Puerto Ricans, Latinos, and the Neoliberal City.* Berkeley: University of California Press, 2004.

Dávila, Arlene. *Latinos Inc.: The Marketing and Making of a People.* New York: New York University Press, 2001.

Dávila, Arlene. *Latino Spin: Public Image and the Whitewashing of Race.* New York: New York University Press, 2008.

Decena, Carlos Ulises. *Tacit Subjects: Belonging and Same-Sex Desire among Dominican Immigrant Men.* Durham, NC: Duke University Press, 2011.

de Certeau, Michel. *The Practice of Everyday Life.* Trans. Steven Rendall. Berkeley: University of California Press, 1984.

De Genova, Nicholas, and Ana Y. Ramos-Zayas. *Latino Crossings: Mexicans, Puerto Ricans and the Politics of Race and Citizenship.* New York: Routledge, 2003.

Delaney, Samuel R. *Times Square Red, Times Square Blue.* New York: New York University Press, 1999.

De León, Arnoldo. *Tejano Community, 1836–1900.* Albuquerque: University of New Mexico Press, 1982.

Deleuze, Gilles, and Félix Guattari. *A Thousand Plateaus.* Trans. Brian Massumi. New York: Continuum, 2004.

Delgado, Celeste Fraser, and José E. Muñoz, eds. *Everynight Life: Culture and Dance in Latin/o America.* Durham, NC: Duke University Press, 2004.

de Oliver, Miguel. "Marketing Latinos as Development Policy: San Antonio and the Reproduction of Underprivilege." *Latino Studies* 2 (2004): 395–421.

DeSipio, Louis. *Counting the Vote: Latinos as a New Electorate.* Charlottesville: University Press of Virginia, 1996.

Diamond, Elin. *Performance and Cultural Politics.* New York: Routledge, 1996.

Diaz Gonzalez, Evelyn. *The Bronx.* New York: Columbia University Press, 2004.

Diebold, David. *Tribal Rites: San Francisco's Dance Music Phenomenon.* Northridge, CA: Time Warp, 1986.

di Leonardo, Micaela. "Introduction: New Global and American Landscapes of Inequality." In *New Landscapes of Inequality: Neoliberalism and the Erosion of Democracy in America*, edited by Jane L. Collins, Micaela di Leonardo, and Brett Williams, 3–19. Santa Fe, NM: School for Advanced Research Press, 2008.

Dinzey-Flores, Zaire Zenit. "*De la Disco al Caserío*: Urban Spatial Aesthetics and Policy to the Beat of Reggaetón." *Centro Journal* 20.2 (2008): 35–69.

Dobrzynski, Judith H. "San Antonio Reduces Aid to the Arts by 15 Percent." *New York Times,* September 13, 1997.

Dolan, Jill. *Geographies of Learning: Theory and Practice, Activism and Performance.* Middletown, CT: Wesleyan University Press, 2001.

Dolan, Jill. "Performance, Utopia and the 'Utopian Performative.'" *Theatre Journal* 53.3 (2001): 455–79.

Dolan, Jill. *Utopia in Performance: Finding Hope at the Theater.* Ann Arbor: University of Michigan Press, 2005.

Dolnick, Sam. "Openly Gay in the Bronx, but Constantly on Guard." *New York Times,* October 16, 2010, A13.

Dominguez, Virginia. "For a Politics of Love and Rescue." *Cultural Anthropology* 15.3 (2000): 361–93.

Dominus, Susan. "Big Visions for Building Don't Include People Inside." *New York Times,* March 10, 2008, B1.

Doty, Alexander. *Making Things Perfectly Queer: Interpreting Mass Culture.* Minneapolis: University of Minnesota Press, 1993.

Duany, Jorge, and Félix V. Matos-Rodríguez. "Puerto Ricans in Orlando and Central Florida." *Hispanic Chamber of Commerce of Metro Orlando.* http://hispanicchamber.net/images/pdf/puerto_ricans-orl.pdf. Accessed on July 20, 2009.

Duberman, Martin. *Stonewall.* New York: Dutton, 1993.

Duggan, Lisa. "The New Homonormativity: The Sexual Politics of Neoliberalism." In *Materializing Democracy: Toward a Revitalized Cultural Politics*, edited by Russ Castronova and Dana D. Nelson, 175–94. Durham, NC: Duke University Press, 2002.

Duggan, Lisa. *The Twilight of Equality? Neoliberalism, Cultural Politics, and the Attack on Democracy.* Boston: Beacon Press, 2008.

Duggan, Lisa, and Nan D. Hunter. *Sex Wars: Sexual Dissent and Political Culture.* 10th anniversary ed. New York: Routledge, 2006.

Duggan, Lisa, and José Esteban Muñoz. "Hope and Hopelessness: A Dialogue." *Women and Performance* 19.2 (2009): 275–83.

Dunning, Jennifer. "New Spin on 'Cinderella': Prince Finds a Dream Guy." *New York Times,* November 5, 1996, C16.

Dyer, Richard. *Only Entertainment.* New York: Routledge, 1992.

Elam, Harry. *Taking It to the Streets: The Social Protest Theater of Luis Valdez and Amiri Baraka.* Ann Arbor: University of Michigan Press, 2001.

Epps, Brad. *Passing Lines: Sexuality and Immigration.* Cambridge, MA: David Rockefeller Center for Latin American Studies, 2005.

Fairbanks, Robert B. "The Texas Exception: San Antonio and Urban Renewal, 1949–1965." *Journal of Planning History* 1.2 (2002): 181–96.

Fairley, Jan. "Dancing Back to Front: *Regeton,* Sexuality, Gender and Transnationalism in Cuba." *Popular Music* 25.3 (2006): 471–88.

Fernandez, Ramona. "Pachuco Mickey." In *From Mouse to Mermaid: The Politics of Film, Gender, and Culture,* edited by Elizabeth Bell, Lynda Haas, and Laura Sells, 236–54. Bloomington: Indiana University Press, 1995.

Fiol-Matta, Licia. "Pop Latinidad: Puerto Ricans in the Latin Explosion, 1999." *Centro Journal* 14.1 (2002): 45.

Flores, Juan. *The Diaspora Strikes Back: "Caribeño" Tales of Learning and Turning.* New York: Routledge, 2009.

Flores, Juan. *Divided Borders: Essays on Puerto Rican Identity.* Houston: Arte Público Press, 1993.

Flores, Juan. *From Bomba to Hip-Hop: Puerto Rican Culture and Latino Identity.* New York: Columbia University Press, 2000.

Flores, Juan. "The Latino Imaginary: Dimensions of Community and Identity." In *Tropicalizations: Transcultural Representations of Latinidad,* edited by Frances Aparicio and Susana Chávez-Silverman, 183–93. Hanover, NH: Dartmouth College Press, 1997.

Flores, Richard. *Los Pastores: History and Performance in the Mexican Shepherd's Play of South Texas.* Washington, DC: Smithsonian Institution Press, 1995.

Flores, Richard. *Remembering the Alamo: Memory, Modernity and the Master Symbol.* Austin: University of Texas Press, 2002.

Florida, Richard. *The Rise of the Creative Class: And How It's Transforming Work, Leisure, Community and Everyday Life.* New York: Perseus, 2002.

Foster, Susan Leigh. "Choreographies of Protest." *Theatre Journal* 55.3 (2003): 395–412.

Francis, Mark, Lisa Cachan, and Lynn Paxson. *Community Open Spaces: Greening Neighborhoods through Community Action and Land Conservation.* Covelo, CA: Island Press, 1984.

Fraser, Nancy. "Rethinking the Public Sphere: A Contribution to the Critique of Actually Existing Democracy." In *Habermas and the Public Sphere,* edited by Craig Calhoun, 109–42. Cambridge: MIT Press, 1992.

Gallop, Jane. *Anecdotal Theory.* Durham, NC: Duke University Press, 2002.

García, Cindy. "Don't Leave Me, Celia! Salsera Homosociality and Pan-Latina Corporealities." *Women and Performance* 18.3 (2008): 199–213.

Gillison, Douglas. "Close-up on Hunts Point." *Village Voice,* February 4, 2003. http://www.villagevoice.com/2003-02-04/nyc-life/close-up-on-hunts-point/. Accessed August 8, 2009.

Ginsburg, Faye. "Saving America's Souls: Operation Rescue's Crusade against Abortion." In *Fundamentalists and the State: Remaking Politics, Economies, and Militants,* edited by Martin Marty and R. Scott Applebee, 557–88. Chicago: University of Chicago Press, 1992.

Giroux, Henry A. *The Mouse That Roared: Disney and the End of Innocence.* Lanham, MD: Rowman & Littlefield, 1999.

Goffman, Erving. *The Presentation of Self in Everyday Life.* New York: Anchor, 1959.

Goodnough. Abby. "Hispanic Vote in Florida: Neither a Bloc Nor a Lock." *New York Times,* October 17, 2004.

Greenberg, Michael R., and Thomas D. Boswell. "Neighborhood Deterioration as a Factor in Intraurban Migration: A Case Study in New York City." *Professional Geographer* 24.1 (1972): 11–16.

Greene, David. "Why Protect Political Art as 'Political Speech?'" *Hastings Communications and Entertainment Law Journal* 27.2 (2004–5): 359–82.

Guerra, Susana M. "Semillas de Milagro." *La Voz de Esperanza* 19.10 (2006–7): 5.

Gutiérrez, Laura G. *Performing "Mexicanidad: Vendidas y Cabareteras" on the Transnational Stage.* Austin: University of Texas Press, 2010.

Guzman, Betsy. *The Hispanic Population: Census 2000 Brief.* Washington, DC: U.S. Government Printing Office, 2001.

Gúzman, Manuel. "Pa' La Escuelita Con Mucho Cuidaò Y Por La Orillita: A Journey through the Contested Terrains of Nation and Sexual Orientation." In *Puerto Rican Jam: Rethinking Colonialism and Nationalism,* edited by Frances Negrón-Muntaner and Ramón Grosfogel, 209–28. Minneapolis: University of Minnesota Press, 1997.

Habermas, Jürgen. *The Structural Transformation of the Public Sphere: An Inquiry into a Category of Bourgeois Society.* Trans. Thomas Burger. Cambridge, MA: The MIT Press, 1989.

Halberstam, Judith. *In Queer Time and Space: Transgender Bodies, Subcultural Lives.* New York: New York University Press, 2005.

Hamera, Judith. *Dancing Communities: Performance, Difference and Connection in the Global City.* Basingstoke: Palgrave Macmillan, 2007.

Hames-García, Michael, and Ernesto Javier Martínez, eds. *Gay Latino Studies: A Critical Reader.* Durham, NC: Duke University Press, 2011.

Harvey, David. *A Brief History of Neoliberalism.* Oxford: Oxford University Press, 2005.

Harvey, David. *Spaces of Hope.* Berkeley: University of California Press, 2000.

Heilburn, Marta, ed. *Inventing the Skyline: The Architecture of Cass Gilbert.* New York: Columbia University Press, 2000.

Herdt, Gilbert, ed. *Moral Panics, Sex Panics: Fear and the Fight over Sexual Rights.* New York: New York University Press, 2009.

Hermalyn, Gary, and Lloyd Ultan. "One Hundred Years of the Bronx." *Bronx County Historical Society Journal* 35.2 (1998): 63–68.

Herring, Scott. *Another Country: Queer Anti-Urbanism.* New York: New York University Press, 2010.

Hewitt, Andrew. *Social Choreography: Ideology as Performance in Dance and Everyday Movement.* Durham, NC: Duke University Press, 2005.

Huerta, Jorge. *Chicano Drama: Performance, Society and Myth.* Cambridge: Cambridge University Press, 2000.

Huerta, Jorge. *Chicano Theater: Themes and Forms.* Ypsilanti, MI: Bilingual Press, 1982.

Hughes, Walter. "In the Empire of the Beat: Discipline and Disco." In *Microphone Fiends: Youth Music and Youth Culture,* edited by Andrew Ross and Tricia Rose, 147–57. New York: Routledge, 1994.

Hutchinson, Sydney. *From Quebradita to Duranguense: Dance in Mexican American Youth Culture.* Tucson: University of Arizona Press, 2007.

Jackson, Shannon. *Social Works: Performing Art, Supporting Publics.* London: Routledge, 2011.

Jacobson, Robin Dale. *The New Nativism: Proposition 187 and the Debate over Immigration.* Minneapolis: University of Minnesota Press, 2008.

Jiménez Román, Miriam. "Looking at That Middle Ground: Racial Mixing as Panacea?" In *A Companion to Latino Studies,* edited by Juan Flores and Renato Rosaldo, 325–36. Malden, MA: Blackwell, 2007.

Johnson, E. Patrick. *Appropriating Blackness: Performance and the Politics of Authenticity.* Durham, NC: Duke University Press, 2003.

Johnson, E. Patrick. "'Quare' Studies, or (Almost) Everything I Know about Queer Studies I Learned from My Grandmother." *Text and Performance Quarterly* 21.1 (2001): 1–25.

Jonnes, Jill. *South Bronx Rising: The Rise, Fall, and Resurrection of an American City.* New York: Fordham University Press, 2002.

Kintz, Linda. *Between Jesus and the Market: The Emotions That Matter in Right-Wing America.* Durham, NC: Duke University Press, 1997.

Kirshenblatt-Gimblett, Barbara. *Destination Cultures: Tourism, Museums, and Heritage.* Berkeley: University of California Press, 1998.

Kisselgoff, Anna. "'Cinderella' Set in a Puerto Rican Ghetto." *New York Times,* February 3, 2003.

Kuryaki, Illya, and The Valderramas. *Leche.* Compact disc. Universal International, 1999.

La Fountain-Stokes, Lawrence M. "Dancing *La Vida Loca:* The Queer Nuyorican Performances of Arthur Avilés and Elizabeth Marrero." In *Queer Globalizations: Citizenship and the Afterlife of Colonialism,* edited by Arnaldo Cruz-Malavé and Martin F. Manalansan, 162–75. New York: New York University Press, 2002.

La Fountain-Stokes, Lawrence M. "A Naked Puerto Rican Faggot from America: An Interview with Arthur Avilés." *Centro Journal* 19.1 (2007): 314–29.

La Fountain-Stokes, Lawrence M. *Queer Ricans: Cultures and Sexualities in the Diaspora.* Minneapolis: University of Minnesota Press, 2009.

La Fountain-Stokes, Lawrence, Lourdes Torres, and Ramón H. Rivera-Servera. "Toward an Archive of Latina/o Queer Chicago: Arts, Politics, and Social Performance." In *Out in Chicago: LGBT History at the Crossroads*, edited by Jill Austin and Jennifer Brier, 127–53. Chicago: Chicago Historical Society, 2011.

Laviera, Tato. *La Carreta Made a U-turn.* Houston: Arte Público Press, 1992.

Lazos Vargas, Sylvia R. "The Immigrant Rights Marches (Las Marchas): Did the 'Gigante' (Giant) Wake Up or Does It Still Sleep Tonight?" *Nevada Law Journal* 7 (2006–7): 780–825.

Limón, José. *Dancing with the Devil: Society and Cultural Poetics in Mexican-American South Texas.* Madison: University of Wisconsin Press 1994.

Lipsitz, George. *Dangerous Crossroads: Popular Music Postmodernism and the Poetics of Place.* London: Verso,1994.

López, Ana M. "Of Rhythms and Borders." In *Everynight Life: Culture and Dance in Latin/o America,* edited by Fraser Delgado and José Esteban Muñoz, 310–44. Durham, NC: Duke University Press, 1997.

Lowenhaupt Tsing, Ana. *Friction: An Ethnography of Global Connection.* Princeton, NJ: Princeton University Press, 2005.

Madison, D. Soyini. *Acts of Activism: Human Rights as Radical Performance.* Cambridge: Cambridge University Press, 2010.

Madison, D. Soyini, and Judith Hamera, eds. *Sage Handbook of Performance Studies.* London: Sage, 2006.

Magaña, Lisa, ed. *Latino Politics and International Relations: The Case of Arizona's Immigration Law SB 1070.* New York: Springer, 2012.

Manalansan, Martin, IV. "Diasporic Deviants/Divas: How Filipino Gay Transmigrants 'Play with the World.'" In *Queer Diasporas,* edited by Marcie Frank, Cindy Patton, and Benigno Sánchez-Eppler, 183–203. Durham, NC: Duke University Press, 2000.

Manalansan, Martin, IV. "Queer Intersections: Sexuality and Gender in Migration Studies." *International Migration Review* 40.1 (2006): 224–49.

Manuel, Carlos. "Review of Club Zarape." *Adelante Magazine,* October 2005. http://www.karambanightclub.com/days_of_week_html/Tuesday.html. Accessed April 20, 2010.

Marquéz, Raquel R., Louis Mendoza, and Steve Blanchard. "Neighborhood Formation on the West Side of San Antonio, Texas." *Latino Studies* 5 (2007): 288–316.

Marshall, Wayne. "From Música Negra to Reggaeton Latino: The Cultural Politics of Nation, Migration and Commercialization." In *Reggaeton,* edited by Raquel Z. Rivera, Wayne Marshall, and Deborah Pacini Hernandez, 19–78. Durham, NC: Duke University Press, 2009.

Martin, Randy. *Critical Moves: Dance Studies in Theory and Politics.* Durham, NC: Duke University Press, 1998.

Massey, Douglas. *New Faces in New Places: The Changing Geography of American Immigration.* New York: Russell Sage Foundation, 2010.

Mendible, Myrna, ed. *From Bananas to Buttocks: The Latina Body in Popular Film and Culture.* Austin: University of Texas Press, 2007.

Messer, Lucas. "Queer Migrant Culture: Undocumented Queer Latinos and Queer Clubs in Phoenix." PhD diss., Arizona State University, 2010.

Miller, Tim, and David Román. "Preaching to the Converted." *Theatre Journal* 47.2 (1995): 169–88.

Molina-Guzmán, Isabel. *Dangerous Curves: Latina Bodies in the Media.* New York: New York University Press, 2010.

Molineu, Harold. *U.S. Policy toward Latin America: From Regionalism to Globalism.* Boulder, CO: Westview Press, 1986.

Monroe, Dianne. "The Art of Defunding: An Examination of the Forces That Caused City Council to Deny Taxpayer Money to the Esperanza Peace and Justice Center." *San Antonio Current,* November 6–12, 1997.

Montejano, David. *Anglos and Mexicans in the Making of Texas, 1836–1896.* Austin: University of Texas Press, 1987.

Moraga, Cherríe. "Chicana Feminism as Theory in the Flesh." In *This Bridge Called My Back: Writings by Radical Women of Color,* edited by Gloria Anzaldúa and Cherríe Moraga. San Francisco: Aunt Lute Press, 1981.

Moraga, Cherríe. *Giving Up the Ghost: Teatro in Two Acts.* Los Angeles: West End Press, 1986.

Moreno, Alfredo Nieves. "A Man Lives Here: Reggaeton's Hypermasculine Resident." In *Reggaeton,* edited by Raquel Z. Rivera, Wayne Marshall, and Deborah Pacini Hernandez, 252–79. Durham, NC: Duke University Press, 2009.

Muñoz, José E. *Disidentifications: Queers of Color and the Performance of Politics.* Minneapolis: University of Minnesota Press, 1999.

Muñoz, José E. "Feeling Brown: Ethnicity and Affect in Ricardo Bracho's *The Sweetest Hangover (and Other STDs)." Theatre Journal* 52.1 (2000): 67–79.

Muñoz, José E. "No es fácil: Notes on the Negotiation of Cubanidad and Exilic Memory in Carmelita Tropicana's *Milk of Amnesia." Drama Review* 39.3 (1995): 76–82.

Nájera, Marcos. "Nájera Nites." *Latino Perspectives,* September 2004.

Navarro, Mireya. "Mad Hot Reggaeton." *New York Times,* July 17, 2005, 9.1.

Negrón-Muntaner, Frances. *Boricua Pop: Puerto Ricans and the Latinization of American Culture.* New York: New York University Press, 2004.

Negrón-Muntaner, Frances. *Brincando el Charco: Portrait of a Puerto Rican.* 1994. Film.

Nowicki, Dan. "Arizona Immigration Law Ripples through History, U.S. Politics." *Arizona Republic,* July 25, 2010.

Ngai, Sianne. *Ugly Feelings.* Cambridge: Harvard University Press, 2005.

Obama, Barack. *The Audacity of Hope: Thoughts on Reclaiming the American Dream.* New York: Crown / Three Rivers Press, 2006.

Oboler, Suzanne. *Ethnic Labels, Latino Lives: Identity and Politics of (Re)presentation in the United States.* Minneapolis: University of Minnesota Press, 1997.

Oliver, Mary Beth. "Race and Crime in the Media: Research from a Media Effects Perspective." In *A Companion to Media Studies,* edited by Angharad N. Valdivia, 421–26. Malden, MA: Blackwell, 2003.

O'Neill, John. "AIDS as a Globalizing Panic." In *Global Culture: Nationalism, Globalization and Modernity,* 329–42. London: Sage, 1990.

Ono, Kent A., and John M. Sloop. *Shifting Borders: Rhetoric, Immigration and California's Proposition 187.* Philadelphia: Temple University Press, 2002.

Ortiz, Fernando. *Cuban Counterpoint: Tobacco and Sugar.* Trans. Harriet de Onis. Durham, NC: Duke University Press, 1995.

Owens, Brent. Director. *Hookers at the Point: Five Years Later.* 2002. Film.

Padilla, Elena. "Puerto Rican Immigrants in New York and Chicago: A Study in Comparative Assimilation." Master's thesis, University of Chicago, 1947.

Padilla, Felix. *Latino Ethnic Consciousness: The Case of Mexican Americans and Puerto Ricans in Chicago.* South Bend, IN: Notre Dame University Press, 1985.

Papayanis, Marilyn Adler. "Sex and the Revanchist City: Zoning Out Pornography in New York." *Environment and Planning D: Society and Space* 18 (2000): 341–53.

Paredez, Deborah. *Selenidad: Selena, Latinos, and the Performance of Memory.* Durham, NC: Duke University Press, 2009.

Pareles, Jon. "Reggaeton Rides the Next Latin Wave." *New York Times,* September 11, 2005, 2.77.

Patton, Cindy. *Globalizing AIDS*. Minneapolis: University of Minnesota Press, 2002.

Patton, Cindy. *Sex and Germs: Politics of AIDS*. Montreal: Black Rose Books, 1988.

Peña, Devon G. *The Terror of the Machine: Technology, Work, Gender and Ecology on the U.S.-Mexico Border*. Austin: CMAS Books, 1997.

Peñaloza, Lisa. "We're Here, We're Queer, and We're Going Shopping! A Critical Perspective on the Accommodation of Gays and Lesbians in the U.S. Marketplace." In *Gays, Lesbians, and Consumer Behavior: Theory, Practice, and Research Issues in Marketing*, edited by Daniel Wardlow, 9–41. Binghampton, NY: Haworth Press, 1998.

Peña-Ovalle, Priscilla. *Dance and the Hollywood Latina: Race, Sex, and Stardom*. New Brunswick, NJ: Rutgers University Press, 2011.

Pérez, Emma. *The Decolonial Imaginary: Writing Chicanas into History*. Bloomington: Indiana University Press, 1999.

Pérez, Gina M. *The Near Northwest Side Story: Migration, Displacement, and Puerto Rican Families*. Berkeley: University of California Press, 2004.

Phelan, Peggy. *Unmarked: The Politics of Performance*. New York: Routledge, 1993.

Protevi, John. *Political Affect: Connecting the Social and the Somatic*. Minneapolis: University of Minnesota Press, 2009.

Quiroga, José. "From Republic to Empire: The Loss of Gay Studies." *GLQ* 10.1 (2003): 133–35.

Quiroga, José. *Tropics of Desire: Interventions from Latino America*. Durham, NC: Duke University Press, 2000.

Ragland, Cathy. *Música Norteña: Mexican Migrants Creating a Nation between Nations*. Philadelphia: Temple University Press, 2009.

Ramírez Berg, Charles. *Latino Images in Film: Stereotypes, Subversion, and Resistance*. Austin: University of Texas Press, 2002.

Ramos Zayas, Ana Y. *National Performances: The Politics of Class, Race, and Space in Puerto Rican Chicago*. Chicago: University of Chicago Press, 2003.

Renáud-González, Barbara. "Remembering the Alamo, Part II." *The Nation*, March 15, 1999. http://www.thenation.com/article/remember-alamo-part-ii?page=0,1. Accessed March 15, 1999.

Ricourt, Milagros, and Ruby Danta. *Hispanas de Queens: Latino Panethnicity in a New York City Neighborhood*. Ithaca, NY: Cornell University Press, 2003.

Rivera, Raquel Z., Wayne Marshall, and Deborah Pacini Hernandez, eds. *Reggaeton*. Durham, NC: Duke University Press, 2009.

Rivera-Servera, Ramón H. "Choreographies of Resistance: Latina/o Queer Dance and the Utopian Performative." *Modern Drama* 157.2 (2004): 269–89.

Rivera-Servera, Ramón H. "Crossing Hispaniola: Cultural Erotics at the Haitian-Dominican Borderlands." In *Performance in the Borderlands*, edited by Ramón H. Rivera-Servera and Harvey Young, 97–127. London: Palgrave, 2011.

Rivera-Servera, Ramón H. "Dancing Reggaetón with Cowboy Boots: Social Dance Clubs and the Politics of Dance in the Latino Southwest." In *Transnational Encounters: Music and Performance at the U.S.-Mexico Border*, edited by Alejandro Madrid, 373–92. London: Oxford University Press, 2011.

Rivera-Servera, Ramón H. "Exhibiting Voice / Narrating Migration: Performance-Based Curatorial Practice in *Azúcar! The Life and Music of Celia Cruz*." *Text and Performance Quarterly* 29.2 (2009): 131–48.

Rivera-Servera, Ramón H. "Latina/o Queer Futurities: Arthur Aviles Takes on the Bronx." *Ollantay Theatre Magazine* 25.29–30 (2007): 127–46.

Rivera-Servera, Ramón H. "Musical Trans(actions) Intersections in Reggaetón." *Trans: Revista Transcultural de Música* 13 (2009). www.sibertrans.com/trans/a62/musi cal-trans-actions-intersection-in-reggaeton.

Roach, Joseph. *Cities of the Dead: Circum-Atlantic Performance.* New York: Columbia University Press, 1996.

Roberts, Katherine, and Richard Levine. "Coors Extends a $300 Million Peace Offering." *New York Times,* November 4, 1984, 4.8.

Rodríguez, Clara E. *Changing Race: Latinos, the Census, and the History of Ethnicity in the United States.* New York: New York University Press, 2000.

Rodríguez, Juana María. *Queer Latinidad.* New York: New York University Press, 2003.

Rodríguez, Richard T. *Next of Kin: The Family in Chicano/a Cultural Politics.* Durham, NC: Duke University Press, 2009.

Román, David. *Acts of Intervention: Performance, Gay Culture, and AIDS.* Bloomington: Indiana University Press, 1998.

Román, David. "Comment—Theatre Journals." *Theatre Journal* 54.3 (2002): xii–xix.

Román, David. "Latino Performance and Identity." *Aztlán* 22.2 (1997): 151–67.

Román, David. *Performance in America: Contemporary U.S. Culture and the Performing Arts.* Durham, NC: Duke University Press, 2005.

Román, David. "Theatre Journals: Dance Liberation." *Theatre Journal* 55.3 (2003): vii–xxiv.

Román, David, and Alberto Sandoval-Sánchez. "Caught in the Web: *Latinidad,* AIDS, and Allegory in *Kiss of the Spider Woman."* In *Everynight Life: Culture and Dance in Latin/o America,* edited by Celeste Fraser-Delgado and José Muñoz, 255–87. Durham, NC: Duke University Press, 2004.

Rooney, Jim. *Organizing the South Bronx.* Albany: State University of New York Press, 1995.

Rúa, Mérida. *A Grounded Identidad: Making New Lives in Chicago's Puerto Rican Neighborhoods.* New York: Oxford University Press, 2012.

Rumbaut, Ruben G. "Origins and Destinies: Immigration to the United States since World War II." *Sociological Forum* 9.4 (1994): 583–621.

Sahd, Brian. "Community Development Corporations and Social Capital." In *Community-Based Organizations: The Intersection of Social Capital and Local Context in Contemporary Urban Society,* edited by Robert Mark Silverman, 85–124. Detroit: Wayne State University Press, 2004.

Sánchez, Graciela I. "La Cultura, la Comunidad, la Familia, y la Libertad." In *Gender on the Borderlands: The Frontiers Reader,* edited by Antonia Castañeda, Susan H. Armitage, Patricia Hart, and Karen Weathermon, 75–86. Lincoln: University of Nebraska Press, 2007.

Sánchez González, Lisa. *Boricua Literature: A Literary History of the Puerto Rican Diaspora.* New York: New York University Press, 2001.

Sandoval Sánchez, Alberto. *José Can You See? Latinos On and Off Broadway.* Madison: University of Wisconsin Press, 1999.

Sandoval Sánchez, Alberto. "Quinceañera: A Latino Queer and Transcultural Party for AIDS." In *The Color of Theater: Race, Culture, and Contemporary Performance,* edited by Roberta Uno and Lucy Mae San Burns, 303–12. New York: Continuum Press, 2002.

Sandoval Sánchez, Alberto, and Nancy Saporta Sternback. *Stages of Life: Transcultural Performance and Identity in U.S. Latina Theatre.* Tucson: University of Arizona Press, 2001.

Sanneh, Kaleefa. "Reggaeton's Rise on Radio Shows Change Isn't Bad." *New York Times,* June 30, 2005, E1.

Sassen, Saskia. *The Global City: New York, London, Tokyo.* Princeton, NJ: Princeton University Press, 1991.

Savran, David. "Choices Made and Unmade." *Theater* 3.2 (2001): 89–95.

Schechner, Richard. *Performance Theory.* New York: Routledge, 1994.

Schneider, Rebecca. *Performance Remains: Art and War in Times of Theatrical Reenactment.* London: Routledge, 2011.

Soto, Sandra K. *Reading Chican@ Like a Queer: The De-mastery of Desire.* Austin: University of Texas Press, 2010.

Stein, Peter. "Criteria for Urban Land Trusts." In *Land-saving Action: A Written Symposium by 29 Experts on Private Land Conservation in the 1980s,* edited by Russell L. Brenneman and Sarah M. Bates, 48–52. Covelo, CA: Conservation Law Foundation of New England / Island Press, 1984.

Sternberg, Ernest. "The Sectoral Cluster in Economic Development Policy: Lessons from Rochester and Buffalo, New York." *Economic Development Quarterly* 5.4 (1991): 342–56.

Storm Roberts, John. *The Latin Tinge: The Impact of Latin American Music on the United States.* New York: Oxford University Press, 1979.

Taylor, Diana. "Opening Remarks" in *Negotiating Performance: Gender, Sexuality and Theatricality in Latin/o America,* edited by Diana Taylor and Juan Villegas, 1–16. Durham, NC: Duke University Press.

Taylor, Diana. "Performance and/as History." *Drama Review* 50.1 (2006): 67–86.

Thornton, Sarah. *Club Cultures: Music, Media, and Subcultural Capital.* Middletown, CT: Wesleyan University Press, 1996.

Tienda, Marta, and Vilma Ortiz. "Hispanicity and the 1980 Census." *Social Science Quarterly* 67.1 (1986): 3–20.

Tongson, Karen. *Relocations: Emergent Queer Suburban Imaginaries.* New York: New York University Press, 2011.

Troyano, Alina. *I, Carmelita Tropicana: Performing between Cultures.* Boston: Beacon Press, 2000.

Turner, Victor. *From Ritual to Theatre: The Human Sciences of Play.* New York: Performing Arts, 1982.

Underiner, Tamara L. "After SB 1070: Art and Activism in Arizona." Paper presented to the Association for Theatre in Higher Education Annual Conference, August 14, 2011.

Uno, Roberta, and Lucy Mae San Burns, eds. *The Color of Theater: Race, Culture, and Contemporary Performance.* New York: Continuum Press, 2002.

Urquijo-Ruiz, Rita E. "Comfortably Queer: The Chicano Gay Subject in Dan Guerrero's ¡*Gaytino!*" *Ollantay Theater Magazine* 25.29–30 (2007): 147–67.

Valdivia, Angharad N. "Is My Butt Your Island? The Myth of Discovery and Contemporary Latina/o Communication Studies." In *Latina/o Communication Studies Today*, edited by Angharad N. Valdivia, 3–26. New York: Peter Lang, 2008.

Ward, Peter M., and Julie A. Dowling. "Spatial Segregation and Housing Patterns of Hispanic Populations in the United States." In *Transforming Our Common Destiny: Hispanics in the US*, edited by Marta Tienda. Forthcoming.

Warner, Michael, ed. *Fear of a Queer Planet*. Minneapolis: University of Minnesota Press, 1993.

Warner, Michael. *Publics and Counterpublics*. New York: Zone, 2005.

Warren, Sarah F. "Art: To Fund or Not to Fund? That is *Still* the Question." *Cardozo Arts and Entertainment Law Journal* 19.1 (2001): 149–81.

Wickstrom, Maurya. "Commodities, Mimesis, and *The Lion King*: Retail Theatre for the 1990s." *Theatre Journal* 51.3 (1999): 285–98.

Wolf, Stacy. *A Problem Like Maria: Gender and Sexuality in the American Musical*. Ann Arbor: University of Michigan Press, 2002.

Wright, Jeremiah. "The Audacity to Hope." 1990. http://www.preachingtoday.com/sermons/outlines/2010/july/theaudacitytohope.html. Accessed February 28, 2011.

Ybarra-Frausto, Tomás. Introduction to *Community, Culture and Globalization*, edited by Don Adams and Arlene Goldbard. New York: Rockefeller Foundation, 2002.

INDEX